THE SOURCES OF THE FAUST TRADITION

FROM SIMON MAGUS TO LESSING

THE SOURCES OF THE FAUST TRADITION

FROM SIMON MAGUS TO LESSING

BY

PHILIP MASON PALMER

and

ROBERT PATTISON MORE

LONDON AND NEW YORK

First published 1936
by Frank Cass

Published 2013 by Routledge
2 Park Square, Milton Park, Abingdon, Oxfordshire OX14 4RN
711 Third Avenue, New York, NY, 10017, USA

First issued in paperback 2016

Routledge is an imprint of the Taylor & Francis Group, an informa business

Library of Congress Catalog Card Number: 66-19729

ISBN 13: 978-1-138-98258-1 (pbk)
ISBN 13: 978-0-7146-2075-6 (hbk)

PREFACE

In an experience of many years in conducting a course in Goethe's *Faust,* trying to present to students of varied types and training the background out of which the drama grew, the compilers of this text have constantly felt the need of a collection of source material which would make that background more real and consequently more interesting.

Whether a student is studying the background of Goethe's *Faust,* or any other subject, it is desirable, both from the point of view of holding his interest and of developing his power of judgment, that he get as much direct contact as possible with the original materials that make up his field of study. But the original materials that are implied in a study of the growth and development of the Faust legend are widely scattered and for the undergraduate often difficult, if not impossible, of access. Furthermore, knowing, as he frequently does, "little Latin and less Greek," it is very questionable whether he can use them if he is able to find them.

The authors have endeavored to bring together in usable form the materials in question. The content and form of the collection have been in part determined by its primary purpose of serving as an aid to students receiving their first serious introduction to Goethe's masterpiece and in part by the trend of Faust research. It is intended to be used as a supplement to the usual scholarly edition in the student's hands.

The authors are deeply grateful to the many who have been helpful with friendly hints and counsel. They wish to acknowledge especially the assistance of

Professors Charles J. Goodwin and Adolph F. Pauli in checking the translations of the Cyprianus and Theophilus selections respectively; the courtesy of the Committee on Rotographs of MSS. and Rare Printed Books of the Modern Language Association of America in supplying a photostatic copy of the British Museum text of the English Faust Book of 1592; and, finally, the kindness of Professor John A. Walz, of Harvard, who, with characteristic thoroughness and patience, looked over the manuscript and gave many welcome suggestions.

P. M. Palmer

R. P. More

Bethlehem, Pa.

CONTENTS

THE SOURCES OF
THE FAUST TRADITION
FROM SIMON MAGUS TO LESSING

I

INTRODUCTION

INTRODUCTION

THE Faust tradition, which finds in Goethe's drama its loftiest and perhaps its final expression, owes its widespread interest to the fact that it became the vehicle of certain fundamental religious and philosophical problems which have ever fascinated and tormented mankind : the relationship between man and the powers of good and evil ; man's revolt against human limitations ; the thirst for knowledge beyond mere information ; the puzzling disparity between the sublimity and the misery of human life. These problems are by no means the exclusive property of the Faust legend for they form, individually or collectively, the background of much of the world's greatest literature. It was the good fortune of the Faust tradition that in its evolution it combined these elements in a peculiarly happy way and that it attracted and inspired the genius of one of the world's greatest poets.

The history of the tradition in folklore and literature parallels that of many another epic theme. Its origin is obscure ; the development irregular and spasmodic, sometimes halting for long periods and then again, as in Goethe's day, proceeding with seven league boots. Generation after generation works at the old story, widening its scope, reforming, reinterpreting until the master-hand gives it its present form.

The beginnings of the legend so far as it concerns the notorious German magician, Doctor Faust, do not antedate the Protestant Reformation. It is in the reaction of the followers of Martin Luther to the unrestrained enthusiasm of the German Humanists, to the Humanist's attitude towards educational, religious and philosophical questions that the beginnings must be sought. This reaction was natural enough in the intellectual dislocation taking place in the Germany of 1500.

Throughout the fifteenth century forces had been at work which, with much else, tended to uproot, or at least reorient many of the intellectual sign-posts of the Middle Ages. There was the break with traditional ways of thinking ; the renewed interest in secular learning ; the establishment of the northern universities ; the rise of individualism ; a general widening of the horizon. But the older Church and the new Protestant group both viewed this development with consternation and something resembling fear. However, it is from the Lutheran circle that the protest arose against inordinate ambition and ungodly speculation,—a protest which found its most popular expression in the old Faust books. That the archconjuror and blowhard Faust should have been selected as the awful example of the results of an attempt to transcend human limitations is perhaps mere chance.

The growth of the legend is an interesting chapter in the history of myth development. For the Faust of the sixteenth century was merely the lodestone about which gathered in time a mass of superstition which in turn is the deposit of centuries. Many of the stories told about Faust are found in the accounts of earlier magicians. Part of the material, like the compact with the devil, is common property of the Christian Church. Other elements can be traced back to Hebrew and Persian sources antedating Christianity.

On the whole, the progress of the legend in folktale, letter, ballad, novel, and play from the earliest Faust book down to Goethe is reasonably clear. Some links in the chain are missing, it is true, as, for example, the text of the old stage play. But even in this case, it is possible, on the basis of the puppet plays and theater programs extant, to piece together the probable action.

On the other hand, the development of the magic elements in the legend, and of the compact with the devil, or perhaps better, the connection, if any, of these elements with earlier legends about magicians, is by no means as clear. Numerous predecessors of the sixteenth century magician were credited with magic powers, among them Solomon, Simon Magus, Virgil, Cyprian, Merlin, Roger Bacon, Robert the Devil, Zyto, various popes, and many lesser lights. Superstition explained the magic powers, which these individuals were reputed to possess, by a compact with Satan or some other evil spirit. The compact takes actual form in the legend of Theophilus and the legend of Proterius. The origins of both the conception of magic and of the compact are dimmed by time and lost in the mazes of occultism and demonology. How much of all this is directly connected with the Faust tradition is a moot question. None of the problems of larger import which distinguish the later forms of the tradition, with the possible exception of the relationship of man to good and evil, are to be found in the so-called predecessors. However, the influence of blood pact and magic art is unmistakable, indirect perhaps but none the less potent. Medieval Europe delighted in tales of magicians and legends of saints who had made compacts with Satan. Witness the large number of tales which contain these motifs and the popularity of such collections as the *Legenda Aurea.*

To map out the course of the tradition in all its ramifications is an almost impossible task owing to the mass of material involved. It is, perhaps, enough if the broad outlines are sketched and the most important documents presented. It is the characteristic which is important and it is to the characteristic that this collection is to be confined. No attempt is made to go into the history of demonology or to trace the development of the devil myth. These are the fields of the folklore specialist or the theologian. Lack of space alone accounts for the omission of the younger Faust books, and the Fausts of Weidmann, Klinger, and Maler Müller.

II

FORERUNNERS OF FAUST

FORERUNNERS OF FAUST

Among the legends which have been regarded as possible forerunners of the sixteenth century Faust tradition the legends of Simon Magus, Cyprian, and Theophilus in particular have attracted the attention of Faust scholars. These legends were widely known throughout medieval Europe and the question of the possible connection of these older legends with the Faust legend has been the subject of much discussion, some scholars arguing for a direct derivation of the Faust legend from the earlier ones, others just as vigorously denying any such derivation. In any event, they are a part of the larger tradition and have for that reason been chosen for fuller presentation.

The legend of Simon Magus and the legend of Cyprian are characteristic magus legends. The magus legend centers round some individual who has a reputation as a magician, and has as its subject matter the career of the magician, his remarkable feats, and his ultimate fate. The Theophilus legend presents the first detailed account of a compact with Satan. The Helladius-Proterius legend is probably older than the Theophilus legend, but the latter was much better known, to judge from the frequency with which it appears in the literature of medieval Europe.

The authors are responsible for the translations of Cyprian and Theophilus. The English translations of the *Legenda Aurea* have been added to show the popular form of the legends as known to the Europe of 1500.

Simon Magus

The first mention of the Simon known through the centuries as Simon Magus is found in Acts viii, 9-13, 18-24. The account there given is repeatedly referred to by Christian writers throughout the history of the Church and the unfortunate sorcerer has gained undying notoriety by lending his name to one of the great vices of the Church — simony.

More important, however, from the point of view of Faust scholars, has been the gradual accretion of legendary material about the person of Simon — a process which began at least as early as the second century. Whether this was due to a confusion of the Simon of the Biblical tale with another and later Simon, also a magician ; likewise whether the Simon legend, as it was evolved, was anti-Pauline propaganda,[1] is of no importance for our particular purpose.

A number of the early church fathers give some account of Simon. Among them may be mentioned Justin Martyr,[2] Tertullian,[3] Irenaeus,[4] Hippolytus,[5] and Arnobius.[6] But the most important and interesting account of Simon Magus in the early Christian literature is in the so-called "Pseudo-Clementine Literature,"[7]

[1] For the theories and arguments on these two points see the articles on Simon Magus in the *Catholic Encyclopedia* and the *Encyclopedia Britannica* (13th ed.).

[2] Justin Martyr (ca. 100 A.D.–ca. 165) was a native of Palestinian Syria. His *First Apology* was written about 150.

[3] Quintus Septimus Florens Tertullianus (ca. 155–ca. 222). Born at Carthage of good family, he received an excellent education and became an able jurist. He became a Christian at a mature age and was one of the greatest of the ancient church writers of the West. The *De Anima* was written in the first decade of the 3rd century.

[4] Irenaeus, a church father of the 2nd century, became Bishop of Lyons in 178. His *Adversus haereses* was written ca. 180.

[5] Hippolytus was born in the second half of the 2nd century. He was a presbyter of the Church at Rome under Bishop Zephyrinus (199–217). In 235 he was transported to Sardinia where he probably died. The *Refutatio omnium haeresium* is also known as *Philosophumena*.

[6] Arnobius, a teacher of rhetoric in Sicca Venera in proconsular Africa under Diocletian. The *Adversus Gentes* was written ca. 303.

[7] The *Clementine Recognitions* and the *Clementine Homilies,* according to modern scholars, probably date from the 4th century. They were of course not written by Clement of Rome. Both are believed to go back to a common source, *The Circuits of Peter,* which may date from approximately the middle of the 3rd century. The *Recognitions* at least, were well known throughout the centuries that follow, as is evidenced by the many surviving manuscripts and the frequent citations by other authors. (Cf. Harnack, *Geschichte der altchristlichen Literatur,* I, 1, pages 212 ff. Leipzig, 1893.)

viz., the *Clementine Homilies,* the *Clementine Recognitions,* and to a minor extent, the *Apostolic Constitutions.* The *Homilies* and *Recognitions* tell the same story which consists largely of an account of the doctrinal disputes between Simon Magus and the Apostle Peter in Asia Minor. Into this is woven the story of Simon and of the family of Clemens Romanus, the ostensible author of the work. The pertinent selections from the *Recognitions* are reprinted below.

No part of the Simon legend appealed more to the imagination than the conflicts between Peter and Simon in Rome, and these were early developed and loomed large in the medieval accounts. Curiously enough none of this feature appears in either the *Recognitions* or the *Homilies* and only a short mention is made of it in the *Apostolic Constitutions.* Fuller accounts are given in other early documents, however, and the selections given below are from two of these, viz., *Acts of the Holy Apostles Peter and Paul,*[8] and *The Teaching of Simon Cephas in the City of Rome.*[9]

The legend was thus fully developed during the first four centuries of our era and the story was of sufficient popularity to survive to the close of the Middle Ages. In the middle of the 12th century, the *Kaiserchronik*[10] tells the legend at considerable length, with some rearrangement of the episodes. Somewhat over a century later, the material is taken

For this reason, and because this version was printed in 1526 (later editions in 1536, 1563, 1570) we have taken our quotations from the *Recognitions.*

8 The *Acts of the Holy Apostles Peter and Paul,* according to Harnack (*Geschichte der altchristlichen Literatur,* II, 2, page 176. Leipzig, 1904) are almost certainly not older than the 4th century.

9 The *Teaching of Simon Cephas in the City of Rome* in the Ante-Nicene Christian Library, Vol. XX, Edinburgh, 1871, is one of a number of documents "attributed to the first three centuries." However, Harnack, *Geschichte der altchristlichen Literatur,* I, 2, page 534, Leipzig, 1893, inclines to the period between 390 and 430.

10 The *Kaiserchronik* is thought to date from about 1141, but to go back to still earlier sources. It is probably Bavarian in origin, being accredited to the Pfaffe Konrad. Many surviving manuscripts, as well as later additions made to the work, are evidence of its popularity.

into the *Legenda Aurea*[11] and its presence in this collection is in itself sufficient evidence of the fact that it must have been widely known throughout the 14th, 15th, and 16th centuries. The story as told in the *Legenda Aurea* is given below as representative of the medieval version of the legend.

I. Clementine Recognitions.[12]
Book II

Chapter 7. "This[13] Simon's father was Antonius, and his mother Rachel. By nation he is a Samaritan, from a village of the Gettones; by profession a magician, yet exceedingly well trained in the Greek literature; desirous of glory, and boasting above all the human race, so that he wishes himself to be believed to be an exalted power, which is above God the Creator, and to be thought to be the Christ, and to be called the *Standing One.* And he uses this name as implying that he can never be dissolved, asserting that his flesh is so compacted by the power of his divinity, that it can endure to eternity. Hence, therefore, he is called the *Standing One,* as though he cannot fall by any corruption.

Chapter 8. "For after that John the Baptist was killed, as you yourself also know, when Dositheus had broached his heresy, with thirty other chief disciples, and one woman, who was called *Luna*[14] — whence also these thirty appear to have been appointed with reference to the number of the days, according to the course

[11] The *Legenda Aurea* is a collection of saints' legends made by Jacobus de Voragine (ca. 1230–ca. 1298) Archbishop of Genoa. The collection became immensely popular. It was one of the earliest books to issue from the press and by 1500 no less than 74 Latin editions had been published. There were further numerous translations into English, French, German, Italian, Low German, Bohemian, etc.

[12] The passages cited are from the translation by Rev. Thomas Smith in the Ante-Nicene Christian Library, Vol. III, Edinburgh, 1871.

[13] Niceta and Aquila, formerly followers of Simon Magus and now disciples of Peter, are describing Simon Magus to Peter. Aquila is speaking.

[14] In the *Homilies,* this woman is called Helena.

of the moon — this Simon, ambitious of evil glory, as we have said, goes to Dositheus, and pretending friendship, entreats him, that if any one of those thirty should die, he should straightway substitute him in room of the dead : for it was contrary to their rule either to exceed the fixed number, or to admit any one who was unknown, or not yet proved ; whence also the rest, desiring to become worthy of the place and number, are eager in every way to please, according to the institutions of their sect, each one of those who aspire after admittance into the number, hoping that he may be deemed worthy to be put into the place of the deceased, when, as we have said, any one dies. Therefore Dositheus, being greatly urged by this man, introduced Simon when a vacancy occurred among the number.

Chapter 9. "But not long after he fell in love with that woman whom they call Luna ; and he confided all things to us as his friends : how he was a magician, and how he loved Luna, and how, being desirous of glory, he was unwilling to enjoy her ingloriously, but that he was waiting patiently till he could enjoy her honourably ; yet so if we also would conspire with him towards the accomplishment of his desires. And he promised that, as a reward of this service, he would cause us to be invested with the highest honours, and we should be believed by men to be gods ; 'Only, however, on condition,' says he, 'that you confer the chief place upon me, Simon, who by magic art am able to show many signs and prodigies, by means of which either my glory or our sect may be established. For I am able to render myself invisible to those who wish to lay hold of me, and again to be visible when I am willing to be seen. If I wish to flee, I can dig through the mountains, and pass through rocks as if they were clay. If I should throw myself headlong from a lofty mountain, I should be borne unhurt to the earth, as if I were held up ; when bound, I can loose myself, and bind those who had bound me ; being shut up in prison, I can make the barriers open of their own accord ; I can render statues animated, so that those who see suppose that they are men. I can make new trees suddenly spring up, and produce sprouts at once. I can throw myself into the fire, and not be burnt ; I can change my countenance, so that I cannot be recognized ; but I can show people that I have two faces. I shall change myself into a sheep or a goat ; I shall make a beard to grow upon little boys ; I shall ascend by flight into the air ; I shall exhibit abundance of gold, and shall make and unmake kings. I shall be worshipped as God ; I shall have divine honours publicly assigned to me, so that an image of me shall be set up, and I shall be worshipped and adored as God. And what need of more words ? Whatever I wish, that I shall be able to do. For already I have achieved many things by way of experiment. In short,' says he, 'once when my mother Rachel ordered me to go to the field to reap, and I saw a sickle lying, I ordered it to go and reap ; and it reaped ten times more than the others. Lately, I produced many new sprouts from the earth, and made them bear leaves and produce fruit in a moment ; and the nearest mountain I successfully bored through.'

Chapter 10. "But when he spoke thus of the production of sprouts and the perforation of the mountain, I was confounded on this account, because he wished to deceive even us, in whom he seemed to place confidence ; for we knew that those things had been from the days of our fathers, which he represented as having been done by himself lately. We then, although we heard these atrocities from him, and worse than these, yet we followed up his crimes, and suffered others to be deceived by him, telling also many lies on his behalf ; and this before he did any of the things which he had promised, so that while as yet he had done nothing, he was by some thought to be God.

Chapter 11. "Meantime, at the outset, as soon as he was reckoned among the thirty disciples of Dositheus, he began to depreciate Dositheus himself, saying that he did not teach purely or perfectly, and that this was the result not of ill intention, but of ignorance. But Dositheus, when he perceived that Simon was depreciating him, fearing lest his reputation among men might be obscured (for he himself was supposed to be the *Standing One*), moved with rage, when they met as usual at the school, seized a rod, and began to beat Simon; but suddenly the rod seemed to pass through his body, as if it had been smoke. On which Dositheus, being astonished, says to him, 'Tell me if thou art the *Standing One,* that I may adore thee.' And when Simon answered that he was, then Dositheus, perceiving that he himself was not the Standing One, fell down and worshipped him, and gave up his own place as chief to Simon, ordering all the rank of thirty men to obey him; himself taking the inferior place which Simon formerly occupied. Not long after this he died.

Chapter 12. "Therefore, after the death of Dositheus, Simon took Luna to himself; and with her he still goes about, as you see, deceiving multitudes, and asserting that he himself is a certain power which is above God the Creator, while Luna, who is with him, has been brought down from the higher heavens, and that she is Wisdom, the mother of all things, for whom, says he, the Greeks and barbarians contending, were able in some measure to see an image of her; but of herself, as she is, as the dweller with the first and only God, they were wholly ignorant. Propounding these and other things of the same sort, he has deceived many. But I ought also to state this, which I remember that I myself saw. Once, when this Luna of his was in a certain tower, a great multitude had assembled to see her, and were standing around the tower on all sides; but she was seen by all the people to lean forward, and to look out through all the windows of that tower. Many other wonderful things he did and does ; so that men, being astonished at them think that he himself is the great God.

Chapter 13. "Now when Niceta and I once asked him to explain to us how these things could be effected by magic art, and what was the nature of that thing, Simon began thus to explain it to us as his associates. 'I have,' said he, 'made the soul of a boy, unsullied and violently slain, and invoked by unutterable adjurations, to assist me ; and by it all is done that I command.' 'But,' said I, 'is it possible for a soul to do these things ?' He answered : 'I would have you know this, that the soul of man holds the next place after God, when once it is set free from the darkness of his body. And immediately it acquires prescience : wherefore it is invoked for necromancy.' Then I answered : 'Why, then, do not the souls of persons who are slain take vengeance on their slayers ?' 'Do you not remember,' said he, 'that I told you, that when it goes out of the body it acquires knowledge of the future ?' 'I remember,' said I. 'Well, then,' said he, 'as soon as it goes out of the body, it immediately knows that there is a judgment to come, and that every one shall suffer punishment for those evils that he hath done ; and therefore they are unwilling to take vengeance on their slayers, because they themselves are enduring torments for their own evil deeds which they had done here, and they know that severer punishments await them in the judgment. Moreover, they are not permitted by the angels who preside over them to go out, or to do anything.' 'Then,' I replied, 'if the angels do not permit them to come hither, or to do what they please, how can the souls obey the magician who invokes them ?' 'It is not,' said he, 'that they grant indulgence to the souls that are willing to come ; but when the presiding angels are adjured by one greater than themselves, they have the excuse of our violence who adjure them, to permit the souls which we invoke to go out: for they do not sin who suffer violence, but we who impose necessity upon them.' Thereupon Niceta, not able longer to refrain, hastily answered, as indeed I also was about to do, only I wished first to get information from him on several points; but, as I said, Niceta, anticipating me, said: 'And do you not fear the day of judgment, who do violence to angels, and invoke souls, and deceive men, and bargain for divine honour to yourself from men? And how do you persuade us that there shall be no judgment, as some of the Jews confess, and that souls are not immortal, as many suppose, though you see them with your very eyes, and receive from them assurance of the divine judgment.'

Chapter 14. "At those sayings of his Simon grew pale; but after a little, recollecting himself, he thus answered: 'Do not think that I am a man of your race. I am neither magician, nor lover of Luna, nor son of Antonius. For before my mother Rachel and he came together, she, still a virgin, conceived me, while it was in my power to be either small or great, and to appear as a man among men. Therefore I have chosen you first as my friends, for the purpose of trying you, that I may place you first in my heavenly and unspeakable places when I shall have proved you. Therefore I have pretended to be a man, that I might more clearly ascertain if you cherish entire affection towards me.' But when I heard that, judging him indeed to be a wretch, yet wondering at his impudence; and blushing for him, and at the same time fearing lest he should attempt some evil against us, I beckoned to Niceta to feign for a little along with me, and said to him: 'Be not angry with us, corruptible men, O thou incorruptible God, but rather accept our affection, and our mind willing to know who God is; for we did not till now know who thou art, nor did we perceive that thou art he whom we are seeking.'

Chapter 15. "As we spoke thus and such like words with looks suited to the occasion, this most vain fellow believed that we were deceived ; and being thereby the more elated, he added also this : 'I shall now be propitious to you, for the affection which you bear towards me as God ; for you loved me while you did not know me, and were seeking me in ignorance. But I would not have you doubt that this is truly to be God, when one is able to become small or great as he pleases ; for I am able to appear to man in whatever manner I please. Now, then, I shall begin to unfold to you what is true. Once on a time, I, by my power, turning air into water, and water again into blood and solidifying it into flesh, formed a new human creature—a boy—and produced a much nobler work than God the Creator. For He created a man from the earth, but I from air—a far more difficult matter ; and again I unmade him and restored him to air, but not until I had placed his picture and image in my bedchamber, as a proof and memorial of my work.' Then we understood that he spake concerning that boy whose soul, after he had been slain by violence, he made use of for those services which he required."

Book VII

Chapter 8. Then[15] said Peter : "Is there then no one of your family surviving ?" I answered : "There are indeed many powerful men, coming of the stock of Caesar ; for Caesar himself gave a wife to my father, as being his relative, and educated along with him, and of a suitably noble family. By her my father had twin sons, born before me, not very like one another, as my father told me ; for I never knew them. But indeed I have not a distinct recollection even of my mother ;

[15] Peter is talking to Clement.

but I cherish the remembrance of her face, as if I had seen it in a dream. My mother's name was Matthidia, my father's Faustinianus,[16] my brothers', Faustinus and Faustus. Now, when I was barely five years old, my mother saw a vision—so I learned from my father—by which she was warned that, unless she speedily left the city with her twin sons, and was absent for ten years, she and her children should perish by a miserable fate.

Chapter 9. "Then my father, who tenderly loved his sons, put them on board a ship with their mother, and sent them to Athens to be educated, with slaves and maid-servants, and a sufficient supply of money; retaining me only to be a comfort to him, and thankful for this, that the vision had not commanded me also to go with my mother. And at the end of a year my father sent men to Athens with money for them, desiring also to know how they did; but those who were sent never returned. Again, in the third year, my sorrowful father sent other men with money, who returned in the fourth year, and related that they had seen neither my mother nor my brothers, that they had never reached Athens, and that no trace had been found of any one of those who had been with them.

Chapter 10. "My father hearing this, and confounded with excessive sorrow, not knowing whither to go or where to seek, went down with me to the harbour, and began to ask of the sailors whether any of them had seen or heard of the bodies of a mother and two little children being cast ashore anywhere, four years ago; when one told one story and another another, but nothing definite was disclosed to us searching in this boundless sea. Yet my father, by reason of the great affection which he bore to his wife and children, was fed with vain hopes, until he thought of placing me under

[16] In the *Homilies*, the sons are named Faustinus and Faustinianus, and the name of the father is Faustus.

guardians and leaving me at Rome, as I was now twelve years old, and himself going in quest of them. Therefore he went down to the harbour weeping, and going on board a ship, took his departure; and from that time till now I have never received any letters from him, nor do I know whether he is alive or dead. But I rather suspect that he also has perished, either through a broken heart or by shipwreck: for twenty years have now elapsed since then, and no tidings of him have ever reached me."

[Peter and Clemens with a number of their friends, visit the island of Aradus to see certain works of art, particularly certain columns and paintings.]

Chapter 13. But when Peter had admired only the columns, being no wise ravished with the grace of the painting, he went out, and saw before the gates a poor woman asking alms of those who went in; and looking earnestly at her, he said: "Tell me, O woman, what member of your body is wanting, that you subject yourself to the indignity of asking alms, and do not rather gain your bread by labouring with your hands which God has given you." But she, sighing, said: "Would that I had hands which could be moved; but now only the appearance of hands has been preserved, for they are lifeless, and have been rendered feeble and without feeling by my gnawing of them." Then Peter said: "What has been the cause of your inflicting so great an injury upon yourself?" "Want of courage," said she, "and naught else; for if I had had any bravery in me, I could either have thrown myself from a precipice, or cast myself into the depths of the sea, and so ended my griefs."

Chapter 14. . . Then Peter: "What thing is it so great, that affects you with so heavy sadness? I should like to know. For if you informed me of the cause, I might be able both to show you clearly, O woman, that souls do live in the infernal regions; and instead of the precipice or the deep sea, I might give you some remedy, that you may be able to end your life without torment."

Chapter 15. Then the woman, hearing this welcome promise, began to say: "It is neither easy of belief, nor do I think it necessary to tell, what is my extraction, or what is my country. It is enough only to explain the cause of my grief, why I have rendered my hands powerless by gnawing them. Being born of noble parents, and having become the wife of a suitably powerful man, I had two twin sons, and after them one other. But my husband's brother was vehemently enflamed with unlawful love towards me; and as I valued chastity above all things, and would neither consent to so great wickedness, nor wished to disclose to my husband the baseness of his brother, I considered whether in any way I could escape unpolluted, and yet not set brother against brother, and so bring the whole race of a noble family into disgrace. I made up my mind, therefore, to leave my country with my two twins, until the incestuous love should subside, which the sight of me was fostering and enflaming; and I thought that our other son should remain to comfort his father to some extent.

Chapter 16. "Now in order to carry out this plan, I pretended that I had had a dream, in which some deity stood by me in a vision, and told me that I should immediately depart from the city with my twins, and should be absent until he should command me to return; and that, if I did not do so, I should perish with all my children. And so it was done. For as soon as I told the dream to my husband, he was terrified; and sending with me my twin sons, and also slaves and maid-servants, and giving me plenty of money, he ordered me to sail to Athens, where I might educate my sons, and that I should stay there, until he who had commanded me to depart should give me leave to return. While I was sailing along with my sons, I was shipwrecked in the night by the violence of the winds, and, wretch that I am, was driven to this place; and when all had perished, a powerful wave caught me, and cast me upon a rock. And while I sat there with this only hope, that haply I might be able to find my sons, I did not throw myself into the deep, although then my soul, disturbed and drunk with grief, had both the courage and power to do it.

Chapter 17. "But when the day dawned, and I with shouting and howling was looking around, if I could even see the corpses of my unhappy sons anywhere washed ashore, some of those who saw me were moved with compassion, and searched, first over the sea, and then also along the shores, if they could find either of my children. But when neither of them was anywhere found, the women of the place, taking pity on me, began to comfort me, every one telling her own griefs, that I might take consolation from the likeness of their calamities to my own. But this saddened me all the more; for my disposition was not such that I could regard the misfortunes of others as comforts to me. And when many desired to receive me hospitably, a certain poor woman who dwells here constrained me to enter into her hut, saying that she had had a husband who was a sailor, and that he had died at sea while a young man, and that, although many afterwards asked her in marriage, she preferred widowhood through love of her husband. 'Therefore,' said she, 'we shall share whatever we can gain by the labour of ours hands.'

Chapter 18. "And, not to detain you with a long and profitless story, I willingly dwelt with her on account of the faithful affection which she retained for her husband. But not long after, my hands (unhappy woman that I was!), long torn with gnawing, became powerless, and she who had taken me in fell into palsy, and now lies at home in her bed; also the affection of those women who had formerly pitied me grew cold. We are both helpless. I, as you see, sit begging; and when I get anything, one meal serves two wretches. Behold, now you have heard enough of my affairs; why do you delay the fulfilment of your promise, to give me a remedy, by which both of us may end our miserable life without torment?"

Chapter 19. While she was speaking, Peter, being distracted with much thought, stood like one thunder-struck; and I Clement coming up, said: "I have been seeking you everywhere, and now what are we to do?" But he commanded me to go before him to the ship, and there to wait for him; and because he must not be gainsayed, I did as he commanded me. But he, as he afterwards told me the whole, being struck with a sort of suspicion, asked of the woman her family, and her country, and the names of her sons; "and straightway," he said, "if you tell me these things, I shall give you the remedy." But she, like one suffering violence, because she would not confess these things, and yet was desirous of the remedy, feigned one thing after another, saying that she was an Ephesian, and her husband a Sicilian, and giving false names to her sons. Then Peter, supposing that she had answered truly, said: "Alas! O woman, I thought that some great joy should spring up to us today; for I suspected that you were a certain woman, concerning whom I lately learned certain like things." But she adjured him, saying: "I entreat you to tell me what they are, that I may know if amongst women there be one more unfortunate than myself."

Chapter 20. Then Peter, incapable of deception, and moved with compassion, began to say: "There is a certain young man among those who follow me for the sake of religion and sect, a Roman citizen, who told me that he had a father and two twin brothers, of whom not one is left to him. 'My mother,' he said, 'as I learned from my father, saw a vision, that she should depart from the Roman city for a time with her twin sons, else they should perish by a dreadful death ; and when she had departed, she was never more seen.' And afterwards his father set out to search for his wife and sons, and was also lost."

Chapter 21. When Peter had thus spoken, the woman, struck with astonishment, fainted. Then Peter began to hold her up, and to comfort her, and to ask what was the matter, or what she suffered. But she at length, with difficulty recovering her breath, and nerving herself up to the greatness of the joy which she hoped for, and at the same time wiping her face, said : "Is he here, the youth of whom you speak ?" But Peter, when he understood the matter, said : "Tell me first, or else you shall not see him." Then she said : "I am the mother of the youth." Then says Peter : "What is his name ?" And she answered : "Clement." Then said Peter : "It is himself ; and he it was that spoke with me a little while ago, and whom I ordered to go before me to the ship." Then she fell down at Peter's feet, and began to entreat him that he would hasten to the ship. Then Peter said : "Yes, if you will promise me that you will do as I say." Then she said : "I will do anything ; only show me my only son, for I think that in him I shall see my twins also." Then Peter said : "When you have seen him, dissemble for a little time, until we leave the island." "I will do so," she said.

Chapter 22. Then Peter, holding her hand, led her to the ship. And when I saw him giving his hand to the woman, I began to laugh ; yet, approaching to do him honour, I tried to substitute my hand for his, and to support the woman. But as soon as I touched her hand, she uttered a loud scream, and rushed into my embrace, and began to devour me with a mother's kisses. But I, being ignorant of the whole matter, pushed her off as a mad woman ; and at the same time, though with reverence, I was somewhat angry with Peter.

Chapter 23. But he said : "Cease : what mean you, O Clement, my son ? Do not push away your mother." But I, as soon as I heard these words, immediately bathed in tears, fell upon my mother, who had fallen down, and began to kiss her. For as soon as I heard, by degrees I recalled her countenance to my memory ; and the longer I gazed, the more familiar it grew to me. . .

[The excursionists then returned to Antaradus, where the rest of the party had been staying, among them Niceta and Aquila, and there Peter gave an account of what had happened.]

Chapter 28. And when Peter said this, Niceta and Aquila suddenly started up, and being astonished, began to be greatly agitated, saying : "O Lord, Thou Ruler and God of all, are these things true, or are we in a dream ?" Then Peter said : "Unless we be mad, these things are true." But they, after a short pause, and wiping their faces, said : "We are Faustinus and Faustus : and even at the first, when you began this narrative, we immediately fell into a suspicion that the matters that you spoke of might perhaps relate to us ; yet again considering that many like things happen in men's lives, we kept silence, although our hearts were struck by some hope. Therefore we waited for the end of your story, that, if it were entirely manifest that it related to us, we might then confess it." And when they had thus spoken, they went in weeping to our mother. . .

[There is introduced into the story "a certain poor old man, a workman," with whom Peter, Clement and his brothers have a long argument on doctrinal matters, for the old man is not a Christian. The discussion ends as follows :]

Book IX

Chapter 32. . . Then said the old man: "You have most fully argued, my son; but I, as I said at the first, am prevented by my own consciousness from according assent to all this incomparable statement of yours. For I know both my own *genesis* and that of my wife, and I know that those things have happened which our *genesis* prescribed to each of us; and I cannot now be withdrawn by words from those things which I have ascertained by facts and deeds. In short, since I perceive that you are excellently skilled in this sort of learning, hear the horoscope of my wife, and you shall find the configuration whose issue has occurred. For she had Mars with Venus above the centre, and the Moon setting in the houses of Mars and the confines of Saturn. Now this configuration leads women to be adulteresses, and to love their own slaves, and to end their days in foreign travel and in waters. And this has so come to pass. For she fell in love with her slave, and fearing at once danger and reproach, she fled with him, and going abroad, where she satisfied her love, she perished in the sea."

Chapter 33. Then I answered: "How know you that she cohabited with her slave abroad, and died in his society?" Then the old man said: "I know it with perfect certainty; not indeed that she was married to the slave, as indeed I had not even discovered that she loved him. But after she was gone, my brother gave me the whole story, telling me that first she had loved himself; but he, being honourable as a brother, would not pollute his brother's bed with the stain of incest. But she, being both afraid of me, and unable to bear the unhappy reproaches (and yet she should not be blamed for that to which her *genesis* compelled her), pretended a dream, and said to me: 'Some one stood by me in a vision, who ordered me to leave this city without delay with my two twins.' When I heard this, being anxious for her safety and that of my sons, I immediately sent away her and the children, retaining with myself one who was younger. For this she said that he had permitted who had given her warning in her sleep."

[As a result of the above speech the old man is recognized as Faustinianus and the whole family is reunited. After a long series of chapters dealing with doctrinal discussions, there is related the following episode.]

Book X

Chapter 53. . . and when it was daybreak, Peter, looking at me and my brothers, said: "I wonder what has befallen your father." And while he was speaking, my father came in, and found Peter speaking to us about him. And when he had saluted he began to apologize, and to explain the reason why he had remained abroad. But we, looking at him, were horrified; for we saw on him the face of Simon, yet we heard the voice of our father. And when we shrank from him, and cursed him, my father was astonished at our treating him so harshly and barbarously. Yet Peter was the only one who saw his natural countenance; and he said to us: "Why do you curse your father?" And we, along with our mother, answered him: "He appears to us to be Simon, though he has our father's voice." Then Peter: "You indeed know only his voice, which has not been changed by the sorceries; but to me also his face, which to others appears changed by Simon's art, is known to be that of your father Faustinianus." And looking at my father, he said: "The cause of the dismay of your wife and sons is this,—the appearance of your countenance does not seem to be as it was, but the face of the detestable Simon appears in you."

Chapter 58. Then, turning to my father he said:

"I gave you leave to salute Appion and Anubion, who, you said, were your friends from boyhood, but not that you should speak with Simon." Then my father said: "I confess I have sinned." Then said Anubion: "I also with him beg and entreat of you to pardon the old man—good and noble man as he is. He was unhappily seduced and imposed upon by the magician in question; for I will tell you how the thing was done. When he came to salute us, it happened that at that very time we were standing around him [i.e. Simon], hearing him tell that he intended to flee away that night, for that he had heard that some persons had come even to this city of Laodicea to apprehend him by command of the emperor, but that he wished to turn all their rage against this Faustinianus, who has lately come hither. And he said to us: 'Only you make him sup with us, and I shall compound a certain ointment, with which, when he has supped, he shall anoint his face, and from that time he shall seem to all to have my countenance. But you first anoint your faces with the juice of a certain herb, that you may not be deceived as to the change of his countenance, so that to all except you he shall seem to be Simon.'

Chapter 59. "And when he said this, I said to him: 'And what advantage will you gain from this deed?' Then Simon said: 'In the first place, that those who are seeking me may lay hold on him, and so give over the search for me. But if he be punished by Caesar, that his sons may have much sorrow, who forsook me, and fled to Peter, and are now his assistants.' Now I confess to you, Peter, what is true. I did not dare then tell Faustinianus; but neither did Simon give us opportunity of speaking with him in private, and disclosing to him fully Simon's design. Meantime, about the middle of the night, Simon has fled away, making for Judaea...

[How Peter turns the trick against Simon by causing

Faustinianus, in the form of Simon, to recant the attacks the magician had made against Peter, is interesting but of no importance from the point of view of the Simon legend.]

II. Acts of the Holy Apostles Peter and Paul.[17]

When, consequently, the people[18] were making a seditious murmuring, Simon, moved with zeal, rouses himself, and began to say many evil things about Peter, saying that he was a wizard and a cheat. And they believed him, wondering at his miracles; for he made a brazen serpent move itself, and stone statues to laugh and move themselves, and himself to run and suddenly to be raised into the air. But as a set-off to these, Peter healed the sick by a word, by praying made the blind to see, put demons to flight by a command; sometimes he even raised the dead. And he said to the people that they should not only flee from Simon's deceit, but also that they should expose him, that they might not seem to be slaves to the devil.

And thus it happened that all pious men abhorred Simon the magian, and proclaimed him impious. But those who adhered to Simon strongly affirmed Peter to be a magian, bearing false witness as many of them as were with Simon the magian; so that the matter came even to the ears of Nero the Caesar, and he gave order to bring Simon the magian before him. And he, coming in, stood before him, and began suddenly to assume different forms, so that on a sudden he became a child, and after a little an old man, and at other times a young man; for he changed himself both in face and stature into different forms, and was in a frenzy, having the devil as his servant.

* * *

17 The citations are from the translation by Walker in the Ante-Nicene Christian Library, Vol. XVI, Edinburgh, 1873.

18 All the events quoted from the *Acts of the Holy Apostles Peter and Paul* take place in Rome.

Then Simon, having gone in to Nero, said: Hear, O good emperor: I am the son of God come down from heaven. Until now I have endured Peter only calling himself an apostle; but now he has doubled the evil: for Paul also himself teaches the same things, and having his mind turned against me, is said to preach along with him; in reference to whom, if thou shalt not contrive their destruction, it is very plain that thy kingdom cannot stand.

* * *

Simon said: I wonder, O good emperor, that you reckon this man of any consequence—a man uneducated, a fisherman of the poorest, and endowed with power neither in word nor by rank. But, that I may not long endure him as an enemy, I shall forthwith order my angels to come and avenge me upon him. Peter said: I am not afraid of thy angels; but they shall be much more afraid of me in the power and trust of my Lord Jesus Christ, whom thou falsely declarest thyself to be.

Nero said: Art thou not afraid, Peter, of Simon, who confirms his godhead by deeds? Peter said: Godhead is in Him who searcheth the hidden things of the heart. Now then, tell me what I am thinking about, or what I am doing. I disclose to thy servants who are here what my thought is, before he tells lies about it, in order that he may not dare to lie as to what I am thinking about. Nero said: Come hither, and tell me what thou art thinking about. Peter said: Order a barley loaf to be brought, and to be given to me secretly. And when he ordered it to be brought, and secretly given to Peter, Peter said: Now tell us, Simon, what has been thought about, or what said, or what done.

Nero said: Do you mean me to believe that Simon does not know these things, who both raised a dead man, and presented himself on the third day after he had been beheaded, and who has done whatever he said he would do? Peter said: But he did not do it before me. Nero said: But he did all these before me. For assuredly he ordered angels to come to him, and they came. Peter said: If he has done what is very great, why does he not do what is very small? Let him tell what I had in my mind, and what I have done. Nero said: Between you, I do not know myself. Simon said: Let Peter say what I am thinking of, or what I am doing. Peter said: What Simon has in his mind I shall show that I know, by my doing what he is thinking about. Simon said: Know this, O emperor, that no one knows the thoughts of men, but God alone. Is not, therefore, Peter lying? Peter said: Do thou, then, who sayest that thou art the Son of God, tell what I have in my mind; disclose, if thou canst, what I have just done in secret. For Peter, having blessed the barley loaf which he had received, and having broken it with his right hand and his left, had heaped it up in his sleeves. Then Simon, enraged that he was not able to tell the secret of the apostle, cried out, saying: Let great dogs come forth and eat him up before Caesar. And suddenly there appeared great dogs, and rushed at Peter. But Peter, stretching forth his hands to pray, showed to the dogs the loaf which he had blessed; which the dogs seeing, no longer appeared. Then Peter said to Nero: Behold, I have shown thee that I knew what Simon was thinking of, not by words, but by deeds; for he, having promised that he would bring angels against me, has brought dogs, in order that he might show that he had not god-like but dog-like angels.

* * *

Simon said: Dost thou believe, O good emperor, that I who was dead, and rose again, am a magician?

For it had been brought about by his own cleverness that the unbelieving Simon had said to Nero : Order me to be beheaded in a dark place, and there to be left slain ; and if I do not rise on the third day, know that I am a magician ; but if I rise again, know that I am the Son of God.

And Nero having ordered this, in the dark, by his magic art he managed that a ram should be beheaded. And for so long did the ram appear to be Simon until he was beheaded. And when he had been beheaded in the dark, he that had beheaded him, taking the head, found it to be that of a ram ; but he would not say anything to the emperor, lest he should scourge him, having ordered this to be done in secret. Thereafter, accordingly, Simon said that he had risen on the third day, because he took away the head of the ram and the limbs—but the blood had been there congealed—and on the third day he showed himself to Nero, and said : Cause to be wiped away my blood that has been poured out ; for, behold, having been beheaded, as I promised, I have risen again on the third day.

* * *

Simon said : Listen, O Caesar Nero, that thou mayst know that these men are liars, and that I have been sent from the heavens : tomorrow I go up into the heavens, that I may make those who believe in me blessed, and show my wrath upon those who have denied me.

* * *

Then Nero ordered a lofty tower to be made in the Campus Martius, and all the people and the dignities to be present at the spectacle. And on the following day, all the multitude having come together, Nero ordered Peter and Paul to be present, to whom also he said : Now the truth has to be made manifest.

Peter and Paul said: We do not expose him, but our Lord Jesus Christ, the Son of God, whom he has falsely declared himself to be.

And Paul, having turned to Peter, said: It is my part to bend the knee, and to pray to God; and thine to produce the effect, if thou shouldst see him attempting anything, because thou wast first taken in hand by the Lord. And Paul, bending his knees, prayed. And Peter, looking stedfastly upon Simon, said: Accomplish what thou hast begun; for both thy exposure and our call is at hand: for I see my Christ calling both me and Paul. Nero said: And where will you go to against my will? Peter said: Whithersoever our Lord has called us. Nero said: And who is your lord? Peter said: Jesus the Christ, whom I see calling us to Himself. Nero said: Do you also then intend to go away to heaven? Peter said: If it shall seem good to Him that calls us. Simon said: In order that thou mayst know, O emperor, that these are deceivers, as soon as ever I ascend into heaven, I will send my angels to thee, and will make thee come to me. Nero said: Do at once what thou sayest.

Then Simon went up upon the tower in the face of all, and, crowned with laurels, he stretched forth his hands, and began to fly. And when Nero saw him flying, he said to Peter: This Simon is true; but thou and Paul are deceivers. To whom Peter said: Immediately shalt thou know that we are true disciples of Christ; but that he is not Christ, but a magician, and a malefactor. Nero said: Do you still persist? Behold, you see him going up into heaven. Then Peter, looking stedfastly upon Paul, said: Paul, look up and see. And Paul, having looked up, full of tears, and seeing Simon flying, said: Peter, why art thou idle? finish what thou hast begun; for already our Lord Jesus Christ is calling us. And Nero hearing them, smiled a little and said: These men see themselves worsted already, and are gone mad. Peter said : Now thou shalt know that we are not mad. Paul said to Peter : Do at once what thou doest.

And Peter, looking stedfastly against Simon, said : I adjure you, ye angels of Satan, who are carrying him into the air, to deceive the hearts of the unbelievers, by the God that created all things, and by Jesus Christ, whom on the third day He raised from the dead, no longer from this hour to keep him up, but to let him go. And immediately, being let go, he fell into a place called Sacra Via, that is, Holy Way, and was divided into four parts, having perished by an evil fate.

III. The Teaching of Simon Cephas in the City of Rome.[19]

...And immediately they sent and fetched Simon the sorcerer ; and the men who were adherents of his opinion said to him : As a man concerning whom we have confidence that there is power in thee to do anything whatsoever, do thou some sign before us all, and let this Simon the Galilaean, who preaches Christ, see [it]. And, whilst they were thus speaking to him, there happened to be passing along a dead person, a son of one of those who were chiefs and men of note and renown among them. And all of them, as they were assembled together, said to him : Whichever of you shall restore to life this dead person, he is true, and to be believed in and received, and we will all follow him in whatsoever he saith to us. And they said to Simon the sorcerer : Because thou wast here before Simon the Galilaean, and we knew thee before him, exhibit thou first the power which accompanieth thee.

Then Simon reluctantly drew near to the dead person ; and they set down the bier before him ; and he

[19] The citation is from the translation by Pratten in the Ante-Nicene Christian Library, Vol. XX, Edinburgh, 1871.

looked to the right hand and to the left, and gazed up into heaven, saying many words: some of them he uttered aloud, and some of them secretly and not aloud. And he delayed a long while, and nothing took place, and nothing was done, and the dead person was [still] lying upon his bier.

And forthwith Simon Cephas drew near boldly towards the dead man, and cried aloud before all the assembly which was standing there: In the name of Jesus Christ, whom the Jews crucified at Jerusalem, and whom we preach, rise up thence. And as soon as the word of Simon was spoken the dead man came to life and rose up from the bier.

IV. Legenda Aurea.[20] Life of S. Peter the Apostle.

That time Simon the enchanter was in Jerusalem, and he said he was first truth, and affirmed that who that would believe in him he would make them perpetual. And he also said that nothing to him was impossible. It is read in the book of S. Clement that he said that he should be worshipped of all men as God, and that he might do all that he would. And he said yet more: When my mother Rachel commanded me that I should go reap corn in the field, and saw the sickle ready to reap with, I commanded the sickle to reap by itself alone, and it reaped ten times more than any other. And yet he added hereto more, after Jerome, and said: I am the Word of God, I am the Holy Ghost, I am Almighty, I am all that is of God. He made serpents of brass to move, and made images of iron and of stone to laugh, and dogs to sing, and as S. Linus saith, he would dispute with S. Peter and show, at a day assigned, that he was God. And

20 The text is taken from *The Golden Legend or Lives of the Saints as Englished by William Caxton.* J. M. Dent and Company, London, 1900. IV, 14-20. Caxton's translation was completed in 1483.

Peter came to the place where the strife should be, and said to them that were there : Peace to you brethren that love truth. To whom Simon said : We have none need of thy peace, for if peace and concord were made, we should not profit to find the truth, for thieves have peace among them. And therefore desire no peace but battle, for when two men fight and one is overcome then is it peace. Then said Peter : Why dreadest thou to hear of peace? Of sins grow battles, where is no sin there is peace ; in disputing is truth found, and in works righteousness. Then said Simon : It is not as thou sayest, but I shall show to thee the power of my dignity, that anon thou shalt adore me ; I am first truth, and may flee by the air ; I can make new trees and turn stones into bread ; endure in the fire without hurting ; and all that I will I may do. S. Peter disputed against all these, and disclosed all his malefices. Then Simon Magus, seeing that he might not resist Peter, cast all his books into the sea, lest S. Peter should prove him a magician, by his books, and went to Rome where he was had and reputed as a god. And when Peter knew that, he followed and came to Rome. The fourth year of Claudius the emperor, Peter came to Rome, and sat there twenty-five years, and ordained two bishops as his helpers, Linus and Cletus, one within the walls, and that other without. He entended much to preaching of the Word of God, by which he converted much people to the faith of Christ, and healed many sick men, and in his preaching always he praised and preferred chastity. He converted four concubines of Agrippa the provost, so that they would no more come to him, wherefore the provost sought occasion against Peter.

After this, our Lord appeared to S. Peter, saying to him : Simon Magus and Nero purpose against thee, dread thee not, for I am with thee, and shall give to thee the solace of my servant Paul, which to-morn shall come in to Rome. Then Peter, knowing that he should not long abide here, assembled all his brethren, and took Clement by the hand and ordained him a bishop, and made him to sit in his own seat. After this, as our Lord had said tofore, Paul came to Rome, and with Peter began to preach the faith of Christ.

Simon Magus was so much beloved of Nero that he weened that he had been the keeper of his life, of his health, and of all the city. On a day, as Leo the pope saith, as he stood tofore Nero, suddenly his visage changed, now old and now young, which, when Nero saw, he supposed that he had been the son of God. Then said Simon Magus to Nero : Because that thou shalt know me to be the very son of God, command my head to be smitten off and I shall rise again the third day. Then Nero commanded to his brother to smite off his head, and when he supposed to have beheaded Simon, he beheaded a ram. Simon, by his art magic went away unhurt, and gathered together the members of the ram, and hid him three days. The blood of the ram abode and congealed. The third day he came and showed him to Nero, saying : Command my blood to be washed away, for lo I am he that was beheaded, and as I promised I have risen again the third day. Whom Nero seeing, was abashed and trowed verily that he had been the son of God. All this saith Leo. Sometime also, when he was with Nero secretly within his conclave, the devil in his likeness spake without to the people. Then the Romans had him in such worship that they made to him an image, and wrote above, this title : To Simon the holy God. Peter and Paul entered to Nero and discovered all the enchantments and malefices of Simon Magus, and Peter added thereto, seeing that like as in Christ be two substances that is of God and man, so are in this magician two substances, that is of man and of the devil. Then said Simon Magus, as S. Marcelle and Leo witness, lest I should suffer any longer this enemy, I shall command my angels that they shall avenge me on him. To whom Peter said : I dread nothing thine angels, but they dread me. Nero said : Dreadest thou not Simon, that by certain things affirmeth his godhead? To whom Peter said : If dignity or godhead be in him let him tell now what I think or what I do, which thought I shall first tell to thee, that he shall not now lie what I think. To whom Nero said : Come hither and say what thou thinkest. Then Peter went to him and said to him secretly : Command some man to bring to me a barley-loaf, and deliver it to me privily. When it was taken to him, he blessed it, and hid it under his sleeve, and then said he : Now Simon say what I think, and have said and done. Simon answered : Let Peter say what I think. Peter answered : What Simon thinketh that I know, I shall do it when he hath thought. Then Simon having indignation, cried aloud : I command that dogs come and devour him. And suddenly there appeared great dogs and made an assault against Peter. He gave to them of the bread that he had blessed, and suddenly he made them to flee. Then said Peter to Nero : Lo! I have showed you what he thought against me, not in words but in deeds, for where he promised angels to come against me he brought dogs, thereby he showeth that he hath none angels but dogs. Then said Simon : Hear ye, Peter and Paul ; if I may not grieve you here, ye shall come where me it shall behoove to judge you. I shall spare you here. Haec Leo. Then Simon Magus, as Hegesippus and Linus say, elate in pride, avaunted him that he can raise dead men to life. And it happed that there was a young man dead, and then Nero let call Peter and Simon, and all gave sentence by the will of Simon that he should be slain that might not arise the dead man to life. Simon then, as he made his incantations upon the dead body, he was seen move his head of them that stood by; then all they cried for to stone Peter. Peter unnethe getting silence said: If the dead body live, let him arise, walk and speak, else know ye that it is a fantasy that the head of the dead man moveth. Let Simon be taken from the bed. And the body abode immovable. Peter standing afar making his prayer cried to the dead body, saying: Young man, arise in the name of Jesu Christ of Nazareth crucified, and anon, he arose living, and walked. Then, when the people would have stoned Simon Magus, Peter said: He is in pain enough, knowing him to be overcome in his heart; our master hath taught us for to do good for evil. Then said Simon to Peter and Paul: Yet is it not come to you that ye desire, for ye be not worthy to have martyrdom, the which answered: That is, that we desire to have, to thee shall never be well, for thou liest all that thou sayest.

Then as Marcel saith: Simon went to the house of Marcel and bound there a great black dog at the door of the house, and said: Now I shall see if Peter, which is accustomed to come hither, shall come, and if he come this dog shall strangle him. And a little after that, Peter and Paul went thither, and anon Peter made the sign of the cross and unbound the hound, and the hound was as tame and meek as a lamb, and pursued none but Simon, and went to him and took and cast him to the ground under him, and would have strangled him. And then ran Peter to him and cried upon the hound that he should not do him any harm. And anon the hound left and touched not his body, but he all torent and tare his gown in such wise that he was almost naked. Then all the people, and especially children, ran with the hound upon him and hunted and chased him out of the town as he had been a wolf. Then for the reproof and shame he durst not come in to the town of all a whole year after. Then Marcel that was disciple of Simon Magus, seeing these great miracles, came to Peter, and was from then forthon his disciple.

And after, at the end of the year, Simon returned and was received again into the amity of Nero. And then, as Leo saith, this Simon Magus assembled the people and showed to them how he had been angered of the Galileans, and therefore he said that he would leave the city which he was wont to defend and keep, and set a day in which he would ascend into heaven, for he deigned no more to dwell in the earth. Then on the day that he had stablished, like as he had said, he went up to an high tower, which was on the capitol, and there being crowned with laurel, threw himself out from place to place, and began to fly in the air. Then said S. Paul to S. Peter: It appertaineth to me to pray, and to thee for to command. Then said Nero: This man is very God, and ye be two traitors. Then said S. Peter to S. Paul: Paul, brother, lift up thine head and see how Simon flyeth. Then S. Paul said to S. Peter when he saw him fly so high: Peter, why tarriest thou? Perform that thou hast begun, God now calleth us. Then said Peter: I charge and conjure you angels of Sathanas, which bear him in the air, by the name of our Lord Jesu Christ, that ye bear ne sustain him no more, but let him fall to the earth. And anon they let him fall to the ground and brake his neck and head, and he died there forthwith.

[The account of the family history of Clement, viz., the dispersion and reuniting of the family, and the transformation of Faustinianus into the likeness of Simon, is likewise recounted in the *Legenda Aurea* under the life of S. Clement.[21] With the exception that the mother's name is here given as Macidiana, the

[21] Cf. Vol. VI, 254-264 in the edition cited in note 20.

facts are related as cited above from the *Clementine Recognitions.*]

Cyprian of Antioch

The legend of Saint Cyprian of Antioch and Saint Justina arose during the fourth century.[1] The first mention of the story in an historical source is in an eulogy of Cyprian of Carthage[2] delivered by Gregory of Nazianzus[3] in Constantinople sometime in September 379 A.D. The Spanish poet Prudentius[4] also mentions the legend in a hymn to Cyprian of Carthage about 400 A.D. Both Gregory and Prudentius confuse the historical Cyprian of Carthage with the legendary magus of Antioch, a confusion which is passed on to later writers.

Cyprian of Antioch was not a bishop of Antioch nor is a Justina of Antioch known to history. The story is probably pure invention although traces of older tales are to be found in it, particularly the so-called *Acta Pauli et Theclae.*[5] The legend has come down

[1] For a detailed study of the literature and development of the legend, see :
Zahn, *Cyprian von Antiochien and die deutsche Faustsage,* Erlangen, 1882.
Reitzenstein, *Cyprian der Magier.* Nachrichten von der K. Gesellschaft der Wissenschaften zu Göttingen, Phil.-hist. Kl. 1917.
Delehaye, *Analecta Bollandiana,* XXXIX. 1921.
Radermacher, *Griechische Quellen zur Faustsage.* Sitzungsberichte der Akademie der Wissenschaften in Wien. Phil.-hist. Kl., Bd. 206, Abhandlung 4. 1927.
Zahn reprints the Greek text of the *Conversio* and German translations of the *Conversio, Confessio,* and the *Martyrium.* Radermacher prints three Greek variants of the *Conversio* with a German translation.

[2] Cyprian of Carthage (200–258). Born at Carthage where he became a teacher of rhetoric. In 246 he was baptized and became Bishop of Carthage in 248 ; beheaded as Christian martyr in 258. He was an important figure in the early development of the church.

[3] Gregory of Nazianzus (ca. 330–390). Greek church father, coadjutor to his father as Bishop of Nazianzus in Cappadocia and later Bishop of Constantinople. Poet, orator and letter writer.

[4] Aurelius Clemens Prudentius. Born 348 in Spain and lived into the beginning of the 5th century. The most important earlier Christian poet.

[5] These *Acta* originally formed a part of the apocryphal *Acta Pauli.* Their author is unknown but they are thought to go back to the 2nd century (cf. Harnack, *Gesch. d. altchristlichen Literatur,* I, 1, page 136 f. ; II, 2, page 314). A translation will be found in the Ante-Nicene Christian Library, XVI, 279.

to us in three Greek versions: *The Conversion of St. Justina and St. Cyprian, The Confession of Saint Cyprian,* and *The Martyrdom of Saint Cyprian and Saint Justina.* According to Radermacher, Reitzenstein and Delehaye the *Conversion* is the oldest form of the legend. Zahn on the contrary believes that the *Confession* is the oldest form and assumes an introduction, corresponding to the *Conversion,* which he thinks has been lost. It has seemed to us that the *Conversion* offers the best version of the story and we have accordingly selected this version for translation.

The popularity of the legend is clear from the many subsequent versions and the many references in the later centuries. Eudocia (A.D. 393–460), wife of the emperor Theodosius the Younger, wrote a poem on the subject, parts of which have been preserved. Simon Metaphrastes[6] gives a combination of the three versions which furnishes a basis for some of the later Latin forms. The *Legenda Aurea* likewise presents a combination of the three original stories together with some additional material. Calderon's[7] drama, *El Magico Prodigioso,* bases its plot upon the version given in the *Legenda Aurea.*

I. Conversion of St. Justina and St. Cyprian.[8]

When our Saviour, Jesus Christ appeared on earth from heaven and the words of the prophets were fulfilled, the whole world was enlightened with the word

[6] Simon Metaphrastes compiled in the second half of the 10th century a collection of saints' legends in Greek. He did for the Byzantine Church much the same that Jacobus de Voragine in his *Legenda Aurea* did for the western Church.

[7] Pedro Calderon de la Barca (1600–1681), Spanish dramatist.

[8] The translation is from the first of the Greek texts published by Radermacher (op. cit.) who gives three variants of the work. This first variant is from the Ms. Paris 1468.

The title actually given in the Radermacher text is *Confession of the Holy Virgin Justina.* However, the document generally carries the title given above.

and, believing in God, the Father Almighty, and in our Lord Jesus Christ, was baptized in the Holy Ghost. Now there was in the city of Antioch near Daphne a maiden named Justina,[9] the daughter of Aidesios and Kledonia. From her nearby window she heard from Praylios, a deacon, of the mighty works of God, of the incarnation of our Lord Jesus Christ, of the prediction of the prophets, of the birth from Mary, of the adoration of the magi and of the appearance of the stars, of the glory of the angels and of His signs and wonders, ———[10] of the power of the cross, of the resurrection from the dead and of the testament to the disciples, of the ascension into heaven and of His resting there, of the seat at the right hand and of the unending kingdom. Seeing and hearing these things from the deacon through the window, the holy virgin could no longer withstand the ardent urging of the Holy Ghost but desired to appear before the deacon face to face, and as she could not, she said to her mother: "Mother, hearken to me, thy daughter. The idols that we worship day by day, which are put together of stones and bits of wood, gold and silver and bones of dead animals, are as nothing. One of the Galileans, if he come upon them, will overcome them all with the word through prayer, without raising a hand." Her mother, engulfed in the subtleties of philosophy, replied: "Let not thy father know of this thought." Justina answered: "Be it known to thee, mother, and to my father, that I seek the Christ whom I learned to know through Praylios, our neighbor, hearing about Him for many days. There is no other god in whom one shall be saved." And having said these things she went away to offer her prayers to Christ by herself.

[9] The name should probably be Justa, as one of the other variants gives it. Compare Chap. 12 of the translation.

[10] There is here a lacuna in the Greek text.

2. Her mother, in bed, told all these things to Aidesios. And when they had lain awake for a long time ———— [11] and when the host (of angels) [12] had now approached, Aidesios sees more than a hundred torchbearers in the fortress and, in their midst, Christ who said to them: "Come unto me and I will give you the Kingdom of Heaven." Aidesios, having seen these things and being astounded at what he had seen, arose at dawn and took his wife and the maiden and went with Praylios into the house of the Lord. And they demanded of him that he bring them to the bishop Optatus. The deacon announced them, and having fallen at the feet of the bishop, they demanded to receive the seal of Christ. But he hesitated until Aidesios told him of his vision of Christ and of the yearning of the maiden for Christ. Aidesios, however, cut off the hair of his head and beard; for he was a priest of the idols. And when he had fallen at the feet of the bishop, the three received the seal of Christ. And then Aidesios, after he had been deemed worthy of the office of a presbyter for a year and six months, departed in Christ.

3. And the holy virgin Justina went without ceasing into the house of the Lord. But a certain learned man, Aglaidas, of noble family and great wealth, an offense in his manner of living and carried away with the error of idolatry, saw the holy maiden going frequently into the house of the Lord, and having fallen in love with her, made advances to her through many women and men, seeking her in marriage. But she dismissed them all in disdain, saying: "I am betrothed to Christ." But the sophist collected a band and lay in wait for her as she went into the house of the Lord, wishing to gain her by force. Her companions

[11] Again a lacuna in the Greek text.

[12] Throughout the translation, the words given in parentheses are not found in the Greek text here used and are supplied from the second variant as given by Radermacher.

cried out and those of her household heard it and, coming out sword in hand, made them disappear. But Aglaidas grasped the maiden in his arms and held her fast. The maiden, however, made the sign of the cross and threw him violently on his back to the earth. And with her fist she beat his ribs and face black and blue, tore his garments and sent him away conquered. And having done these things, like unto her model, Thekla, she proceeded into the house of the Lord.

4. Aglaidas, enraged, went to Cyprian the magician[13] and agreed to pay him two talents of gold as if the latter were able by his magic to capture the holy virgin — not knowing, poor wretch, that the power of Christ is insuperable. But Cyprian with his magic arts summoned a demon. The demon came and said: "Why hast thou summoned me?" Cyprian replied: "I love a maid of the Galileans. Tell me whether thou art able to procure her for me." The wretched demon gave his promise as though he had what he did not have. Cyprian says: "Tell me of thy deeds that I may have confidence in thee." The demon says: "I became an apostate from God in obedience to my father; I threw the heavens into confusion; I cast down angels from on high; I deceived Eve; I deprived Adam of the delights of Paradise; I taught Cain to murder his brother; I stained the earth with blood; I caused thorns and thistles to grow; I assembled theatres; I caused adulteries; I brought together processions; I caused idolatry; I taught the people[14] to make a calf; I prompted the crucifixion of Christ; I made cities to tremble; I tore down walls; I divided houses. Hav-

[13] In the *Confession of Saint Cyprian*, Cyprian gives a quite lengthy account of his training as a magician. He tells of his devotion from childhood to the various Greek mysteries, e.g., the mysteries of Apollo, Mithras, Demeter, Pallas Athena, etc. As a young man he studied in Egypt and later among the Chaldeans before coming to Antioch. He was a master of the elements, of demonology, of prophecy.

[14] i.e. the people of Israel.

ing done these things, how can I be powerless against her? Take, therefore, this philtre and besprinkle the house of the maid from without and I will go and instill in her the spirit of my father [15] and straightway she will give ear unto thee."

5. The holy virgin rose at the third hour of the night and made her prayers to God. And as she perceived the onset of the demon and the ardent desire of her reins, she aroused herself to her Master and when she had sealed her whole body with the power of Him who bore the cross, she said with a loud voice: "O almighty God, O Father of Thy beloved son, Jesus Christ, Thou who hast cast into Tartarus the murderous serpent and saved those who were captured by it, Thou who alone hast spread out the heavens and established the earth, Thou who hast lifted up the torch of the sun and given light to the moon, Thou who hast formed man of earth in Thine own image and stamped him with Thine allwise spirit and placed him in the rapture of Paradise in order that he might enjoy the things created by Thee, who hast not abandoned him when he was banished from them through the guile of the serpent, but, O friend of man, didst call him back through Thy crossbearing power and, having healed his wounds, didst bring him into perfect health through Christ by whom the world has been established, the canopy of heaven spread out, the earth established and the waters stored up and all things recognize Thee as the true God over all, may it be Thy will to save Thy servant through Him and let temptation not touch me! For Thee and Thine only begotten son, Jesus Christ, I agreed to remain a maid." And when she had said these things and had sealed her whole body with the seal of Christ, she breathed upon the demon and put him to confusion.

6. But the demon went away in disgrace and stood

[15] Radermacher's third version has: "the spirit of lasciviousness."

before the face of Cyprian. Cyprian says: "Where is she for whom I sent thee? And why did I lie awake and thou hast missed the goal?" And the demon says: "Ask me not for I cannot tell thee. I saw a sign and I trembled in fear." But Cyprian mocked at him and, trusting in his magic arts, summoned a stronger demon. And the latter, boasting likewise, says to Cyprian: "I knew of thy command and of the incompetence of that demon. For that reason my father sent me to put an end to thy plight. Take this philtre, therefore, and besprinkle her house round about and I will come and prevail over her." Cyprian took the philtre and did as the demon had told him. But when the demon came into the house of the virgin, the holy maid rose at the sixth hour of the night and said her prayers to God, saying: "At midnight I arose to give thanks to Thee for the judgments of Thy righteousness.[16] O Lord God of mercy, Thou law of those in the air and protector of those under the heavens and terror of those under the earth, who didst put the devil to shame and exalted the sacrifice of Abraham, who hast overthrown Baal and slain the dragon through Thy faithful Daniel and made known to the Babylonians the power of Thy divinity, who hast ruled over all things through Thine only begotten son, Jesus Christ; who hast enlightened those things which before were dark and given life to the members which were dead; who hast made rich the poor and set free those who were enslaved to death—be not unmindful of me, Thy maidservant, Thou holy and kindly king, but keep my members unspotted in purity and maintain the torch of my virginity unextinguished in order that I may go in with my bridegroom Christ and may give back in purity the flesh which Thou didst commit to me as a pledge in Christ, for Thine is the glory through Him for ever and ever, Amen." And

[16] Cf. Psalms 119, 62.

when she had thus prayed she rebuked the demon in Christ and sent him away confounded.

7. But the demon, defeated in those things of which he had boasted, stood before Cyprian. And Cyprian says: "Where is she for whom I sent thee?" The demon says: "I have been defeated and cannot say. For I saw a sign and trembled with fear." Cyprian, at a loss, called a stronger demon, the father of all demons, and said to him: "What is this weakness of you demons, that thy whole power has been overcome?" The demon says: "I will presently deliver her to thee. Be thou ready." Cyprian says: "What is the token of thy victory?" The demon said: "I will agitate her with divers fevers and after six days I will appear to her at midnight and will make her ready."

8. So the demon went away and appeared to the holy virgin in the form of a maiden. And when she had seated herself on the couch, she said to the holy maid of God: "I also wish to discipline my body with thee today, for I was sent by Christ to live the life of a virgin. Tell me, what is this struggle for virginity and what is the reward? For I see that thou art much wasted away." The holy maid says to the demon: "The reward is great, the struggle small." But the demon said: "How was it then that Eve was a virgin in Paradise, while she lived with Adam, but was afterward persuaded, bore children and attained to a knowledge of the good and the world was stocked with children?" But when the demon was urgent that they pass out by the door, she became thoughtful and very much disturbed and recognized who it was who tempted her and she hastened to her prayers and, sealing herself with the sign of Christ, she breathed upon the demon and sent him away confounded. Recovering from her confusion, she put an end to her distress, saying: "I glorify Thee,

O Christ, Thou who dost preserve those oppressed by the enemy and dost guide Thy servants in the light according to Thy father's will, who drivest away with the rays of justice the spirits that cause trouble in the night. Grant that I be not overcome by the enemy. Nail fast my flesh to the fear of Thee and have mercy on me through Thy law and glorify Thy name, O Lord."

9. Deeply ashamed, the demon appeared before Cyprian. Cyprian says to him : "Thou wast conquered by one girl. What power is the source of her victory?" The demon says: "I cannot tell thee, for I saw a sign and I trembled with fear. Wherefore also I withdrew. If thou wilt know, swear to me and I will tell thee." Cyprian said: "How shall I swear to thee?" The demon said: "By the great powers which abide with me." Cyprian says: "By thy great powers, I will not depart from thee." (The demon, taking courage, says: "I saw the sign of the crucified One and I trembled with fear." Then Cyprian says: "Is the crucified One then greater than thou?" The demon says: "He is greater than all.) For whatsoever mistakes we make or whatsoever things we bring to pass here we shall receive our reward in the world to come. For there is a brazen fork and it is heated and placed on the neck of (the sinner, whether angel or) man; and thus with the hissing of fire the angels of the crucified One lead him to the tribunal and render unto each according to his works." Cyprian says: "Therefore I will also make haste to become a friend of the crucified One in order that I may not be subjected to such condemnation." The demon says: "Thou hast sworn to me and breakest thou thine oath?" Cyprian says: "I despise thee and fear not thy powers. For during (this) night I have been convinced that ye were overcome by the prayers and entreaties of the virgin and by the making of the sign of the crucified

One, with which I seal myself and depart from thee." And saying these things he crossed himself and said: "Glory be to Thee, O Christ. Get thee hence, demon. For I seek after Christ." And the demon went away discomfited.

10. But Cyprian, having piled up his books, put them on youths[17] and, having come into the house of the Lord and fallen at the feet of the blessed Anthimus, says: "O servant of the blessed Christ, I too desire to serve as a soldier of Christ and to be inscribed in the book of the living." But the holy bishop, believing that he wished to tempt him, said to him: "Be content, O Cyprian, with them that are outside. Spare the church of Christ. For His power is invincible." Cyprian says: "I also am convinced that it is invincible. For during this night I sent demons to the holy virgin Justina. And I recognized her prayers and that she overcame the demons with the seal of Christ. Take therefore the books with which I did evil and burn them in the fire and have mercy on me." The bishop was persuaded and burned his books and blessed him and sent him away, saying: "Hasten, my son, into the house of prayer." And Cyprian went into his house and shattered all his idols and all night long he beat his breast, saying: "How shall I dare to appear before the power of Christ, when I have done so many evil things? Or how shall I bless Him with the mouth with which I have cursed holy men, calling on unclean demons. Therefore will I strew ashes on the ground and fall down upon them silently, and beg for God's mercy."

11. And when it was dawn,—it was the great Sabbath[18]—he went into the house of the Lord. As he proceeded slowly on his way, he prayed, saying: "O Lord, if I am worthy to be called a perfect servant of

[17] Radermacher (op. cit., p. 104) believes the text is here corrupted and suggests "donkeys" instead of "youths."

[18] i.e. the Sabbath before Easter.

Thine, grant me as I enter Thy house to hear a prophetic word from Thy holy scriptures." And as he entered, the psalmist David said unto him: "Behold, O Lord: keep not silence: be not far from me."[19] And again from Hosea: "Behold, my servant shall deal prudently."[20] (And again David: "Mine eyes prevented the night watches, that I might meditate in thy word."[21]) And again Isaiah: "Fear not, Jacob my servant and beloved Israel, whom I have chosen."[22] And again the apostle Paul: "Christ has redeemed us from the curse of the law, being made a curse for us."[23] Then the psalmist David: "Who can utter the mighty acts of the Lord? who can shew forth all his praise?"[24] Then the light of the Gospels. Then the sermon of the bishop. Then the prayers of the catechumens.

12. The deacon bade the catechumens withdraw. Cyprian remained seated and Asterius the deacon said to him: "Go outside." Cyprian said: "I have become a servant of the crucified One and dost thou cast me out?" The deacon says: "Thou art not yet become perfect." Cyprian replieth: "My Christ liveth who hath put to shame the demons, saved the virgin and had mercy on me. Therefore I will not go out unless I am become perfect." Asterius then brought the matter to the bishop. And the bishop bade him come and when he had examined him thoroughly according to the law and had prayed with such fervor that creation was shaken, he took him and baptized him. And on the eighth day he became a reader and expounder of the divine mysteries of Christ, and on the twenty-fifth day subdeacon and doorkeeper of the divine mysteries of the sacred court, and on the fiftieth day deacon of

[19] Cf. Psalms 35, 22.
[20] Cf. Isaiah 52, 13. The reference to Hosea is in error.
[21] Cf. Psalms 119, 148.
[22] Cf. Isaiah 44, 2.
[23] Cf. Galatians 3, 13.
[24] Cf. Psalms 106, 2.

Christ. And grace against demons was with him and he healed all suffering. He turned many away from the mad worship of idols and persuaded them to become Christians. And when the year was passed he became the bishop's coadjutor, occupying for sixteen years a seat in the presbytery. Then the blessed Anthimus convoked the bishops of the cities round about, consulted with them concerning that which was expedient for the church, and then resigned to him the episcopal see. Within a few days the sainted Anthimus departed in Christ, commending his flock to him. And when he had put his affairs in order, the sainted Cyprian appointed the holy virgin to the position of deaconess and called her Justina and made her mother of a convent. But Cyprian enlightened many and turned them away from every heresy and added them to the flock of Christ.[25] To whom be glory and power for ever and ever, Amen.

II. Of S. Justina[26]

Justina the virgin was of the city of Antioch, daughter of a priest of the idols. And every day she sat at a window by a priest which read the gospel, of whom at the last she was converted. And when the mother of her had told it unto her father in his bed, Jesu Christ appeared to them with his angels, saying: Come to me, I shall give to you the kingdom of heaven. And when he awoke, anon they did them to be baptized with their daughter. And this virgin was strongly grieved and vexed of Cyprian, and at the last she converted him to the faith of Jesu Christ. And Cyprian from his childhood had been an enchanter, for

[25] *The Martyrdom of Saint Cyprian and Saint Justina* gives a variant ending of the legend. Cyprian and Justina are seized and the demand is made that they renounce their Christian faith. When they refuse, they are tortured and finally beheaded. Their remains are taken to Rome and there interred.

[26] From *The Golden Legend or Lives of the Saints as Englished by William Caxton*. J. M. Dent, London, 1900. V, 166-172.

from the time that he was seven years old he was consecrated by his parents to the devil. And he used the craft of necromancy, and made women to turn into juments and beasts as them seemed, and many other things semblable. And he was covetous of the love of Justina, and burnt in the concupiscence of her, and resorted to his art magic that he might have her for himself, or for a man named Acladius, which also burnt in her love. Then he called a devil to him, to the end that he might by him have Justina, and when the devil came he said to him : Why hast thou called me ? And Cyprian said to him : I love a virgin, canst thou not so much that I may have my pleasure of her ? And the devil answered : I that might cast man out of Paradise, and procured that Cain slew his brother, and made the Jews to slay Christ, and have troubled the men, trowest thou I may not do that thou have a maid with thee, and use her at thy pleasure ? Take this ointment and anoint withal her house withoutforth, and I shall come and kindle her heart in thy love, that I shall compel her to assent to thee. And the next night following the devil went and enforced him to move her heart unto unlawful love. And when she felt it, she recommended herself devoutly to God, and garnished her with the sign of the cross, and the devil, all afraid of the sign of the cross, fled away from her, and came again to Cyprian and stood before him. And Cyprian said to him : Why hast thou not brought to me this virgin ? And the devil said : I see in her a sign which feared me, that all strength is failed in me. Then Cyprian left him, and called another devil more stronger than he was. And he said : I have heard thy commandment and have seen the non-power of him, but I shall amend it and accomplish thy will. Then the devil went to her, and enforced to move her heart in love, and inflame her courage in things not honest.

And she recommended her to God devoutly, and put from her that temptation by the sign of the cross, and blew on the devil, and threw him anon away from her. And he fled all confused and came tofore Cyprian, and Cyprian said to him : Where is the maid that I sent thee for ? and the devil said : I acknowledge that I am overcome and am rebutted, and I shall say how, for I saw in her a sign horrible, and lost anon all my virtue. Then Cyprian left him, and blamed him, and called the prince of the devils. And when he was come he said : Wherefore is your strength so little, which is overcome of a maid ? Then the prince said to him : I shall go and vex her with great fevers, and I shall inflame more ardently her heart, and I shall arouse and bedew her body with so ardent desire of thee that she shall be all frantic ; and I shall offer to her so many things that I shall bring her to thee at midnight. Then the devil transfigured himself in the likeness of a maid, and came to this holy virgin, and said : I am come to thee for to live with thee in chastity, and I pray thee that thou say what reward shall we have for to keep us so. And the virgin answered : The reward is great, and the labour is small. And the devil said to her : What is that then that God commanded when he said : Grow and multiply and replenish the earth ? Then, fair sister, I doubt that if we abide in virginity that we shall make the word of God vain, and be also despising and inobedient, by which we shall fall into a grievous judgment, where we shall have no hope of reward, but shall run in great torment and pain. Then by the enticement of the devil the heart of the virgin was smitten with evil thoughts, and was greatly inflamed in desire of the sin of the flesh, so that she would have gone thereto, but then the virgin came to herself, and considered who that it was that spake to her. And anon she blessed her with the sign of the cross, and blew against the devil, and anon he vanished away and melted like wax, and incontinent she was delivered from all temptation.[27] A little while after, the devil transfigured him in the likeness of a fair young man, and entered into her chamber, and found her alone in her bed, and without shame sprang into her bed and embraced her, and would have had a done with her. And when she saw this she knew well that it was a wicked spirit, and blessed her as she had done tofore, and he melted away like wax.[28] And then by the sufferance of God she was vexed with axes and fevers. And the devil slew many men and beasts, and made to be said by them that were demoniacs that, a right great mortality should be throughout all Antioch, but if Justina would consent wedlock and have Cyprian. Wherefore all they that were sick and languishing in maladies lay at the gate of Justina's father and friends, crying that they should marry her and deliver the city of that right great peril. Justina then would not consent in no wise, and therefore everybody menaced her. And in the sixth year of that mortality she prayed for them, and chased and drove thence all that pestilence. And when the devil saw that he profited nothing, he transumed and transfigured him in the form of Justina for to defoul the fame of Justina, and in mocking Cyprian he advanced him that he had brought to him Justina. And came to him in the likeness of her, and would have kissed him as if she had languished for his love. And when Cyprian saw him and supposed that it had been Justina, he was all replenished with joy and said : Thou art welcome, Justina, the fairest of all women ; and anon as Cyprian named Justina, the devil might not suffer the name, but as soon as he heard it he vanished

27 The following episode is, as far as known, an invention of Jacobus de Voragine.

28 The rest of the account of the temptation of Justina follows the story told by Cyprian in *The Confession of St. Cyprian.*

away as a fume or smoke. And when Cyprian saw him deceived, he was all heavy and sorrowful, and was then more burning and desirous in the love of Justina, and woke long at the door of the virgin, and as him seemed he changed him sometimes into a bird by his art magic, and sometimes into a woman, but when he came to the door of the virgin he was neither like woman or bird, but appeared Cyprian as he was. Acladius, by the devil's craft, was anon turned into a sparrow, and when he came to the window of Justina, as soon as the virgin beheld him, he was not a sparrow, but showed himself as Acladius, and began to have anguish and dread, for he might neither fly ne leap, and Justina dreading lest he should fall and break himself, did do set a ladder by which he went down, warning him to cease of his woodness, lest he should be punished as a malefactor by the law. Then the devil, being vanquished in all things, returned to Cyprian, and held him all confused tofore him, and Cyprian said to him : And how art not thou overcome, what unhappy is your virtue that ye may not overcome a maid, have ye no might over her, but she overcometh you and breaketh you all to pieces? Tell me, I pray thee, in whom she hath all this great might and strength. And the devil said : If thou wilt swear to me that thou wilt not depart from me ne forsake me, I shall show to thee her strength and her victory ; to whom Cyprian said : By what oath shall I swear? And the devil said : Swear thou by my great virtues that thou shalt never depart from me. And Cyprian said : I swear to thee by thy great virtues that I shall never depart from thee. Then the devil said to him, weening to be sure of him : This maid maketh the sign of the cross, and anon then we wax feeble and lose all our might and virtue, and flee from her, like as wax fleeth from the face of the fire. And Cyprian said then to him : The crucified God is then greater than thou? And the devil said: Yea, certainly he is greater than all others, and all them that we here deceive, he judgeth them to be tormented with fire inextinguishable. And Cyprian said: Then ought I to be made friend of him that was crucified, lest I fall hereafter into such pains. To whom the devil said: Thou hast sworn by the might and virtues of my strengths, the which no man may forswear, that thou shalt never depart from me. To whom Cyprian said: I despise thee, and forsake thee and all thy power, and renounce thee and all thy devils, and garnish and mark me with the sign of the cross, and anon the devil departed all confused.

Then Cyprian went to the bishop, and when the bishop saw him he weened that he were come to put the christian men in error, and said: Let it suffice unto thee, Cyprian, them that be without forth, for thou mayst nothing prevail against the church of God, for the virtue of Jesu Christ is joined thereto, and is not overcome. And Cyprian said: I am certain that the virtue of our Lord Jesu Christ is not overcome, and then he recounted all that was happened, and did him to be baptized of him. And after, he profited much, as well in science as in life. And when the bishop was dead, Cyprian was ordained bishop, and placed the blessed virgin Justina with many virgins in a monastery, and made her abbess over many holy virgins. S. Cyprian sent then epistles to martyrs and comforted them in their martyrdom.

[29] The earl of that country heard of the fame and renomee of Cyprian and Justina, and he made them to be presented tofore him and demanded them if they would do sacrifice. And when he saw that they abode steadfastly in the faith of Jesu Christ, he commanded

[29] The version of the final fate of Cyprian and Justina that follows has as its source *The Martyrdom of St. Cyprian and St. Justina.*

that he should be put in a caldron full of wax, pitch, and grease, burning and boiling. And all this gave to them marvellous refreshing, and did to them no grief ne pain. And the priest of the idols said to the provost of that place: Command me, sire, to stand and to be tofore the caldron, and I shall anon overcome all their virtue. And then he came tofore the caldron and said: Great is the god Hercules, and Jupiter the father of gods. And anon the great fire issued from under the caldron and anon consumed and burnt him. Then Cyprian and Justina were taken out of the caldron and sentence was given against them, and they were both beheaded together. And their bodies were thrown to hounds and were there seven days, and after they were taken up and translated to Rome, and as it is said, now they rest at Placentia. And they suffered death in the seventh calends of October, about the year of our Lord two hundred and eighty, under Diocletian.

Theophilus of Adana [1]

The most popular and most widely spread of the magus legends down to approximately 1500 was that of Theophilus of Adana. This legend, which is one of the first tributes to the Virgin Mary, was originally written in Greek, probably between 650 and 850 A.D. Thirteen Greek manuscripts, some of which are comparatively late, are listed by Radermacher in his *Griechische Quellen zur Faustsage*. The Greek

[1] For a detailed study of the development and literature of the legend see: Sommer, *De Theophili cum diabolo foedere*. Dissertation. Halle, 1844.

Dasent, *Theophilus in Icelandic, Low German and other tongues*. London, 1845.

Petsch, *Theophilus, Mittelniederdeutsches Drama in drei Fassungen*. Heidelberg, 1908.

Frank, *Rutebeuf, Le Miracle de Theophile*. Paris, 1925.

Plenzat, *Die Theophiluslegende in den Dichtungen des Mittelalters*. Germanische Studien. Berlin, 1926.

Radermacher, *Griechische Quellen zur Faustsage*. Sitzungsberichte der Akademie der Wissenschaften in Wien. Phil.-hist. Kl., Bd. 206, Abhandlung 4. 1927.

manuscripts vary considerably in length and content. Three of the longest are known as the "Eutychianus" texts as they all end with a short paragraph in which one Eutychianus claims to have written down the account of Theophilus. According to his story he was a member of Theophilus' household and a scribe of the church at Adana. Most of the Theophilus scholars are of the opinion that Eutychianus was more probably a scribe who elaborated the original legend and added the final paragraph in order to make the whole more plausible. The date of the story is given as 537 in the *Legenda Aurea.* From the mention of the "Persian invasions" it is possible that this date is approximately correct, although it may be placed as late as 600.

It was through the medium of Latin translations that the Theophilus legend spread throughout Western Europe. The oldest Latin version which we possess was translated toward the end of the ninth century by a priest who called himself Paulus Diaconus of Naples. His translation follows in the main the Eutychianus texts—particularly the Vienna manuscript of the Eutychianus version. There is evidence, however, that Paulus used two or more manuscripts or followed a manuscript that has not come down to us. This translation served as the basis of about two thirds of the later versions of Theophilus. For this reason the version of Paulus Diaconus has been chosen for translation into English, rather than one of the Greek versions.

Before 1500 the Theophilus story had been carried into practically all the nations of Europe. We have more than twenty-five different versions in Latin alone, one of which, that in the *Legenda Aurea,* is sufficient guarantee of the spread of the legend. Then there are a number of versions in French, English, German, Italian, Spanish, Dutch, Anglo-Saxon, Icelandic, and Swedish.

I. A MIRACLE OF THE VIRGIN MARY CONCERNING THEOPHILUS THE PENITENT

by

EUTYCHIANUS

Translated into Latin by Paulus Diaconus Neapoleos[2]

Chapter I. Theophilus' departure from the pious life; his denial of Christ and Mary.

BEFORE the invasion of the detestable Persians into the Roman commonwealth, it came to pass that there lived in a city called Adana, in the second district of the Cilicians, a certain steward of God's holy church, named Theophilus, who was distinguished by his morals and mode of living. Quietly and with all moderation he managed most excellently the sheepfold of Christ and the business pertaining to the church, so that the bishop, because of his happy discretion, depended upon him in all business of the church and of the people in general. Wherefore all, great and small, were grateful to him and esteemed him highly. For to the orphans, the naked[3] and the needy he administered alms very prudently.

2. And it came to pass that at God's summons the bishop of that city died and, inasmuch as all the clergy and all the people esteemed the steward highly and recognized his diligence, they resolved immediately and by common consent to make him bishop. And when their solemn resolution was made known, they sent it to the metropolitan. When he received the petition

[2] This translation is based on the version of Paulus Diaconus found in the *Acta Sanctorum,* Paris edition, 1863–1883. February, Vol. I, 489-493. We have also made use of the Latin text edited by Petsch in his *Theophilus* and of the Greek originals published by Radermacher (op. cit.).

[3] Petsch gives *viduis* 'widows' instead of *nudis*. The wording in section 6, where the thought is repeated, makes this emendation a likely one.

and when the virtues of the steward had been made clear, he agreed to grant the petition and, directing that the steward nominated should be promoted to be bishop, ordered him to be summoned. When the metropolitan's letter had been received, Theophilus at first delayed his going, asking everyone not to compel him to become bishop, asserting that he was satisfied to remain steward and protesting that he was unworthy of an office of such honor. But as the people insisted, he was taken by the arm, led to the metropolitan and received with joy. The consecration was to begin but the vicar, prostrating himself on the floor and embracing the feet of the metropolitan, prayed that no such thing should be done to him, protesting that he was wholly unworthy of the rank of bishop and that he was conscious of his own sins. And when he had for a long time lain prostrate on the floor at the metropolitan's feet, he was given three days time to consider. And then, after the third day, the metropolitan summoned him and began to admonish him and praise his shrewdness. But nevertheless the steward protested that he was unworthy to ascend the steps of such a throne. The metropolitan, therefore, seeing him so persistent in his obstinacy and seeing that he was loath to consent, dismissed him and promoted another man worthy of this church to conduct the office of bishop.

3. Then after the bishop was ordained and they had returned to their own city, certain of the clergy urged that Theophilus be removed from his office and that the bishop ordain a new steward. When this was done Theophilus, having retired from his former office, took care of his own house only. Therefore the cunning enemy and envious foe of the human race, seeing this man living modestly and passing the time in good deeds, made his heart to beat with perverse thoughts, instilling into him jealousy of the steward's power and the desire of honor, and inclined him toward such

abominable and wicked counsels that he sought not for divine but human glory and strove for vain and transitory honor more than divine — so much so that he even demanded the aid of sorcerers.

4. Now there was in that city a certain wicked Jew, a practicer of all sorts of diabolical arts, who had already plunged many into the deep pit of perdition by his unchristian counsels. And the wretched steward, incited by vain glory, fell to turning over in his mind confusedly the lust of this world and was consumed by the desire of honor. So with all haste he proceeded by night to the aforesaid Jew and, knocking at the door, sought admission. Then the Jew, hateful to God, seeing him thus broken, called him into the house and said to him: "Why hast thou come to me?" And Theophilus ran up and threw himself at his feet and answered: "I beseech thee to aid me, for my bishop has disgraced me and has wrought this against me." The detestable Jew replied: "Come to me tomorrow evening at this hour and I will lead thee to my master and he will help thee in that thou hast desired." Hearing this the vicar was rejoiced and did as he was told, going to him in the middle of the night. And in truth the wicked Jew did lead him to the Circus of the city and said to him: "Whatsoever thou seest or whatsoever sound thou hearest, be not afraid and do not make the sign of the cross." After Theophilus on his part had promised this, the Jew showed him suddenly creatures clad in white robes, with a multitude of candlesticks, uttering loud cries, and, seated in their midst, the prince. It was the devil and his minions. The hapless Jew, holding the steward by the hand, led him to this infamous assembly. And the devil said to him: "Why hast thou brought this man to us?" He replied: "My master, I have brought him because he has been falsely judged by his bishop and has asked for thy help." The devil then

said: "How shall I give help to him, a man serving his God? But if he will be my servant and be counted among our hosts, I will aid him so that he may do more than before and rule over all, even the bishop." And the perverted Jew said to the wretched steward: "Didst thou hear what he hath said to thee?" And he replied: "I have heard and whatsoever he shall say to me, I will do so long as he helps me." And he began to kiss the feet of the prince and to implore him. The devil said to the Jew: "Let him deny the son of Mary and those things which are offensive to me,[4] and let him set down in writing that he denieth absolutely, and whatsoever he may desire he shall obtain from me, so long as he denieth." Then Satan entered into the steward and he replied: "I deny Christ and His mother." And making a written statement and putting wax on it, he sealed it with his own ring and the two went away rejoicing greatly at his perdition.

5. On the morrow, however, after the steward had been recalled with all honor from his retirement and after the man who had been promoted had been ingloriously removed, the bishop, moved methinks by divine providence, reappointed the former steward and in the presence of all the clergy and the people offered him authority over the management of the holy church and likewise over all its possessions and over all the people. And the steward was given twice as much preferment as he had had before and again elevated to honor, so that the bishop cried out that he had sinned because he had demoted so worthy and perfect a person and had promoted one who was useless and less worthy. When this same steward had been ordained, he began to set things in order and to be lifted above all, everyone obeying him with fear and trembling and serving him for a short while. The Jew, execrable in

[4] The text of Petsch has: 'Let him deny the son of Mary and Mary herself, for they are offensive to me.' This agrees with the Greek version.

very truth, frequently betook himself secretly to the steward and said to him: "Hast thou observed how thou hast obtained benefit and speedy relief from me and my master in that thou didst pray for?" And then he replied: "I recognize it and am altogether thankful for thy assistance."

Chapter II. Penitence of Theophilus. Hope of forgiveness obtained from the virgin mother of God.

6. And when he had remained a short time in such vanity and in the deep pit of denial, God, the Creator of all and our Redeemer, who doth not desire the death of sinners but rather their conversion and life, mindful of his former way of living and in what manner he had served God's holy church, and that he had ministered abundantly to the widows, the orphans and the needy, did not despise His creature but granted him the conversion of repentance. And having turned away in his heart from such arrogance and denial and having regained a state of sobermindedness, he began to humble his spirit and to be troubled by the things which he had done and he devoted himself to fasting, prayers, and vigils,—reflecting on many things and seeing himself cheated of salvation, meditating on the torments of eternal fire and the fire that is not quenched and the passing of the soul,[5] the gnashing of teeth and the worm that dieth not. Turning over all these things in his mind, with fearful apprehension, groaning and with bitter tears he said: "Oh miserable wretch that I am, what have I done and what have I wrought? Whither shall I turn now, I who am laden with luxury, in order that I may make my soul safe? Where shall I, unhappy sinner, go, I who have denied my Christ and His holy mother and have made myself

[5] The translation is according to the arrangement of Petsch.

a servant of the devil through an impious pact in my own handwriting? Who, thinkest thou, will be able to retrieve that from the hand of the destroyer, the devil, and succor me? Why did I have to become acquainted with that vilest of Jews who should be burned?—For this same Jew had been condemned a short time before by law and judge.—Why indeed? Thus they are rewarded, who forsake our Lord and Master and follow after the devil.[6] For what did it profit me, the temporal advantage and the vain arrogance of this world? Woe to me wretch, in what manner have I lost the light and entered into darkness? I was well off, when I had retired to the management of mine own affairs. Why have I sought for the sake of vain glory and empty fame to consign my wretched soul to Gehenna? What aid shall I pray for, who am cheated of aid by the devil? I, who am guilty of this thing, I am the cause of my soul's perdition, the betrayer of my salvation. Woe to me, in what manner I am carried off I do not know. Woe to me, what shall I do? To whom shall I go? What shall I reply on the day of judgment when all shall be naked and open? What shall I say in that hour when the just will be crowned while I will be condemned? And with what assurance shall I stand before that royal and awful tribunal? Whom shall I implore? Whom shall I entreat in that tribulation? Or on whom may I call in that hour of need, when all are concerned with their own affairs and not those of others? Who will pity me? Who will aid me? Who will protect me? Who will be my patron? Verily no one. There no one helps but all render an account for themselves. Woe to my wretched soul! By what means hast thou been enslaved? How hast thou been cast down? In what way alienated and shaken? By what sort of ruin art thou fallen?

[6] The translation is according to the punctuation of Petsch.

By what shipwreck overwhelmed? By what mire art thou enveloped? In what haven wilt thou now find shelter? To what remedy wilt thou have recourse? Woe to me, miserable one, who, having stumbled and fallen into the abyss, am unable to rise!"

7. And while he disputed these things with his own soul and while these seeds of salvation were being sown in his heart, God, who is alone pious and merciful, who despises not His own creature but is a staff to him, encompassed him with the following thoughts. Then the steward said: "Although I know that I have denied the son of God, born of the holy immaculate ever virgin mother Mary, our Lord Jesus Christ, and Mary herself, through that Jew whom I came to know in an evil moment, nevertheless I shall go to that same mother of the Lord, holy, glorious, resplendent, and her alone I shall entreat with all my heart and soul and I will pray and fast in her holy temple without ceasing, until I obtain mercy through her on the day of judgment." And again he said: "But with what lips I may presume to pray for her loving kindness I know not. For I know that I have woefully transgressed by denying her. Or how shall I begin my confession? In what sort of heart or what state of conscience shall I put my faith and try to move my impious tongue and soiled lips? Or for what sins shall I first do penance or seek forgiveness? And if in rashness I shall have presumed to do this, wretch that I am, fire from heaven descending will consume me because the world even now will not suffer the evil that I, wretched creature, have done. Alas poor soul, rise from the darkness that hath laid hold on thee, and falling down before her, call upon the mother of our Lord Jesus Christ, because she, in truth, hath power to impose healing penance for such sin."

8. And pondering these things in his mind, now that the troublesome stumbling blocks of this world

had been abandoned, with good courage, great zeal, and ready will, in that holy and venerable church of our immaculate glorious ever virgin Mary, he prostrated himself before her. And he offered up prayers and entreaties without ceasing day and night and devoted himself sedulously to fasting and vigils, in order that, having turned away from such misdeeds, he might be redeemed and saved from that dangerous deceiver and wicked dragon and from the denial he had made. For forty days and forty nights he fasted and prayed and entreated our protectress, the mother of the Lord, our Saviour.

9. And verily, after the passing of the days there appeared manifest unto him in the middle of the night that all-abiding aid and ready protection of those Christians who watch for her, that true refuge of those who flock to her, that path of those who are lost, that redemption of captives, that light of those in the darkness, the truest refuge of the afflicted, the consolation of those in trial, our Lady and in very truth mother of Christ, saying to him: "Why, O man, dost thou persist with rashness and pride in asking that I aid thee, thou man who hast denied my son, the Saviour of the world, and me? And how can I beseech Him to forgive thee the evil thou hast done? With what eyes shall I look into the merciful countenance of my son, whom thou hast denied, and presume to entreat Him for thy sake? With what assurance can I appeal to Him, when thou hast renounced Him? Or in what wise shall I stand before that fearsome tribunal and presume to open my mouth to ask for His most compassionate clemency? For I will not suffer to see my son defamed by insults. Granted, O man, that the sins which thou hast committed against me can in some degree find forgiveness forasmuch as I do so devoutly love all Christians, particularly those who flock to my temple with upright faith and pure con-

science. These I approve of and aid in every way and I warm them with my arms and encompass them with bowels of mercy. But I cannot bear to hear or see revilers of my son because they need much struggle and suffering and contrition of heart to obtain His mercy. For He is an exceeding compassionate and very just and pious judge."

10. And the man in turn replied and said unto her: "My Lady, ever blessed, thou art the shelter of mankind, the haven and prop of those who take refuge in thee. I know, my Lady, verily I know that I have sinned grievously against thee and against Him who was born from thee, our Lord, and am not worthy to ask thy grace. But having an example in those who have previously sinned against thy son, our Lord, and have won remission of their sins through penitence, I presume for that reason to approach thee. For if it were not through penitence, Rahab the prostitute had not been saved; if it were not by penitence, how did David, falling into the pit of fornication and homicide after receiving the gift of prophecy, after being made king, and after the testimony of the Lord, obtain not only indulgence for his great sins but likewise the gift of prophecy anew by showing his repentance by his words? If it were not by penitence, how was it that the blessed Peter, prince of apostles, first of the disciples, pillar of the church, who received from God the keys of the kingdom of heaven, who denied Christ, the Lord, not once or twice but thrice, obtained through his bitter weeping both indulgence for so great a sin and received even greater honor than before and was made shepherd of the Lord's sheepfold? If it were not by penitence, how did He exalt Zacchaeus, himself the chief of the publicans and a false accuser? If it were not through penitence, how was the blessed Paul transformed from a persecutor into a chosen vessel? If it were not through penitence, how did the apostle

command him who had committed fornication among the Corinthians to be forgiven, saying: 'Lest Satan should get an advantage of him?' If it were not by penitence, how did Cyprian, who had done so many evil things, who cut open pregnant women and was completely entangled in infamy, hasten to penitence and, greatly strengthened by Saint Justina, receive not only remission of such great sins[7] but likewise obtain the crown of martyrdom? Wherefore I too, a miserable sinner, approach thee, trusting in the evidence of the penitence of so many and praying for thy divine pity that thou mayest deign to extend to me the right hand of protection and to grant me indulgence for my sins through thy son, our Lord Jesus Christ, against whom I, poor wretch, have sinned.

11. In short, while he was thus confessing, our sainted and venerable Lady, who alone is chaste, who alone is holy and blessed in soul and body, who alone hath eloquence before Christ whom she bore, the consolation of the sorrowful, the comfort of the afflicted, the cloak of the naked, the staff of the aged, the strong protection of those who hasten to her, who giveth warmth to the Christians encompassed by her holy bowels of compassion, said to him: "Confess to me, O man, that the son whom I bore and whom thou hast denied is Christ, the Son of the living God, who will come to judge the quick and the dead, and I will entreat Him for thee and support thee." And the steward replied: "How shall I presume, my ever blessed Lady, I who am unhappy and unworthy, who have a sordid and polluted mouth, who have denied thy son and our Lord, and have been tripped up by the vain desires of this world? And not this alone, but I have also defiled that which I had for the relief of my soul,—I mean the holy cross and the holy bap-

[7] The *Acta Sanctorum* has 'cantorum malorum.' We have accepted the emendation of Petsch, 'tantorum malorum.'

tism which I received—by signing that writ of most bitter abnegation." Then the holy and immaculate virgin Mary, mother of God, said: "Only do thou come and acknowledge Him, for He is merciful and will accept the tears of thy repentance, just as of all those who come to Him in purity and in truth. For because of this He, though He is God, deigned to receive incarnation through me, with no weakening of the essence of His deity, in order that He might redeem mankind."

12. Then the happy man, with reverence and with fitting prayer, wept with bowed head and confessed and said: "I believe in, I worship and glorify our Lord Jesus Christ, one of the Holy Trinity, Son of the living God, who was born ineffably of the Father before the ages, but descended in recent times from heaven and was incarnated the true God by the Holy Ghost through thee, the holy and immaculate virgin Mary, and came forth for the salvation of man. I acknowledge Him to be the perfect God and the perfect man, who condescended to suffer on account of us sinful men, to be spat upon and beaten with blows and to have His hands stretched upon the living tree, like a good shepherd laying down His life for us sinners. He was buried and rose again, ascended into heaven in the flesh which He received from thee, His most chaste and true mother, and shall come again in His sacred glory to judge the quick and the dead and to render to each according to his works. He hath no need of an accuser for when our works have been brought to trial our consciences accuse or excuse us, and fire shall test of what sort the work of each one is. I confess these things with my soul, my heart, and my body. I worship, adore and embrace them and with this my prayerful pledge, made with all the strength of my soul, bring me, holy and immaculate virgin, mother of God,

to thy son, our Lord, and do not detest or despise the prayer of a sinner who hath been ravished, tripped up and betrayed, but deliver me from the iniquity which hath seized upon me and from the blast of the whirlwind which possesseth me, who am deprived of the grace of the Holy Spirit." And when he had said this, receiving as it were some amends from him, the holy mother of God, the hope and stay of Christians, the redemption of those who have gone astray, and the true way of those who flee to her, the fountain[8] of the hesitating, who intercedes for sinners, who is the refuge of the poor, the consolation of the poor in spirit and the mediator between God and man, said to him: "Behold, I believe thee because of the baptism thou hast received through my son, Jesus Christ, our Lord, and because of the exceeding great compassion which I have with you Christians, and I will approach Him and, falling down at His feet, will ask Him for thee how far He will accept thee."

Chapter III. Theophilus' sins forgiven. The writ returned. Death of Theophilus.

13. And when this vision had appeared and the day was done, the immaculate virgin mother of God departed from him. And for three days more the steward prayed and beat his face violently against the floor in that same venerable temple, remaining without food and flooding the place with tears; nor did he go to rest but regarded continually the pure light and the ineffable countenance of our glorious Lady, Mary the mother of God, from whom he expected hope of salvation. Wherefore once again she who is alone the true protection, the sole consolation of those who flee

[8] The text reads 'fons fluctuantium.' In view of the Greek text, it should probably be 'pons fluctuantium,' "the support of those who are tossed on the waves."

to her, the only light-shedding cloud, who was nourished in the holy of holies, appeared unto him with joyful face and cheerful eyes and with gentle voice thus addressed him: "Man of God, sufficient is thy penitence which thou hast shown to the Saviour of all and God the Creator. For the Lord doth accept thy tears and granteth thy prayers for my sake if only thou wilt observe these things in thy heart toward Christ, the son of the living God, until the day of thy death." Then he replied: "Surely I will give heed, my Lady, that I may not neglect thy words; because, after God, I have thee as protection and support and, trusting in thy help, I shall not disregard what I have promised and confessed. For I know, I know that there is none other protection for mankind except thee, thou ever blessed one. For who, O my Lady, immaculate virgin, hath set his hope on thee and been confounded? Or what man hath prayed for the omnipotence of thy help and hath been forsaken? Wherefore I too, a sinner and prodigal, call upon thee to bestow the never failing fountain of thy loving kindness, the bowels of thy compassion upon me, erring and deceived man, who am plunged in the deep mire. Give order that I may receive back that accursed writ of denial and the wicked compact, which I did sign, from him who deceived me, the devil, because it is this which doth so sorely torment my wretched soul."

14. And again, therefore, with much wailing and exceeding great lamentation the aforesaid man earnestly besought her who is the sole hope of us all and the salvation of our souls and prayed to the holy ever virgin Mary. And verily after three days more the blessed Mary delivered unto him, in a vision as it seemed, that bond of apostasy with the seal of wax upon it, just as he had given it. When he rose from

his sleep the aforesaid steward found the bond upon his breast and, filled with joy at the outcome, he trembled so that the joints of all his members were almost loosed.

15. And verily on the next day, when it was the Lord's day, he went into the holy catholic church. And after the reading of the holy gospel, he threw himself at the feet of the most holy bishop and told him in minute detail of all that had been done by that execrable and pernicious Jew and sorcerer; of his own arrogance and denial and the compact made because of the vain glory of this world; of his confession to our Lord and Master Jesus Christ and his penitence through miracles; and then of the unfailing fountain of the immaculate mother of God, by whose aid he even received back again that writing of most infamous denial. And holding it forth to the most holy bishop, he delivered the signed compact into his hands and all wondered, both clergy and laity, women and children. And he demanded that that most evil and horrible writing should be read in public in the presence of all. And all the people knew what had befallen him and in what manner the writing of denial had been returned to him.

16. Wherefore the bishop also exclaimed and said: "Come, all ye faithful, let us glorify our true Lord Jesus Christ! Come all and behold these wondrous miracles! Come, all ye chosen of Christ, and behold Him who doth not desire the death of the sinner but instead conversion and eternal life. Come and behold the tears which wash away sins. Come, my dearly beloved, and witness the tears which blot out the wounds of evil deeds and show the soul whiter than the snow. Come and see the tears flow which transport souls to God. Come and behold the tears which obtain remission of sins. Come, all ye Christians, and

consider the tears which take away the wrath of God. Come and witness of how much avail are the sighs of the soul and a contrite heart. Who doth not marvel, my brothers, at the unspeakable patience of God? Who is not amazed at the ineffable compassion and charity of God toward us sinners? For Moses, the lawgiver, fasting for forty days, received graven tablets from God; and this our brother, biding for forty days in the venerable temple of the immaculate and glorious ever virgin Mary, hath received from God, through fasting and prayer, the grace which he had lost by his apostasy. Let us with him also glorify the Lord who hath so mercifully given ear to the penitence of him who hath sought refuge in Him through the intervention of the immaculate ever virgin Mary, the mother of God, who is a mighty mediator between God and man, the truest hope of those in despair and the refuge of the afflicted. She hath made milder the curse of human nature. She is the true door of eternal life at which all of us sinners knock and it is opened unto us. She beareth our prayers to Him whom she bore, our Lord, and receiveth indulgence for our sins. Therefore, holy mother of God, be thou mindful also of us who watch for thee with pure faith and who take refuge in thee. Forsake not thine humble sheep-fold but pray for it to the Lord, the compassionate, and intercede for us that it may be preserved in prosperity and without calumny. For in thee we Christians place our hope and to thee we flee; to thee we lift up our eyes both day and night. For we greet and glorify thee and Him who was born of thee and was made incarnate through thee, our Lord Jesus Christ. And what shall I now speak or say or what manner of praise or glory shall we offer to our Lord God, Jesus Christ the omnipotent, who was born of thee? Glorious in truth are Thy works, O Lord, and tongue doth not suffice to tell of the splendor of Thy miracles. Glorious in truth are Thy works, O Lord, most fitting are the words of the Gospel: 'Bring forth the best robe and put it on him and put a ring on his hand and shoes on his feet and bring hither the fatted calf and kill it; and let us eat and be merry: for this our brother was dead and is alive again, he was lost and is found.'"

17. And after the steward had arisen, the bishop asked him to burn that most evil document, which was done. And when the people saw the accursed writing and bond of denial burned with fire, they began to shout with many tears: "Kyrie eleison!" And the bishop, making a sign with his hand that they should be silent, said: "Peace be with you!" And he began to celebrate the solemn rites of the mass. After the service was completed and when the communion had been partaken of, the face of the venerable steward shone like the sun. And all who saw the sudden transfiguration of the man glorified God the more, who alone worketh such miracles.

18. And coming to the venerable temple of the mother of God, who delivered him from that execrable sin, he partook of a little food and then, dissolved in body, he was overcome by weakness at the place where he is now buried, even there where he saw that blessed vision. And he bent his head, remaining as it were transfixed in that place. After three days had passed, he kissed the brothers and delivered his blessed soul into the hands of the Son of God and the immaculate ever virgin Mary. He distributed all his possessions to the poor, wisely disposing of them and glorifying God by such a confession, and departed to the Lord, in whom is the glory, now and forever, throughout all the ages of ages. *Amen.*

II. The Legend of Theophilus from The Nativity of Our Lady.[9]

In the year of our Lord five hundred and thirty-seven, there was a man named Theophilus which was vicar of a bishop, as Fulbert saith, that was bishop of Chartres. And this Theophilus dispended all wisely the goods of the church under the bishop; and when the bishop was dead, all the people said that this vicar should be bishop. But he said the office of vicar sufficed him, and had liefer that than to be made bishop, so there was there another bishop made, and Theophilus was against his will put out of his office. Then he fell in despair, in such wise that he counselled with a Jew how he should have his office again, which Jew was a magician, and called the devil, and he came anon. Then Theophilus, by commandment of the devil, renied God and his Mother, and renounced his christian profession, and wrote an obligation with his blood[10] and sealed it with his ring, and delivered it to the devil, and thus he was brought into his office again. And on the morn Theophilus was received into the grace of the bishop by the procuration of the devil, and was re-established in the dignity of his office. And afterwards, when he advised himself, he repented and sor-

[9] From *The Golden Legend or Lives of the Saints as Englished by William Caxton.* J. M. Dent, London, 1900. V, 109-110.

[10] The blood-pact which Caxton apparently attributes to Fulbert of Chartres is not in Paulus Diaconus. According to Grace Frank (op. cit., p. 35) it is not in Fulbert nor in Gautier de Coincy, a source of Rutebeuf. The pact does not appear in the 1479 edition of the *Legenda Aurea* of de Voragine. In Rutebeuf's *Theophile,* which was written between 1254 and 1285, the blood-pact is mentioned; likewise in the *Hohes Lied* of Brun von Sconebeck, which was written before 1267. Plenzat (op. cit.) says that Brun's mention of the blood-pact is the first reference to it on German soil. Ludorff, *Anglia* VII, 77, and Strohmayer, *Romania* XXIII, 605, think that the blood-pact is the result of the influence of other legends. It would appear from the evidence presented that the blood-pact entered the Theophilus legend in the 13th century.

rowed sore of this that he had done, and ran with great devotion unto the Virgin Mary, with all devotion of his thought, praying her to be his aid and help. And then on a time our blessed Lady appeared to him in a vision, and rebuked him of his felony, and commanded him to forsake the devil, and made him to confess Jesu Christ to be son of God, and to knowledge himself to be in purpose to be a christian man, and thus he recovered the grace of her and of her son. And in sign of Pardon that she had gotten him, she delivered to him again his obligation that he had given to the devil, and laid it upon his breast so that he should never doubt to be servant of the devil, but he enjoyed that he was so delivered by our blessed Lady. And when Theophilus had heard all this he was much joyful, and told it to the bishop and tofore all the people that was befallen him, and all marvelled greatly and gave laud and praising unto the glorious virgin, our Lady, S. Mary. And three days after he rested in peace.

III

THE HISTORICAL FAUST

THE HISTORICAL FAUST[1]

The documentary evidence which is generally advanced for the existence of a historical Faust is of varying value. The mixture of legendary matter with material that is really authentic is inevitable and increases as we get into the second half of the sixteenth century. Nor is it always easy to sift out the one from the other. Such evidence as we get from Tritheim, Conrad Mutianus Rufus, the account book of the Bishop of Bamberg, Kilian Leib, the Nuremberg and Ingolstadt records, Luther's *Tischreden,* and Philip von Hutten is first hand and genuinely historical, though Tritheim brings in some material that is probably hearsay. The evidence from the matriculation records of the University of Heidelberg is certainly historical but the question remains whether the "Johannes Faust ex Simern" is Faust the magician. In other cases the evidence is partly hearsay, but it is well to remember that the authors were frequently scholarly men and should be given credit for using due caution in what they wrote. To this group belong the *Waldeck Chronicle,* Joachim Camerarius, Begardi, Gast, Gesner, the *Zimmerische Chronik,* Wier, Lercheimer, and Philipp Camerarius. The evidence of Manlius would seem to belong somewhere between the two groups in view of the fact that he claims to be quoting Melanchthon

[1] For a discussion of the historical Faust see :

Erich Schmidt, "Faust und das sechzehnte Jahrhundert." *Charakteristiken* I. Berlin, 1886.

Erich Schmidt, "Faust und Luther." *Berichte der Berliner Akademie,* XXV (1896), 567 ff.

Georg Witkowski, "Der historische Faust." *Deutsche Zeitschrift für Geschichtswissenschaft,* 1896–97, pp. 298 ff.

Robert Petsch, "Der historische Doktor Faust." *Germanisch-Romanische Monatsschrift,* II (1910), 99 ff.

Carl Kiesewetter, *Faust in der Geschichte und Tradition.* Leipzig, 1893. 2nd ed. Berlin, 1921.

Harold George Meek, *Johann Faust.* London, 1930.

who speaks, in part at least, from first hand knowledge. The Erfurt stories as told by Hogel seem at first sight to be distinctly legendary. This impression is strengthened by the fact that we find the same stories in the so-called Erfurt chapters in the enlarged Spies Faust Book. And yet there is reason to believe that Hogel uses as his direct source an older Erfurt chronicle whose author knew at first hand the events he is recounting. The historical value of Hogel cannot, therefore, be ignored.[2] What is offered in the *Explicationes* of Melanchthon, and by Lavater is decidedly hearsay.

The problems raised by all this material are not solved when it has been judged along the lines just indicated. The question still remains whether all these references are to one individual or whether there was more than one personage at the basis of the stories. Erich Schmidt held to the former view ; Robert Petsch believes there were two Fausts. The matter is, of course, one for the personal judgment of the reader.

The Faust of history, as he emerges from the letters, diaries, and records of his contemporaries between 1507, when he is first mentioned, and approximately 1540, when all mention of him as still living ceases, remains at best a shadowy figure. That he was widely known, fairly well educated, and extensively travelled ; that he had pretty generally an evil reputation ; that he was a braggart, a vagabond, and something of a mountebank ; that his contemporaries had a great contempt for him not unmixed with fear, all this may be inferred from the extant documents without too much stretching of the imagination.

The widespread interest aroused among contemporaries and succeeding generations by the historical Faust and the legends connected with his name is attested

[2] For a discussion of the historical value of Hogel see Szamatólski, *Euphorion*, II, 39-57.

by the vast number of references to the alleged magician appearing in the various European literatures. The most complete collection of these references was made by Alexander Tille,[3] who, with unbelievable patience and industry, gathered together almost 450 separate items which he published in Berlin between 1898 and 1901. Some ninety additional references, discovered since Tille's collection was printed, have been published in the *Jahrbuch der Sammlung Kippenberg*, Vols. 1, 4, 8, and 9.

I. Letter of Johannes Tritheim [4] to Johannes Virdung.[5]

—The man of whom you wrote me, George Sabellicus, who has presumed to call himself the prince of necromancers, is a vagabond, a babbler and a rogue, who deserves to be thrashed so that he may not henceforth rashly venture to profess in public things so execrable and so hostile to the holy church. For what, other than

Homo [6] ille de quo mihi scripsisti Georgius Sabellicus, qui se principem necromanticorum ausus est nominare, gyrouagus, battologus, et circuncellio est, dignus qui uerberibus castigetur, ne temere deinceps tam nefanda et ecclesiae sanctae contraria publice audeat profiteri. Quid enim sunt aliud tituli quos sibi

[3] Alexander Tille (1866–1912), *Die Faustsplitter in der Literatur des sechzehnten bis achtzehnten Jahrhunderts.* Berlin, 1898–1901.

[4] Johannes Tritheim (1462–1516), physicist, humanist, writer. Abbot of the monastery at Sponheim near Kreuznach from 1485 to 1506. Then, after a short stay in Berlin, abbot of the monastery of St. James at Würzburg. Tritheim combined great learning with an inclination to the fantastic, which led to a considerable reputation as a magician.

[5] Johannes Virdung of Hasfurt was mathematician and astrologer to the Elector of the Palatinate, and a professor at Heidelberg.

[6] For the original text of this selection and of many others cited here we are indebted to Alexander Tille's remarkably complete collection of scattered references to Faust in European literatures entitled: *Die Faustsplitter in der Literatur des sechzehnten bis achtzehnten Jahrhunderts.* Berlin, 1898-1901.

This passage is Tille No. 1.

symptoms of a very foolish and insane mind, are the titles assumed by this man, who shows himself to be a fool and not a philosopher? For thus he has formulated the title befitting him: Master George Sabellicus, the younger Faust, the chief of necromancers, astrologer, the second magus, palmist, diviner with earth and fire, second in the art of divination with water. Behold the foolish temerity of the man, the madness by which he is possessed, in that he dares to call himself the source of necromancy, when in truth, in his ignorance of all good letters, he ought to call himself a fool rather than a master. But his wickedness is not hidden from me. When I was returning last year from the Mark Brandenburg, I happened upon this same man in the town of Gelnhausen, and many silly things were told me about him at the inn,—things promised by him with great rashness on his part. As soon as he heard that I was there, he fled from the inn and could not be persuaded to come into my presence. The description of his folly, such as he gave to you and which we have mentioned, he also sent to me through a certain

assumit, nisi stultissimae ac uesanae mentis inditia, qui se fatuum non philosophum ostendit? Sic enim titulum sibi conuenientem formauit. Magister Georgius Sabellicus, Faustus iunior. fons necromanticorum, astrologus, magus secundus, chiromanticus, agromanticus, pyromanticus, in hydra arte secundus. Vide stultam hominis temeritatem, quanta feratur insania, ut se fontem necromantiae profiteri praesumat, qui vere omnium bonarum literarum ignarus fatuum se potius appellare debuisset quam magistrum. Sed me non latet eius nequitia. Cum anno priore de Marchia Brandenburgensi redirem, hunc ipsum hominem apud Geilenhusen oppidum inueni, de quo mihi plura dicebantur in hospitio friuola, non sine magna eius temeritate ab eo promissa. Qui mox ut me adesse audiuit, fugit de hospitio, et a nullo poterat persuaderi, quod se meis praesentaret aspectibus. Titulum stulticiae suae qualem dedit ad te quem memorauimus, per quendam ciuem

citizen. Certain priests in the same town told me that he had said, in the presence of many people, that he had acquired such knowledge of all wisdom and such a memory, that if all the books of Plato and Aristotle, together with their whole philosophy, had totally passed from the memory of man, he himself, through his own genius, like another Hebrew Ezra,[7] would be able to restore them all with increased beauty. Afterwards, while I was at Speyer, he came to Würzburg and, impelled by the same vanity, is reported to have said in the presence of many that the miracles of Christ the Saviour were not so wonderful, that he himself could do all the things which Christ had done, as often and whenever he wished. Towards the end of Lent of the present year he came to Kreuznach and with like folly and boastfulness made great promises, saying that in alchemy he was the most learned man of all times and that by his knowledge and ability, he could do whatever

ad me quoque destinauit. Referebant mihi quidam in oppido sacerdotes, quod in multorum praesentia dixerit, tantam se omnis sapientiae consecutum scientiam atque memoriam, ut si uolumina Platonis et Aristotelis omnia cum tota eorum philosophia in toto perisset ab hominum memoria, ipse suo ingenio uelut Ezras alter Hebraeus, restituere uniuersa cum praestantiore ualeret elegantia. Postea me Neometi existente Herbipolim uenit, eademque uanitate actus in plurimorum fertur dixisse praesentia, quod Christi Saluatoris miracula non sint miranda, se quoque omnia facere posse quae Christus fecit quoties et quandocunque uelit. In ultima quoque huius anni quadragesima uenit Stauronesum, et simili stulticiae gloriosus de se pollicebatur ingentia, dicens se in Alchimia omnium qui fuerint unquam esse perfectissimum, et scire atque posse quicquid

[7] Cf. Eusebius, *Ecclesiastical History*, tr. by K. Lane, London, 1926. Vol. I, V, viii, 461 : "— for when the Scriptures had been destroyed in the captivity of the people in the days of Nebuchadnezzar, and the Jews had gone back to their country after seventy years, then in the time of Artaxerxes, the king of the Persians, he (God) inspired Ezra, the priest of the tribe of Levi, to restore all the sayings of the prophets who had gone before, and to restore to the people the law given by Moses." Quoted by Eusebius from Irenaeus.

anyone might wish. In the meantime there was vacant in the same town the position of schoolmaster, to which he was appointed through the influence of Franz von Sickingen,[8] the magistrate of your prince and a man very fond of mystical lore. Then he began to indulge in the most dastardly kind of lewdness with the boys and when this was suddenly discovered, he avoided by flight the punishment that awaited him. These are the things which I know through very definite evidence concerning the man whose coming you await with such anticipation. When he comes to you, you will find him to be not a philosopher but a fool with an overabundance of rashness.—Würzburg, the 20th day of August. A.D. 1507.

homines optauerint. Vacabat interea munus docendi scholasticum in oppido memorato, ad quod Francisci ab Sickingen Baliui principis tui, hominis mysticarum rerum percupidi promotione fuit assumptus, qui mox nefandissimo fornicationis genere cum pueris uidelicet uoluptari coepit, quo statim deducto in lucem fuga poenam declinauit paratam. Haec sunt quae mihi certissimo constant testimonio de homine illo, quem tanto uenturum esse desyderio praestolaris. Cum uenerit ad te, non philosophum, sed hominem fatuum et nimia temeritate agitatum inuenies.—Ex herbipoli uicesima die mensis Augusti. Anno Christianorum 1507.

II. Extract from the Matriculation Records of Heidelberg University.[9]

Nach einem Inscriptions-Verzeichnisse der philosophischen Fakultät zu Heidelberg war ein Johann Faust im Jahre 1509 bei ihr als lernendes Mitglied eingeschrieben. Ein „Johann Faust" kommt in den *actis philosoph. Heidelb.*, tom. III, fol. 36, a unter dem

[8] Franz von Sickingen (1481–1523), imperial counsellor, chamberlain and general, greatest of the "free knights," friend of Ulrich von Hutten and by him interested in humanism. Supporter of the Reformation.

[9] Scheible, *Kloster*, Vol. XI, p. 330.

Decanate des Mag. Laurentius Wolff von Speier, Baccalaureus der Theologie im Jahre 1509, als der erste unter denen vor, die am 15. Januar 1509 ad baccalaureatus gradum de via moderna ordine, quo supra notatum, admissi sunt. Er ist mit den Worten angeführt: „Johannes Faust ex Simern." Auszer ihm stehen in derselben Promotion noch 15 andere. Dem Namen ist, wie einigen andern Promovirten, *d* vorausgesetzt, was nach des Herrn geh. Kirchenraths Ullmann Erklärung, dem ich diese Mittheilung verdanke, so viel als dedit, „er hat bezahlt," bedeutet, und ein Beweis für die Wohlhabenheit dieses Faust ist. Die Via moderna ist die nominalistische Richtung gegenüber der realistischen, welche damals als eine neue oder reformatorische beliebt war. Nach andern historischen Nachrichten, auf die wir hingewiesen haben, wird Faust auch Hedebergensis (vielleicht so viel als Heidelbergensis) genannt und trieb sich auch in der Rheinpfalz herum.

III. Letter of Conrad Mutianus Rufus[10] to Heinrich Urbanus.[11]

—Eight days ago there came to Erfurt a certain soothsayer by the name of George Faust, the demigod of Heidelberg, a mere braggart and fool. His claims,

Venit[12] octauo abhinc die quidam Chiromanticus Ephurdiam nomine Georgius Faustus, Helmitheus Hedebergensis,[13] merus

[10] Conrad Mutianus Rufus (1471–1526). Canon of the Church of St. Mary's at Gotha. His real name was Konrad Muth. He led a studious life as a humanist and philosopher and was ranked by the humanists with Erasmus and Reuchlin, despite the fact that he never published any of his writings.

[11] Heinrich Urbanus, student and later friend of Mutianus Rufus, and through him interested in humanism. From about 1505 he was steward of the Cistercian cloister Georgenthal at Erfurt.

[12] Tille, No. 2.

[13] The Latin phrase 'Helmitheus Hedebergensis' is unintelligible. Christian August Heumann (cf. Tille, page 587) surmises that 'Helmitheus' is a misspelling for "Hemitheus." H. Düntzer (cf. Scheible's *Kloster*, V, 36) suggests "Hedelbergensis" instead of 'Hedebergensis.' These emendations are

like those of all diviners, are idle and such physiognomy has no more weight than a water spider. The ignorant marvel at him. Let the theologians rise against him and not try to destroy the philosopher Reuchlin.[14] I heard him babbling at an inn, but I did not reprove his boastfulness. What is the foolishness of other people to me?—October 3, 1513.

ostentator et fatuus. Eius et omnium diuinaculorum vana est professio, et talis physiognomia leuior typula. Rudes admirantur. in eum theologi insurgant. Non conficiant philosophum Capnionem. Ego audiui garrientem in hospitio, Non castigaui iactantiam. quid aliena insania ad me?—V. Nonas Octobris MDXIII.

IV. From the Account Book of the Bishop of Bamberg,[15] 1519–1520.

The annual accounts of Hans Muller, chamberlain, from Walpurgis[16] 1519 to Walpurgis 1520.

Entry on February 12, 1520, under the heading "Miscellaneous."

Hansen[17] mullers Camermeysters Jarrechnung von walburgis fonffzehenhundert vnd jm Neunzehetten bisz widerumb auff walburgis fonffzehenhundert vnd jm Zweintzigisten Jarn.

Eintrag vom 12. Febr. 1520 unter Pro Diversis:

generally accepted. Franz Babinger (*Alemania* 41, 1914), basing his argument on Kilian Lieb's report (see V, page 89 of this work) argues for the reading "Helmsteten(sis) Hedelbergensis," which would mean "from Helmstedt near Heidelberg."

[14] Johann Reuchlin (1455–1522). Capnio was the Greek form of his name. He was learned in jurisprudence and languages (especially Greek and Hebrew). For many years he was in the service successively of Count Eberhard of Württemberg, Johann von Dalberg at Heidelberg, and Duke Ulrich of Württemberg. In 1519 he became Professor of Greek and Hebrew at Ingolstadt and from 1521 held the same chair at Tübingen. In 1511 he was involved in a bitter quarrel with the theological faculty at Cologne.

[15] George III Schenk of Limburg was Bishop of Bamberg from 1502 to 1522.

[16] i.e. May 1st.

[17] Tille, No. 3.

10 gulden given and presented as a testimonial to Doctor Faust, the philosopher, who made for my master a horoscope or prognostication. Paid on the Sunday after Saint Scholastica's Day [18] by the order of his reverence.

Item x guld[en] geben vnd geschenckt Doctor Faustus ph[ilosoph]o zuuererung hat m[einem] g[nedigen] Herrn ein natiuitet oder Indicium gemacht, Zalt am Sontag nach stolastice Jussit R[everendissi]mus.

V. From the Journal of Kilian Lieb,[19] July 1528.

George Faust of Helmstet said on the fifth of June that when the sun and Jupiter are in the same constellation prophets are born (presumably such as he). He asserted that he was the commander or preceptor of the order of the Knights of St. John at a place called Hallestein [20] on the border of Carinthia.

Georgius [21] faustus helmstetensis [22] quinta Junii dicebat, quando sol et Jupiter sunt in eodem unius signi gradu, tunc nascuntur prophete (utpote sui similes). Asserebat se commendatorem seu praeceptorem domunculae Johannitarum in confiniis carintiae, quod appelletur hallestein.

[18] Saint Scholastica's Day fell on Friday, February 10, 1520.

[19] Kilian Leib was the prior of Rebdorf in Bavaria.

[20] Hallestein. According to Schottenloher (see below) this is probably Heilenstein in Styria which at one time was the seat of the Knights of St. John.

[21] The extract is from Leib's entry for July, 1528. The original journal of Leib is in the Staatsbibliothek in Munich. It has been published by Karl Schottenloher, *Der Rebdorfer Prior, Kilian Leib, und sein Wettertagebuch von 1513 bis 1531*. Gotha, 1913, Friedrich Andreas Perthes A-G. (Sonderabdruck der Beiträge zur Bayrischen Geschichte). The passage cited will be found on pp. 92-93 of this reprint.

[22] 'helmstetensis.' Schottenloher connects this with Mutianus Rufus' "Helmitheus Hedebergensis" and concludes that Faust was born in Helmstedt near Heidelberg.

VI. From the Records of the City of Ingolstadt.

(a) Minute on the actions of the city council in Ingolstadt.

Today, the Wednesday after St. Vitus' Day,[23] 1528. The soothsayer shall be ordered to leave the city and to spend his penny elsewhere.

(b) Record of those banished from Ingolstadt.

On Wednesday after St. Vitus' Day, 1528, a certain man who called himself Dr. George Faust of Heidelberg was told to spend his penny elsewhere and he pledged himself not to take vengeance on or make fools of the authorities for this order.

(a) Ratsprotokoll[24] über die obrigkeitlichen Beschlüsse in Ingolstadt:

Anheut Mitwoch nach viti 1528. Dem Wahrsager soll befohlen werden, dass er zu der Stadt auszieh und seinen Pfennig anderswo verzehre.

(b) Protokoll der aus Ingolstadt Verwiesenen:

Am Mitwoch nach viti 1528 ist einem der sich genannt Dr. Jörg Faustus von Heidelberg gesagt, dass er seinen Pfennig anderswo verzehre, und hat angelobt, solche Erforderung für die Obrigkeit nicht zu ahnden noch zu äffen.

VII. Entry in the Records of the City Council of Nuremberg. May 10, 1532.

Safe conduct to Doctor Faust, the great sodomite[25] and necromancer, at Fürth[26] refused.

The junior Burgomaster.

Doctor fausto[27] dem groszen Sodomiten und Nigromantico zu furr glait ablainen. Bürgermeister junior

[23] St. Vitus' Day fell on Monday, June 15, 1528.

[24] Tille, No. 4.

[25] Cf. Tritheim's account of Faust's experience as a teacher in Kreuznach, No. I, p. 86.

[26] We have followed the suggestion of Neubert, *Vom Doctor Faustus zu Goethes Faust*, Leipzig, 1932, p. 16, that 'zu furr' is to be interpreted as "zu Fürth."

[27] Cited from Neubert, op. cit., p. 16. The original is in the Bavarian State Archives in Nuremberg. Cf. the above with Manlius' story of Faust's narrow escape from arrest in Nuremberg, No. XVIII, p. 102 f.

VIII. From the Waldeck Chronicle.

Francis I by the grace of God, son of Philip II[28] by his second marriage, Bishop of Münster, on June 25, 1535, invested the city of Münster which had been occupied by the Anabaptists and captured it with the aid of princes of the Empire under the leadership of Hensel Hochstraten. John of Leyden,[29] the boastful pretender, who called himself King of Israel and Zion, was executed together with Knipperdollinck and Krechting, their bodies being torn with red-hot pincers, enclosed in iron cages and suspended from the tower of St. Lambert's Church on the 23rd of January, 1536. It was at this time that the famous necromancer Dr. Faust, coming on the same day from Corbach,[30] prophesied that the city of Münster would surely be captured by the bishop on that very night.

Franciscvs I.[31] Dei gratia, filius Philippi II. ex secundo matrimonio natus, Episcopus Monasteriensis, qui anno 1535. 25 Jun. vrbem Münster ab Anabaptistis occupatam, obsidione cinxit, & auxilio procerum imperii, ductore Henselino Hochstraten expugnauit, de Johanne de Leiden farcinatore, qui se Regem Israelis & Sionis nominabat, Knipperdillingio & Krechtio supplicia sumsit, quorum corpora candentibus igne forcipibus lacerata, & ferreis inclusa caueis e turri St. Lamberti suspensa sunt, 23 Jan. an. 1536. quo tempore insignis ille Nigromanticus D. Faustus eo ipso die Corbachii diuertens, praedixit, fore nimirum, vt eadem nocte vrbs Münster ab Episcopo expugnetur.

28 i.e. Philip II, Count of Waldeck.

29 John of Leyden, originally a tailor, became a leader of the Anabaptist movement in Münster and set up there the "Kingdom of Zion" proclaiming himself king. Krechting was his chancellor. Knipperdollinck was mayor of Münster during the Anabaptist régime.

30 A small town in the principality of Waldeck, about eighty miles southeast of Münster.

31 The text is taken from the *Jahrbuch der Sammlung Kippenberg*, I (1921), p. 322.

IX. Letter of Joachim Camerarius[32] to Daniel Stibar.[33]

—I owe to your friend Faust the pleasure of discussing these affairs with you. I wish he had taught you something of this sort rather than puffed you up with the wind of silly superstition or held you in suspense with I know not what juggler's tricks. But what does he tell us, pray? For I know that you have questioned him diligently about all things. Is the emperor victorious? That is the way you should go about it.—Tübingen, the 13th of August, 1536.

—Faustus[34] enim tuus facit, ut tecum lubeat ista disserere, qui utinam docuerit te potius aliquid ex hac arte, quam inflauerit uentulo uanissimae superstitionis, Aut nescio quibus praestigijs suspensum tenuerit. Sed quid ille ait nobis tandem? Quid etiam? Scio enim te diligenter de omnibus percontatum. Caesar ne uincit? Ita quidem fieri necesse est.—Tubingae. Jd. Sextil. Anno Christi MDXXXVI.

X. From the Tischreden of Martin Luther.[35]

God's word alone overcomes the fiery arrows of the devil and all his temptations.

Gottes Wort[36] allein vberwindet des Teufels fewrige pfeile vnd alle anfechtungen.

[32] Joachim Camerarius (1500–1574). His real name was Joachim Liebhard. 1518, teacher of Greek at Erfurt. 1521, he went to Wittenberg where he became a friend of Melanchthon. 1526, became teacher of Greek at the Gymnasium in Nuremberg. 1535, was called to Tübingen to reform the university. 1541, called to Leipzig for the same purpose. Camerarius' importance is beyond dispute. He was the best philologist of his time; and he wrote many works, mostly in the field of philology, but also of history and biography. He enjoyed an international reputation.

[33] Daniel Stibarus was a city councilman of Würzburg.

[34] Tille, No. 5.

[35] Martin Luther (1483–1546), reformer and founder of the Protestant church. The *Tischreden* were published in Eisleben by Aurifaber in 1566. They give the comments and discussions of Luther in the informal circle of his family, friends, and acquaintances, as they had been recorded by Aurifaber himself and by numerous other intimates of Luther. The passage quoted is found in Chap. 1, § 47 of the Aurifaber edition of 1566.

[36] Tille, No. 15.

When one evening at the table a sorcerer named Faust was mentioned, Doctor Martin said in a serious tone: "The devil does not make use of the services of sorcerers against me. If he had been able to do me any harm he would have done it long since. To be sure he has often had me by the head but he had to let me go again."

DA vber Tisch zu abends eines Schwartzkünstlers Faustus genant gedacht ward / saget Doctor Martinus ernstlich / der Teufel gebraucht der / zeuberer dienst wider mich nicht / hette er mir gekont vnd vermocht schaden zu thun / er hette es lange gethan. Er hat mich wol offtmals schon bey dem kopff gehabt / aber er hat mich dennoch mussen gehen lassen.

XI. From the Tischreden of Martin Luther.

Mention was made of magicians and the magic art, and how Satan blinded men. Much was said about Faust, who called the devil his brother-in-law, and the remark was made: "If I, Martin Luther, had given him even my hand, he would have destroyed me; but I would not have been afraid of him,—with God as my protector, I would have given him my hand in the name of the Lord."

De ludificatoribus[37] et arte magica fiebat mentio, quomodo Sathan homines excaecaret. Multa dicebant de Fausto, welcher den Teufel seinen schwoger hies, und hat sich lassen horen: "Wenn ich, Martin Luther, im nur die handt gereicht hette, wolt er mich vorterbet haben; aber ich wolde in nicht gescheuet haben, porrexissem illi manus in nomine Domini, Deo protectore."

[37] This quotation is not in the Aurifaber collection. It was taken down by Antonius Lauterbach in 1537 and first published by E. Kroker, *Luthers Tischreden in der Mathesischen Sammlung*, Leipzig, 1903, p. 422. Our text is from Walz, "An English Faustsplitter," *Modern Language Notes*, Vol. XLII (1927), p. 361.

XII. From the Index Sanitatis of Philipp Begardi.[38]

There is another well-known and important man whom I would not have mentioned were it not for the fact that he himself had no desire to remain in obscurity and unknown. For some years ago he traveled through almost all countries, principalities and kingdoms, and himself made his name known to everybody and bragged much about his great skill not only in medicine but also in chiromancy, nigromancy, physiognomy, crystal gazing, and the like arts. And he not only bragged but confessed and signed himself as a famous and experienced master. He himself avowed and did not deny that he was and was called Faust and in addition signed himself "The philosopher of philosophers." The number of those who complained to me that they were cheated by him was very great. Now his promises were great like those of Thessalus[39]; likewise his fame

Es wirt[40] noch eyn namhafftiger dapfferer mann erfunden : ich wolt aber doch seinen namen nit genent haben / so wil er auch nit verborgen sein / noch vnbekant. Dann er ist vor etlichen jaren vast durch alle landtschafft / Fürstenthuomb vnnd Königreich gezogen / seinen namen jederman selbs bekant gemacht / vnd seine grosse kunst / nit alleyn der artznei / sonder auch Chiromancei / Nigramancei / Visionomei / Visiones imm Cristal /vnd dergleichen mer künst / sich höchlich berümpt. Vnd auch nit alleyn berümpt, sonder sich auch eynen berümpten vnd erfarnen meyster bekant vnnd geschriben. Hat auch selbs bekant / vnd nit geleugknet / dasz er sei / vnnd heysz Faustus, domit sich geschriben Philosophum Philosophorum etc. Wie vil aber mir geklagt haben, dasz sie von jm seind betrogen worden, deren ist eyn grosse zal gewesen. Nuon sein verheyssen ware auch grosz / wie des Tessali : der-

[38] Philipp Begardi was city physician in Worms. The *Index Sanitatis* is of the year 1539.

[39] Thessalus was a Greek physician of the first century A.D. He lived in Rome during the reign of Nero and was buried there. He considered himself superior to his predecessors but Galen, while often mentioning him, always does so in terms of contempt.

[40] Tille, No. 6.

as that of Theophrastus.[41] But his deeds, as I hear, were very petty and fraudulent. But in taking or — to speak more accurately — in receiving money he was not slow. And afterwards also, on his departure, as I have been informed, he left many to whistle for their money. But what is to be done about it? What's gone is gone. I will drop the subject here. Anything further is your affair.

gleichen sein rhuom / wie auch des Theophrasti : aber die that / wie ich noch vernimm, vast kleyn vnd betrüglich erfunden : doch hat er sich imm gelt nemen, oder empfahen (das ich auch recht red) nit gesaumpt / vnd nachmals auch imm abzugk / er hat / wie ich beracht / vil mit den ferszen gesegnet. Aber was soll man nuon darzuothuon, hin ist hin / ich wil es jetzt auch do bei lassen /luog du weiter / was du zuschicken hast.

XIII. Letter from Philipp von Hutten[42] to His Brother Moritz von Hutten.

Here you have a little about all the provinces so that you may see that we are not the only ones who have been unfortunate in Venezuela up to this time; that all the abovementioned expeditions which left Sevilla before and after us perished within three months.

Hie habt[43] ihr von allen Gubernationen ein wenig, damit ihr sehet, dasz wir hie in Venezola nicht allein biszher unglücklich gewest sein, diese alle obgemelte Armata verdorben seind jnnerhalb 3. Monathe, vor und nach uns zu Sevilla aus-

41 Theophrastus, i.e., Philippus Aureolus Paracelsus Theophrastus Bombastus von Hohenheim (1493–1541), physician and chemist. Bombastic in fact as well as by name, inclined to charlatanism, suspected of supernatural powers and himself promoting the suspicion, he is nevertheless credited by modern scholarship with genuine service in the fields of medicine, chemistry, and pharmacy.

42 Philipp von Hutten (1511–1546) was one of the leaders of the Welser troops in Venezuela, where he met his death. The letter would seem to indicate that Faust had made predictions concerning the fortunes of the expedition in Venezuela.

43 Tille, No. 7.

Therefore I must confess that the philosopher Faust hit the nail on the head, for we struck a very bad year. But God be praised, things went better for us than for any of the others. God willing I shall write you again before we leave here. Take good care of our dear old mother. Give my greetings to all our neighbours and friends, especially Balthasar Rabensteiner and George von Libra, William von Hessberg and all my good comrades. Pay my respects to Herr N of Thüngen, my master's brother. Done in Coro in the Province of Venezuela on January 16th, 1540.

gefahren, dasz ich bekennen musz, dasz es der Philosophus Faustus schier troffen hat, dann wir ein fast böszes Jahr antroffen haben, aber Gott hab Lob ist uns fast unter allen andern am besten gangen. Will euch ob Gott will ehe wir hie ausziehen weiter schreiben. Bitt euch unser liebes alts Mutterle laszen befohlen seyn. Grüszt mir all unsere Nachbaren und Freund, insonderheit Balthasar Rabensteinern und Jorg von Libra, Wilhelm von Heszberg und alle gute Gesellen, Sagt auch Herrn N von Thüngen meines gnl. Herrn Bruder mein Dienst. Datum in Coro der Provinzen Venezola im etc. 40. Jahr den 16. Jan.

XIV. From the Sermones Convivales of Johannes Gast.[44]

Concerning the Necromancer Faust

He puts up at night at a certain very rich monastery, intending to spend the night there. A brother places before him some ordinary wine of indifferent quality

De Fausto necromantico.[45]

Diuertitur sub noctem in coenobium quoddam, ualde diues, pernoctaturus illic. Fraterculus apponit illi uile uinum, pen-

[44] Johannes Gast († 1572) was a Protestant clergyman at Basle. His *Sermones Convivales* were very popular. The quotation is from the second volume, published in 1548.

[45] Tille, No. 8.

and without flavor. Faust requests that he draw from another cask a better wine which it was the custom to give to nobles. Then the brother said: "I do not have the keys, the prior is sleeping, and it is a sin to awaken him." Faust said: "The keys are lying in that corner. Take them and open that cask on the left and give me a drink." The brother objected that he had no orders from the prior to place any other wine before guests. When Faust heard this he became very angry and said: "In a short time you shall see marvels, you inhospitable brother." Burning with rage he left early in the morning without saying farewell and sent a certain raging devil who made a great stir in the monastery by day and by night and moved things about both in the church and in the cells of the monks, so that they could not get any rest, no matter what they did. Finally they deliberated whether they should leave the monastery or destroy it altogether. And so they wrote to the Count Palatine concerning the misfortune in which they were involved. He took the monastery under his own protection and ejected the monks to whom he furnishes supplies from year to year and uses what is left for

dulum, ac nihil gratiae habens. rogat Faustus ut ex uase altero hauriat melius uinum, quod nobilibus dare consueuerat. Fraterculus mox dixit, Claues non habeo, Prior dormit, quem exuscitare piaculum est. Faustus inquit, Claues iacent in isto angulo, has accipe, et uas illud ad sinistrum latus aperi, et adfer mihi potum. Fraterculus renuit, sibi non esse commissum a Priori aliud uinum hospitibus proponere. Faustus ijs auditis, iratus dixit, Videbis breui momento mira inhospitalis fratercule. Abijt summo mane insalutato hospite, ira accensus, ac immisit satanam quendam furibundum, die noctuque in coenobio perstrepentem, omnia mouentem tam in ecclesia quam in ipsis habitationibus monachorum, adeo ut quietem nullam habere possint, quodcunque negotium attentarent. Tandem deliberarunt, an coenobium esset relinquendum, aut omnino pereundum. Palatino itaque scripserunt de infortunio illo, quo tenebantur. Qui coenobium in suam recepit defensionem, abiectis monachis,

himself. It is said that to this very day, if monks enter the monastery, such great disturbances arise that those who live there can have no peace. This the devil was able to bring to pass.

Another Story about Faust

At Basle I dined with him in the great college and he gave to the cook various kinds of birds to roast. I do not know where he bought them or who gave them to him, since there were none on sale at the time. Moreover I never saw any like them in our regions. He had with him a dog and a horse which I believe to have been demons and which were ready for any service. I was told that the dog at times assumed the form of a servant and served the food. However, the wretch was destined to come to a deplorable end, for he was strangled by the devil and his body on its bier kept turning face downward even though it was five times turned on its back. God preserve us lest we become slaves of the devil.

quibus alimenta praestat in singulos annos, reliqua sibi seruat. Aiunt quidam, etsi adhuc hodie monachi coenobium intrent, tantas turbationes fieri, ut quietem incolentes habere non possint. Hoc nouit satan instituere.

Aliud de Fausto exemplum.

Basileae cum illo coenatus sum in collegio magno, qui uarij generis aues, nescio ubi emerat, aut quis dederat, cum hoc temporis nullae uenderentur, coquo ad assandum praebuerat. quales etiam ego nunquam in nostris regionibus uiderim. Canem secum ducebat et equum, Satanas fuisse reor, qui ad omnia erant parati exequenda. Canem aliquando serui formam assumere, et esculenta adferre, quidam mihi dixere. Atqui miser deplorandum finem sortitus est, nam a satana suffocatus, cuius cadauer in feretro facie ad terram perpetuo spectans, etsi quinquies in tergum uerteretur. Dominus custodiat nos, ne satanae mancipia fiamus.

XV. From the Explicationes Melanchthoniae,[46] Pars II.

There [in the presence of Nero] Simon Magus tried to fly to heaven, but Peter prayed that he might fall. I believe that the Apostles had great struggles although not all are recorded. Faust also tried this at Venice. But he was sorely dashed to the ground.

Ibi[47] [coram Nerone] Simon Magus subuolare in caelum: sed Petrus precatus est vt decideret. Credo Apostolos habuisse magna certamina, etiamsi non omnia sunt scripta. Faustus Venetiis etiam hoc tentauit. Sed male allisus solo.

XVI. From the Explicationes Melanthoniae, Pars IV.

The devil is a marvellous craftsman, for he is able by some device to accomplish things which are natural but which we do not understand. For he can do more than man. Thus many strange feats of magic are recounted such as I have related elsewhere concerning the girl at Bologna. In like manner Faust, the magician, devoured at Vienna another magician who was

Diabolus[48] est mirabilis artifex; potest enim aliqua arte efficere, quae sunt naturalia, quae nos non scimus. Denn er kan mehr, den die menschen konnen. Sicut narrantur multa magica prodigiosa, vt alias dixi de puella Bononiensi: Item Faustus magus deuoravit alium Magum Viennae, qui post

[46] Philipp Melanchthon (Greek for Schwarzert) (1497–1560) was a co-worker of Luther and after him the most important figure in the German Reformation. From 1518 on he was professor of the Greek language and literature at Wittenberg. After Luther's death he became the head of the Protestant church.

The *Explicationes Melanchthoniae*, or *Postilla Melanthoniana*, as they are called in the Bretschneider and Bindseil edition of Melanchthon's works, were published by Christopher Pezelius, a former student of Melanchthon, in 1594 ff., and they reproduce Melanchthon's commentaries on the Scriptures, delivered between 1549 and 1560.

[47] Tille, No. 9.

[48] Tille, No. 10.

discovered a few days later in a certain cave. The devil can perform many miracles; nevertheless the church has its own miracles.

paucos dies inuentus est in quodam specu. Der Teuffel kan viel wunderlichs dings: tamen Ecclesia habet propria quaedam miracula.

XVII. From the Epistolae Medicinales of Conrad Gesner.[49] Letter from Gesner to Johannes Crato[50] of Krafftheim.

Oporinus[51] of Basle, formerly a disciple and companion of Theophrastus,[52] narrates some wonderful things concerning the latter's dealings with demons. Such men practice vain astrology, geomancy, necromancy, and similar prohibited arts. I suspect indeed that they derive from the Druids who among the ancient Celts were for some years taught by demons in underground places. This has been practiced at Salamanca in Spain down to our own day. From that school came those

Oporinus Basileae[53] olim discipulus Theophrasti, et familiaris fuit, is mira de eius cum daemonibus commercio praedicat. Astrologiam vanam, Geomantiam, Necromantiam, et hiusmodi artes prohibitas exercent. Equidem suspicor illos ex Druidarum reliquijs esse, qui apud Celtas veteres in subterraneis locis a daemonibus aliquot annis erudiebantur: quod nostra memoria in Hispania adhuc Salamancae factitatum constat.

[49] Conrad Gesner (1516–1565), a Swiss teacher, physician, and scholar. His scholarly activity was enormous. His main fields were zoology and botany, but he did tremendous work also in medicine, in philology, and in the editing and translating of Greek and Latin writers. His writings in these fields are encyclopedic.

The letter quoted is dated Zurich, August 16, 1561.

[50] Johannes Crato was Physician in Ordinary of the Emperor, Ferdinand I.

[51] Johannes Oporinus (1507–1568), a Swiss teacher, physician, and in later years publisher and bookseller. The name Oporinus is a translation of Herbst or Herbster.

[52] See note (41), page 95.

[53] Tille, No. 11.

commonly called "wandering scholars," among whom a certain Faust, who died not long since, is very celebrated.

Ex illa schola prodierunt, quos vulgo scholasticos vagantes nominabant, inter quos Faustus quidam non ita pridem mortuus, mire celebratur.

XVIII. From the Locorum Communium Collectanea of Johannes Manlius.[54]

I knew a certain man by the name of Faust from Kundling,[55] which is a small town near my birthplace. When he was a student at Cracow he studied magic, for there was formerly much practice of the art in that city and in that place too there were public lectures on this art. He wandered about everywhere and talked of many mysterious things. When he wished to provide a spectacle at Venice he said he would fly to heaven. So the devil raised him up and then cast him down so that he was dashed to the ground and almost killed. However he did not die.

A few years ago this same John Faust, on the day before his end, sat very downcast in a certain village

Noui[56] quendam nomine Faustum de Kundling, quod est paruum oppidum, patriae meae uicinum. Hic cum esset scholasticus Cracouiensis, ibi magiam didicerat, sicut ibi olim fuit eius magnus usus, et ibidem fuerunt publicae eiusdem artis professiones. Vagabatur passim, dicebat arcana multa. Ille Venetijs cum uellet ostendere spectaculum, dixit se uolaturum in coelum. Diabolus igitur subuexit eum, et afflixit adeo, ut allisus humi pene exanimatus esset : sed tamen non est mortuus.

Ante paucos annos idem Ioannes Faustus, postremo die sedit

[54] Johannes Manlius (Mennel) of Ansbach was at one time a student under Melanchthon. In the *Locorum Communium Collectanea* (1563), Manlius gives extracts and quotations "from the lectures of D. Philipp Melanchthon and accounts of other most learned men." The passages cited are quoted from Melanchthon.

[55] i.e. Knittlingen, not far from Bretten, Melanchthon's birthplace.

[56] Tille, No. 12.

in the Duchy of Württemberg. The host asked him why, contrary to his custom and habit, he was so downcast (he was otherwise a most shameful scoundrel who led a very wicked life, so that he was again and again nigh to being killed because of his dissolute habits). Then he said to the host in the village: "Don't be frightened tonight." In the middle of the night the house was shaken. When Faust did not get up in the morning and when it was now almost noon, the host with several others went into his bedroom and found him lying near the bed with his face turned toward his back. Thus the devil had killed him. While he was alive he had with him a dog which was the devil, just as the scoundrel[57] who wrote "De vanitate artium" likewise had a dog that ran about with him and was the devil. This same Faust escaped in this town of Wittenberg when the good prince Duke John had given orders to arrest him. Likewise in Nuremberg he escaped. He was just beginning to dine when he became restless and immediately rose and paid the host

admodum moestus in quodam pago ducatus Vuirtenbergensis. Hospes ipsum alloquitur, cur moestus esset praeter morem et consuetudinem (erat alioqui turpissimus nebulo, inquinatissimae uitae, ita ut semel atque iterum pene interfectus sit propter libidines) ibi dixit hospiti in illo pago: Ne perterrefias hac nocte. Media nocte domus quassata est. Mane cum Faustus non surgeret, et iam esset fere meridies, hospes adhibitis alijs, ingressus est in eius conclaue, inuenitque eum iacentem prope lectum inuersa facie, sic a diabolo interfectus. Viuens, adhuc, habebat secum canem, qui erat diabolus, sicut iste nebulo qui scripsit De uanitate artium etiam habebat canem, secum currentem, qui erat diabolus. Hic Faustus in hoc oppido Vuittenberga euasit, cum optimus princeps dux Ioannes dedisset mandata de illo capiendo. Sic Norimbergae etiam euasit, cum iam inciperet prandere, aestuauit, surgitque statim, soluens quod

[57] i.e. Cornelius Heinrich Agrippa von Nettesheim (1486–1535), author, physician, and philosopher. He, like so many others, was also suspected of being a sorcerer.

what he owed. He had hardly got outside the gate when the bailiffs came and inquired about him.

The same magician Faust, a vile beast and a sink of many devils, falsely boasted that all the victories which the emperor's armies have won in Italy had been gained by him through his magic. This was an absolute lie. I mention this for the sake of the young that they may not readily give ear to such lying men.

hospiti debebat. uix autem uenerat ante portam, ibi ueniunt lictores, et de eo inquirunt.

Idem Faustus magus, turpissima bestia, et cloaca multorum diabolorum, uane gloriabatur de se omnes uictorias, quas habuerunt Caesariani exercitus in Italia, esse partas per ipsum sua magia. idque fuit mendacium uanissimum. Id enim dico propter iuuentutem, ne statim talibus uanis hominibus assentiantur.

XIX. From the Zimmerische Chronik.[58]

That the practice of such art [soothsaying] is not only godless but in the highest degree dangerous is undeniable, for experience proves it and we know what happened to the notorious sorcerer Faust. After he had practiced during his lifetime many marvels about which a special treatise could be written, he was finally killed

Das aber[59] die pratik solcher Kunst [des Weiszagens] nit allain gottlos, sonder zum höchsten sorgclich, das ist unlaugenbar, dann sich das in der erfarnus beweist, und wissen, wie es dem weitberüempten schwarzkünstler, dem Fausto, ergangen. Derselbig ist nach vilen wunderbarlichen sachen, die er bei seinem leben geiebt, darvon auch ein besonderer tractat wer zu

[58] The *Zimmerische Chronik* is a Swabian chronicle of the 16th century. The authors were Count Froben Christoph von Zimmern (†1566 or 1567) and his secretary Hans Müller (†ca. 1600). The work centers about the history of the Swabian noblemen who later became the Counts of Zimmern. It contains an invaluable store of legends and folklore.

[59] Tille, No. 13.

at a ripe old age by the evil one in the seigniory of Staufen in Breisgau.

(After 1539). About this time also Faust died in or not far from the town of Staufen in Breisgau. In his day he was as remarkable a sorcerer as could be found in German lands in our times. He had so many strange experiences at various times that he will not easily be forgotten for many years. He became an old man and, as it is said, died miserably. From all sorts of reports and conjectures many have thought that the evil one, whom in his lifetime he used to call his brother-in-law, had killed him. The books which he left behind fell into the hands of the Count of Staufen in whose territory he died. Afterwards many people tried to get these books and in doing so in my opinion were seeking a dangerous and unlucky treasure and gift. He sent a spirit into the monastery of the monks at Luxheim [60] in the Vosges mountains which they could

machen, letzstlich in der herrschaft Staufen im Preisgew in groszem alter vom bösen gaist umbgebracht worden.

[Nach 1539.] Es ist auch umb die zeit der Faustus zu oder doch nit weit von Staufen, dem stetlin im Breisgew, gestorben. Der ist bei seiner zeit ein wunderbarlicher nigromanta gewest, als er bei unsern zeiten hat mögen in deutschen landen erfunden werden, der auch sovil seltzamer hendel gehapt hin und wider, das sein in vil jaren nit leuchtlichen wurt vergessen werden. Ist ain alter mann worden und, wie man sagt, ellengclichen gestorben. Vil haben allerhandt anzeigungen und vermuetungen noch vermaint, der bös gaist, den er in seinen lebzeiten nur sein schwager genannt, habe ine umbbracht. Die büecher, die er verlasen, sein dem herren von Staufen, in dessen herrschaft er abgangen, zu handen worden, darumb doch hernach vil leut haben geworben und daran meins erachtens ein sorgclichen und unglückhaftigen schatz und gabe begert. Den münchen zu Lüxheim im Wassichin hat er ain gespenst in das closter verbannet, desen sie in vil jaren nit haben

[60] Compare the story cited above from Johannes Gast on page 96 ff.

not get rid of for years and which bothered them tremendously,—and this for no other reason than that once upon a time they did not wish to put him up over night. For this reason he sent them the restless guest. In like manner, it is said, a similar spirit was summoned and attached to the former abbot of St. Diesenberg by an envious wandering scholar.

künden ab kommen und sie wunderbarlich hat molestirt, allain der ursach, das sie ine einsmals nit haben wellen übernacht behalten, darumb hat er inen den unrüebigen gast geschafft, zu gleich wie man sagt, das dem vorigen apt von S. Diesenberg auch ain sollichs gespenst von ainem neidigen varenden schueler seie zugerüst und angehenkt worden.

XX. From the *De Praestigiis Daemonum* of Johannes Wier.[61]

John Faust was born in the little town Kundling and studied magic in Cracow, where it was formerly taught openly; and for a few years previous to 1540 he practiced his art in various places in Germany with many lies and much fraud, to the marvel of many. There was nothing he could not do with his inane boasting and his promises. I will give one example of his art on the condition that the reader will first promise not

Ioannes Faustus[62] ex Kundling oppidulo oriundus, Cracouiae magiam, ubi olim docebatur palam, didicit eamque paucis annis ante quadragesimum supra sesquimillesimum, cum multorum admiratione, mendacijs et fraude multifaria in diuersis Germaniae locis exercuit. Inani iactantia et pollicitationibus nihil non potuit. Exemplo uno artem ea conditione Lectori

[61] Johannes Wier (1515–1588) was a Dutch physician and particularly known as an opponent of the prosecution of witches. The *De Praestigiis Daemonum* (1st ed. 1563) was an appeal to the emperor and princes in Wier's campaign against superstition. The passages relating to Faust appear for the first time in the fourth edition (1568). For a study of the historical value of what Wier has to say, see the introduction to van't Hooft, *Das Holländische Volksbuch vom Doktor Faust.* Hague, 1926.

[62] Tille, No. 17.

to imitate him. This wretch, taken prisoner at Batenburg on the Maas, near the border of Geldern, while the Baron Hermann was away, was treated rather leniently by his chaplain, Dr. Johannes Dorstenius, because he promised the man, who was good but not shrewd, knowledge of many things and various arts. Hence he kept drawing him wine, by which Faust was very much exhilarated, until the vessel was empty. When Faust learned this, and the chaplain told him that he was going to Grave, that he might have his beard shaved, Faust promised him another unusual art by which his beard might be removed without the use of a razor, if he would provide more wine. When this condition was accepted, he told him to rub his beard vigorously with arsenic, but without any mention of its preparation. When the salve had been applied, there followed such an inflammation that not only the hair but also the skin and the flesh were burned off. The chaplain himself told me of this piece of villainy more than once with much indignation. When another acquaintance of mine, whose beard was black and whose face was rather dark and showed signs of melancholy

ostendam, ut se non imitaturum, mihi prius fidem faciat. Hic scelestus ergo captus Batoburgi in Mosae ripa ad Geldriae fines, barone Hermanno absente, mitius ab eius sacellano D. Ioanne Dorstenio tractabatur, quod huic uiro bono nec callido, plurium rerum cognitionem artesque uarias polliceretur. Hinc et tamdiu uinum, quo Faustus unice afficiebatur, prompsit ille, donec uas euacuaretur. Quod ubi Faustus intelligeret, atque Grauiam sibi abeundum esse, ut raderetur barba diceret alter, uinum is si adhuc curaret, artem denuo promittit singularem, qua citra nouaculae usum, tolleretur barba. Conditione accepta, arsenico confricari eam citra ullam praeparationis mentionem iubet : abhibitaque illinitione tanta successit inflammatio, ut non modo pili, sed et pellis cum carne exurerentur. Cum stomacho idem ille mihi facinus hoc non semel recensuit. Alius mihi non incognitus, barba nigra, reliqua facie sub obscura, et melancholiam attestante (spleneticus etenim erat)

(for he was splenetic), approached Faust, the latter exclaimed: "I surely thought you were my brother-in-law and therefore I looked at your feet to see whether long curved claws projected from them": thus comparing him to the devil whom he thought to be entering and whom he used to call his brother-in-law. He was finally found dead near his bed in a certain town in the Duchy of Württemberg, with his face turned towards his back; and it is reported that during the middle of the night preceding, the house was shaken.

quum Faustum accederet, incunctanter hic ait: Profecto te sororium meum esse existimabam, propterea et pedes tuos mox obseruabam, num longae et incuruae in ijs prominerent ungulae: ita hunc daemoni assimilans, quem ad se ingredi arbitraretur, eundemque sororium appellare consueuit. Hic tandem in pago ducatus Vvirtenbergici inuentus fuit iuxta lectum mortuus inuersa facie, et domo praecedenti nocte media quassata, ut fertur.

XXI. From the Von Gespänsten of Ludwig Lavater.[63]

To this very day there are sorcerers who boast that they can saddle a horse on which they can in a short time make great journeys. The devil will give them all their reward[64] in the long run. What wonders is the notorious sorcerer Faust said to have done in our own times.

Noch hütt[65] by tag sind schwartzkünstler / die sich vszthuond / sy könnind ein rossz sattlen vff den sy in kurtzer yl grosse reisen mögind vollbringen. Den selbigen wirt / wenn es lang vmbhin gadt / der tüfel ritt vnd rossz lon / beschlecht und sattelgelt mit einanderen geben. Was wunder sol zuo vnseren zyten Faustus der verrümpt zauberer getriben haben?

[63] Ludwig Lavater (1527–1586), for many years preacher and finally head of the Protestant church in Zurich. His work *Von Gespänsten* (1569) was very popular and was also translated into French and Italian.

[64] Literally: pay for course and steed, and money for shoeing and saddle.

[65] Tille, No. 18.

XXII. From the Chronica von Thüringen und der Stadt Erffurth of Zacharias Hogel.[66]

a) It was also probably about this time [1550] that those strange things happened which are said to have taken place in Erfurt in the case of the notorious sorcerer and desperate brand of hell, Dr. Faust. Although he lived in Wittenberg, yet, just as his restless spirit in other instances drove him about in the world, so he also came to the university at Erfurt, rented quarters near the large Collegium, and through his boasting brought it to pass that he was allowed to lecture publicly and to explain the Greek poet Homer to the students. When, in this connection, he had occasion to mention the king of Troy, Priam, and the heroes of the Trojan war, Hector, Ajax, Ulysses, Agamemnon,

a) Ferner[67] mag es auch wol umb diese Zeit [1550] und Jahre geschehen seyn, was sich zu Erffurt mit dem beruffenen Schwartzkünstler und verzweifelten hellebrandt Doctor Fausten vor ebenthewr sol zu getragen haben. derselbige, wiewol er zu Wittenberg wohnte, iedoch wie er mit seinem unruhigen geiste sonsten immerdar in der welt herumb vagirte, also fand er sich auch zu Erffurt bey der Universitet ein, mietete bey dem groszen Collegio in der nähe ein, erlangte mit seinem groszsprechen so viel, dz er sich auf offentlicher cadethra hören dorfte lassen, und den Griechischen Poëten Homerum den Studenten ercklären ; und indem er hierbey des Königs zu Troja Priami und derer Kriegs helden Hectors, Aiax, Ulyssen, Agamemnons und mehr anderer zu erwehnen anlasz hatte, beschrieb er sie jede wie sie aus gesehen hatten.

[66] Hogel's chronicle was written in the 17th century. Its source, however, is the Reichmann-Wambach chronicle of the middle of the 16th century. This latter work is now lost. The parts relating to Faust were entered in the chronicle by Wolf Wambach, who continued the work which had been begun by his brother-in-law Reichmann. The story of the efforts of the monk Klinge to convert Faust probably came to Wambach fairly directly. For a discussion of the historical value of Hogel's work, see Szamatólski, *Euphorion,* II, 39 ff.

[67] Tille, No. 26.

and others, he described them each as they had appeared. He was asked (for there are always inquisitive fellows and there was no question as to what Faust was) to bring it to pass through his art, that these heroes should appear and show themselves as he had just described them. He consented to this and appointed the time when they should next come to the auditorium. And when the hour had come and more students than before had appeared before him, he said in the midst of his lecture that they should now get to see the ancient Greek heroes. And immediately he called in one after the other and as soon as one was gone another came in to them, looked at them and shook his head as though he were still in action on the field before Troy. The last of them all was the giant Polyphemus, who had only a single terrible big eye in the middle of his forehead. He wore a fiery red beard and was devouring a fellow, one of whose legs was dangling out of his mouth. The sight of him scared them so that their hair stood on end and

Wurde gebeten, (wie es denn vorwitzige bursche gibt, und was hinter ihm stack, nicht gar verborgen war,) er wolte es durch seine kunst dahin bringen, dz sie ckämen, und sich also sehen möchten laszen, wie er sie ihnen gleichsam vorgemahlt hatte. dz sagte er ihnen zu, bestimte sie auf die nechste zeit ins auditorium, und sagte, da die stunde kommen, und sich mehr Studenten, als zuvorn, bey ihm eingestellet hatten, mitten in seiner lection, nur ietzt solten sie die alten Griechischen helden zu sehen bekommen. Flugs rief er einen nach dem andern hinein, und trat ietzt dieser, darnach ein ander, wenn jener wieder hinaus war, zu ihnen daher, sahe sie an, und schüttelte seinen kopf, wie wenn er noch vor Troja im feldt agirte. Der letzte unter allen war der Riese Polyphemus, der nur ein einig schrecklich grosz auge mitten an seiner Stirn hatte, trug sich mit einem langen fewerrohten Barte, frasz an einem Kerl, und liesz deszen schenckel zum maule herauszoten; schreckte sie mit seinem anblicke, dz ihnen allen die haar gen berge stunden, und wie D. Faust ihm hinaus zu gehen

when Dr. Faust motioned him to go out, he acted as though he did not understand but wanted to grasp a couple of them too with his teeth. And he hammered on the floor with his great iron spear so that the whole Collegium shook, and then he went away.

Not long afterward the commencement for masters was held and [at the banquet given in connection therewith], in the presence of the members of the theological faculty and of delegates from the council, the comedies of the ancient poets Plautus and Terence were discussed and regret was expressed that so many of them had been lost in times gone by, for if they were available, they could be used to good advantage in the schools. Dr. Faust listened to this and he also began to speak about the two poets and cited several quotations which were supposed to be in their lost comedies. And he offered, if it would not be held against him, and if the theologians had no objections, to bring to light again all the lost comedies and to put them at their disposal for several hours, during which time they

winckte, thäte er, wie wenn ers nicht verstünde, [und] sondern ihrer auch ein bohr mit seinen zähnen anfaszen wolte : stiesz mit seinem groszen eisernen spiesz auf den Erdboden, dz sich dz gantze Collegium davon erschütterte, und machte sich drauf wieder davon.

Nicht lange darnach ward eine promotio Magistrorum gehalten, undt bey derselben [dabey angestelleten prandio] in beyseyn derer von der Theologischen Facultet und des Rahts Gesandten, von der alten Poëten Plauti und Terentii comoedien discurrirt, und geklagt, dz derenselben so gar viel vor zeiten schon verlohren weren worden, derer man sich doch, wenn man sie haben könte, mit nutz bey den Schulen wol brauchen könte. D. Faust hörte zu, hub auch an von beiden Poëten zu reden, erzehlte etliche Sprüche, die in ihren verlohrnen Comoedien stehen solten, und erbot sich, wo es ihm ohn gefahr, [seyn], und den Herrn Theologen nicht zu wieder seyn solte, die verlorne Comoedien alle wieder an dz liecht zu bringen und vorzulegen auf etliche stunden lang, da sie

would have to be copied quickly by a goodly number of students or clerks, if they wanted to have them. After that they would be able to use them as they pleased. The theologians and councilmen, however, did not take kindly to the proposal: for they said the devil might interpolate all sorts of offensive things into such newly found comedies. And after all, one could, even without them, learn enough good Latin from those which still existed. The conjurer accordingly could not exhibit one of his masterpieces in this connection.

He was accustomed to spend a good deal of his time while he was in Erfurt at the Anchor House of Squire N. in the Schlössergasse, entertaining him and his guests with his adventures. Once, when he had gone to Prague in Bohemia, a group of such guests gathered at the inn and, because they desired to have him present, begged mine host to tell them where he was. And one of the guests jokingly called Faust by name and begged him not to desert them. At that

von etlichen vielen studenten oder schreibern geschwinde müsten abgeschrieben werden, wenn man sie haben wolte, und nachfolgends möchte man ihrer nützen, wie man wolte. Die Theologen und Rahtsherren aber lieszen ihnen solchen vorschlag nicht gefallen: denn, sagten sie, der Teufel möchte in sollche newerfundene Comoedien allerley ärgerliche sachen mit einschieben, und man könte doch ja auch ohn dieselben aus denen, die noch vorhanden weren, gnung gut Lattein lernen. Dorfte also der Teufelsbanner hierinnen kein meisterstück sehen laszen.

Sonsten pflegte er sich die Zeit über, weil er zu Erffurt war, viel und oft in der Schlöszergaszen zum Encker bey Juncker N. aufzuhalten, und ihn samt seiner geselschaft mit seinen ebenthewren zu belustigen. Er war aber einsmals gen Prag in Böhmen gefahren, und nichts destoweniger hette ihn solche gesellschaft, da sie inmittelst daselbsten beysammen war, gern bey sich gehabt, der wirt mochte gleich sagen, wo er war: undt rief ihn einer schertzweise mit nahmen, und bat ihn, er

instant someone in the street knocks at the door. The servant runs to the window, looks out and asks who is there. And behold, there, before the door, stands Dr. Faust, holding his horse as though he had just dismounted, and says: "Don't you know me? I am he whom they have just called." The servant runs into the room and reports. The host refuses to believe it, saying that Dr. Faust was in Prague. In the meantime he knocks again at the door and master and servant again run to the window, see him, and open the door, and he is given a cordial welcome and immediately led in to the guests. The host's son takes his horse, saying that he will give it plenty of feed, and leads it into the stable. The squire immediately asks Dr. Faust how he had returned so quickly. "That's what my horse is for," says Dr. Faust. "Because the guests desired me so much and called me, I wanted to oblige them and to appear, although I have to be back in Prague before morning." Thereupon they drink to his health in copious draughts, and when he asks

wolte sie nicht verlaszen. Indem klopft eines auf der gaszen an die thür. Der Hauszknecht laüfft ans fenster, [und] guckt, und fraget, wer da sey. Sihe da steht D. Faust vor der thür, helt sein pferd bey der hand, wie wenn er erst abgestiegen were, und spricht: kennest mich nicht? ich bins, den sie ietzt geruffen haben. der Knecht laüfft in die Stube, und sagts. der [Herr] Wirt wils nicht glauben, denn D. Faust sey ja zu Prag. Indem pocht er noch einmal an die thür. da lauft herr und knecht wieder ans fenster, sehen ihn, machen auf, und wird er schön empfangen, und bald zun gästen geführt. des Wirts sohn nimt sein Pferd, sagt, er wolle ihm schon futter gnung geben, und führts in stall. D. Fausten fragt der Juncker bald, wie er so geschwinde wiederkommen sey. Da ist mein Pferd gut dazu, sagt D. Faust: weil mich die herrn Gäste so sehr begehrt, und mir geruffen, hab ich ihnen wilfahren und erscheinen wollen, wiewol ich noch vor morgen wieder zu Prag seyn musz. drauf trincken sie ihm einen guten rausch zu, und, wie er sie fragt, ob sie auch gern

them whether they would also like to drink a foreign wine, they answer: "Yes." He asks whether it shall be Reinfal,[68] Malmsey, Spanish, or French wine. And when one of them says: "They are all good," he asks for an auger and with it makes four holes in the table and closes them with plugs. Then he takes fresh glasses and taps from the table that kind of wine which he names and continues to drink merrily with them. In the meantime the son runs into the room and says: "Doctor, your horse eats as though he were mad; he has already devoured several bushels of oats and continually stands and looks for more. But I will give him some more until he has enough." "Have done," says the doctor, "he has had enough; he would eat all the feed in your loft before he was full." But at midnight the horse utters a shrill neigh so that it is heard throughout the entire house. "I must go," says the doctor, but tarries a little until the horse neighs

einen frembden Wein mögen trincken, sagen sie, Ja. Er fragt, ob es Rheinfal, Malvasier, Spanischer oder Frantzenwein seyn solle. Da spricht einer [corrigiert aus: So spricht da], Sie sind alle gut, Bald fordert er ein börl, macht damit in dz Tischblat vier löcher, stopft sie alle mit pflöcklein zu, nimmt frische gläser, und zäpft aus dem tischblatt jenerley Wein hinein, welchen er nennet, und trinckt mit ihnen darvon lustig fort. Indeszen läuft der Sohn im Hause in die stube; spricht, Herr Doctor, ewer Pferd friszt wie wenns toll were: es hat mir schon etliche scheffel haber [gefressen] verschluckt, steht und sicht stets, wo sein mehr sey; ich wil ihm doch noch mehr geben, dz es satt habe. Last dz bleiben, sagt der Doctor, es hat gnung bekommen, es fräsze euch alle ewer futter vom boden, ehe es voll würdt. Zur Mitternacht aber thut dz Pferd ein hellen Schrey, dz man es durch dz gantze hausz hört. Ich musz fort, sagt der Doctor; läszt sich doch halten ein wenig, bis es zum andern, und letzt zum drittenmal schreyet.

68 An Istrian wine highly esteemed in Germany in the middle ages. The derivation of the word is uncertain but the form Rheinfall is merely the result of popular etymology. The earliest German form of the word is "raival" from the Latin "vinum rivale."

a second and finally a third time. Thereupon he goes, takes his leave of them outside, mounts his horse and rides up the Schlössergasse. But the horse in plain sight rises quickly into the air and takes him back through the air to Prague. After several weeks he comes again from Prague to Erfurt with splendid gifts which had been given to him there, and invites the same company to be his guests at St. Michael's. They come and stand there in the rooms but there is no sign of any preparation. But he knocks with a knife on the table. Soon someone enters and says: "Sir, what do you wish?" Faust asks, "How quick are you?" The other answers: "As an arrow." "No," says Dr. Faust, "you shall not serve me. Go back to where you came from." Then he knocks again and when another servant enters and asks the same question, he says: "How quick are you?" "As the wind," says he. "That is something," says Dr. Faust, but sends him out again too. But when he knocked a third time, another entered and, when he was asked the same ques-

drauf geht er fort, nimt drauszen seinen abschied von ihnen, setzt sich aufs Pferd, reitet die Schlössergasse hinaufwerts. dz Pferd aber schwingt sich zusehens eilends in die höhe, und führt ihn durch die luft gen Prag wider zu. Nach etlichen Wochen komt er wider von Prag gen Erffurt mit herlichen ihm dort verehrten presenten, bittet jene Geselschaft zu sich bei S. Michaël zu gast. Sie kommen, und stehen da nun in der Stuben : da ist aber gar keine Zuschickung nicht. Er aber klopft mit einem meszer an den tisch. Bald tritt einer hinein, und sagt: herr, was [ist?] wolt ihr? Er fragt: Wie behende bistu? Jener antwortet: Wie ein Pfeil. O nein, sagt D. Faust, du dienst mir nicht. gehe wieder hin, wo du bist herkommen. Darnach klopft er aber, und wie ein ander diener hineintritt, und fragt gleichfals, spricht er : wie schnell bistu denn? Wie der Wind, sagt jener. Es ist wol etwas, spricht D. Faust, läst ihn aber auch wieder hinausgehen. Wie er aber zum drittemal klopfte, da trat einer hinein, und sagte, als er auch so gefragt wird, er were so geschwinde, als der

tion, said he was as quick as the thoughts of man. "Good," said Dr. Faust, "you'll do." And he went out with him, told him what he should do, and returned again to his guests and had them wash their hands and sit down. Soon the servant with two others brought in three covered dishes each, and this happened four times. Thirty six courses or dishes were served, therefore, with game, fowl, vegetables, meat pies and other meat, not to mention the fruit, confections, cakes, etc. All the beakers, glasses, and mugs were put on the table empty. Soon Dr. Faust asked each one what he wished to drink in the way of beer and wine and then put the cups outside of the window and soon took them back again, full of just that fresh drink which each one wanted to have. The music which one of his servants played was so charming that his guests had never heard the like, and so wonderful as if several were playing in harmony on harmoniums, fifes, cornets, lutes, harps, trumpets, etc. So they made merry until broad daylight. What was to be the outcome? The man played so many tricks that

Menschen Gedancken weren. da recht, sagte D. Faust, du wirsts thun : gieng mit hinaus, befahl ihm, wz er thun solte, gieng wieder zu seinen gästen, liesz sie waszer nehmen, und sich setzen. Bald brachte der diener selb dritte, von ieder drey gedeckte schüszeln voll : und dz geschah viermal : wurden also 36. gerichte oder schüszeln aufgetragen, mit wildpret, vogeln, gemüszen, Pasteten und anderm fleische, ohn des obsts confects, kuchen, etc. Alle becher, [und] gläser und Kandeln wurden leer auf den tisch gesetzt : bald fragte D. Faust, wz einer wolte trincken von bier und wein, setzte drauf dz geschirr vors fenster ; und bald nahm ers wieder voll eben des getränckes frisch, welches man haben wolte. Die music, so einer seiner diener spielte, war beides so lieblich, dz dergleichen von den gästen nie gehört worden, und so wunderlich, wie wenn ihr etliche auff positiven, querchpfeiffen, zincken, lauten, harfen, posaunen etc. zusammen stimmeten. So waren sie bis an den hellen morgen lustig. Wz solte geschen? Es machte

the city and country began to talk about him and many of the nobility of the country came to Erfurt to him. People began to worry lest the devil might lead the tender youth and other simpletons astray, so that they also might show a leaning towards the black art and might regard it as only a clever thing to do. Since the sorcerer attached himself to the squire in the Anchor House, who was a papist, therefore the suggestion was made that the neighboring monk, Dr. Klinge, should make an effort to tear him from the devil and convert him. The Franciscan did so, visited him and spoke to him, at first kindly, then sternly; explained to him God's wrath and the eternal damnation which must follow on such doings; said that he was a well educated man and could support himself without this in a godly and honorable way: therefore he should stop such frivolity, to which he had perhaps been persuaded by the devil in his youth, and should beg God for forgiveness of his sins, and should hope in this way to obtain that forgiveness of his sins which

der mann der poszen so viel, dz die Stadt und dz land von ihm schwatzte, und manche vom Adel auf dem lande ihm gen Erffurt nachzogen, und begunte sich die sorge zu finden, es möchte der Teufel die zarte jugent und andere einfeltige verführen, dz sie auch zur Schwartzen kunst lust bekämen, und sie vor eine geschwindigkeit nur halten möchten. Nun sich dann der Zäuberer zum Juncker im Encker, so ein Papist war, hielte. Als ward anleitung gegeben, dz sich doch der benachbarte mönch D. Klinge an ihm versuchen möchte, ob er ihn vom Teufel reiszen und bekehren möchte. Dieser Franciscaner thäts, fand sich mit herbey, redte erst freundlich, so dann hart mit ihm: erklärte ihm gottes zorn und ewig verdamnis, so ihm auf solchem wesen stünde: sagte, er were ein fein gelehrter mann und könte sich mit got und ehren wol nehren sonsten: drumb solte er sich solcher leichfertigkeit, dazu er vielleicht in seiner Jugend, durch den Teufel bereden hatte laszen, abthun, und Gott seine Sünde abbitten: solte hoffen, er würde also vergebung seiner Sünde erlangen, die

God had never yet denied anyone. Dr. Faust said: "My dear sir, I realize that you wish me well; I know all that, too, which you have just told me. But I have ventured so far, and with my own blood have contracted with the devil to be forever his, with body and soul: how can I now retract? or how can I be helped?" Dr. Klinge said: "That is quite possible, if you earnestly call on God for grace and mercy, show true repentance and do penance, refrain from sorcery and community with the devils, and neither harm nor seduce any one. We will hold mass for you in our cloister so that you will without a doubt get rid of the devil." "Mass here, mass there," said Dr. Faust. "My pledge binds me too absolutely. I have wantonly despised God and become perjured and faithless towards Him, and believed and trusted more in the devil than in Him. Therefore I can neither come to Him again nor obtain any comfort from His grace which I have forfeited. Besides, it would not be honest nor would it redound to my honor to have it said that

Gott keinem noch verschlossen hette. D. Faust sagte: Mein lieber Herr, ich erkenne, dz ihrs gerne gut mit mir sehen möchtet: weisz auch dz alles wol was ihr mir ietzt vorgesagt habt: Ich hab mich aber so hoch verstiegen, und mit meinem eigenen blut gegen dem Teufel verschrieben, dz ich mit leib und Seel ewig sein seyn will: wie kan ich denn nu zurück? oder wie kan mir geholfen werden? D. Kling sprach: Dz kan wol geschehen, wann ihr Gott umb gnade und barmhertzigkeit ernstlich anruft, wahre rew und busz thut, der Zauberey und gemeinschaft mit den Teufeln euch enthaltet, und niemanden ärgert, noch verführt: wir wollen in unserm Kloster vor euch Mesz halten, dz ihr wol solt des Teufels loszwerden. Mesz hin, Mesz her, sprach D. Faust: meine zusage bindet mich zu hart: so hab ich gott muthwillig verachtet, bin meineydig und trewlosz an ihm worden, dem Teufel mehr gegläubet und vertrawt, denn ihm: darumb ich zu ihm nit wieder kommen, noch seiner gnaden, die ich verschertzt, mich getrösten kann: zu dem were es nicht ehrlich: noch mir

I had violated my bond and seal, which I had made with my own blood. The devil has honestly kept the promise that he made to me, therefore I will honestly keep the pledge that I made and contracted with him." "Well," says the monk, "then go to, you cursed child of the devil, if you will not be helped, and will not have it otherwise." Thereupon he went to his Magnificence, the Rector, and reported it to him. The council was also informed and took steps so that Dr. Faust had to leave. So Erfurt got rid of the wicked man.

However, this affair with the aforesaid sorcerer probably took place in this year or shortly before or afterwards, during the lifetime of Dr. Klinge.

b) Also the Lord God afflicted Dr. Klinge, the above mentioned obdurate monk and abbot in the Franciscan cloister in Erfurt, so that he despaired of his life. But he recovered again and, because it was reported to him that they said of him in the city that

rühmlich nachzusagen, dz ich meinem brief und Siegel, dz doch mit meinem blut gestellet, wiederlauffen solte : so hat mir der Teufel redlich gehalten, wz er mir hat zugesagt, darumb wil ich ihm auch wieder redlich halten, wz ich ihm hab zugesagt und verschrieben habe. Ey, sagt der mönch, so fahre immerhin, du verfluchtes Teufelskindt, wenn du dir ie nicht wilt helfen laszen, und es nicht anderst haben. Gieng drauf von ihm zum magnifico Rectore und zeigte es ihm an. Hierauf ward der Raht auch von der sachen berichtet, und von ihm verschaffung gethan, dz D. Faust den stab förder setzen musste, und ward also Erffurt des bösen menschen losz.

doch mag sich dieses mit solchem Zäuberer in diesem Jahr, oder kurtz vorher oder hernach bey D. Klingen lebzeit noch zugetragen haben

b) Auch grif Gott der Herr obgedachten verstockten Mönch und Guardian im Franziscaner Kloster zu Erfurt D. Klingen mit schwerer Krankheit an, dasz er sich seines Lebens erwegte. Er kam aber wieder auf, und weil ihm vorbracht worden, man hette von ihm in der Stadt ausgesprengt, alsz

he had become Lutheran, he wrote and published his book called *Catechismus Catholicus*, printed in 1570 in Cologne. And in the introduction he bore witness that he would remain in the doctrine which he had preached in Erfurt for thirty-six years. And this was the monk who wanted to turn and convert the notorious Dr. Faust from his evil life. Dr. Klinge however died in the year 1556 on the Tuesday after Oculi,[69] on which Sunday he had still preached in the church of Our Lady. And he lies buried in that church opposite the chancel, where his epitaph may be seen.

ob er Lutherisch were worden, schrieb und publicierte er deshalben sein Buch Catechismus Catholicus genant, und anno 1570 zu Cöln gedruckt, und bezeugt er in der Vorrede er wolte bey der lehre, die er nu 36 Jahr zu Erfurt gepredigt, bleiben, etc. Und disz der Mönch gewesen, der den berufenen D. Fausten von seinen bösen leben ablencken und bekehren hat wollen: welcher D. Klinge aber hernach anno 1556 am Dienstage nach Oculi gestorben: an welchem Sontage er noch zu unserer lieben frawen gepredigt hatte, und liegt drumb alda gegen der Cantzel über begraben, da man sein Grabschrift siehet.

XXIII. From the Christlich Bedencken of Augustin Lercheimer.[70]

He was born in a little place called Knittlingen, situated in Württemberg near the border of the Palat-

Er ist [71] bürtig gewesen auss eim flecken, genant Knütling, ligt im Wirtemberger lande an der Pfältzischen grentze. War

[69] 'Oculi' is the fourth Sunday before Easter.

[70] Augustin Lercheimer von Steinfelden (1522–1603) was professor of Greek at Heidelberg from 1563 to 1579. From 1579 to 1584 he held the same chair at Neustadt on the Hardt. From 1584 to his death he was again at Heidelberg as professor of mathematics. His name was really Herman Witekind, originally Wilcken. He assumed the pseudonym Lercheimer in his work *Christlich bedencken und erinnerung von Zauberey* (Heidelberg, 1585; 3rd edition, Speyer, 1597).

[71] Tille, No. 48.

inate. For a time he was schoolmaster in Kreuznach under Franz von Sickingen : he had to flee from there because he was guilty of sodomy. After that he travelled about the country with his devil ; studied the black art at the university in Cracow ; came to Wittenberg and was allowed to stay there for a time, until he carried things so far that they were on the point of arresting him, when he fled. He had neither house nor home in Wittenberg or elsewhere ; in fact he had no permanent abode anywhere, but lived like a vagabond, was a parasite, drunkard, and gourmand, and supported himself by his quackery. How could he have a property at the outer gate in the Scheergasse in Wittenberg, when there never was any suburb there, and therefore also no outer gate ? nor was there any Scheergasse there.

* * *

ein zweile schulmeister vnder Frantz von Sickinge bey Creutzenach : von dannen muste er verlauffen von wegen begangener sodomia. Fuhr darnach mit seinem teufel in landen vmmher, studierte die schwartze kunst auff der hohen schule zu Craco : Kam gen Wittenberg, ward ein zeitlang alda gelitten, biss ers zu grob machete dass man jn gefenglich wolte eynziehen, da macht er sich dauon. Hatte weder Hauss noch Hof zu Wittenberg oder anderswo, was nirgent daheim lebte wie ein lotterbube, war ein schmorotzer, frass sauff vnd ernehrete sich von seiner gauckeley. Wie konte er hauss vnd hof da haben beym eussern thor in der scheer gassen, da nie keine vorstatt gewesen vnd derhalben auch kein eusser thor ? auch ist nie kein scheergasse da gewesen.

* * *

In the third edition of his work, from which our quotations are taken, Lercheimer added a vehement denunciation of the Spies Faust book, resenting as he did the unknown author's assertion that the magician had been brought up in Wittenberg, had received his degrees at the university there, and had resided in the city. Lercheimer himself had matriculated at Wittenberg in 1546.

For a complete discussion of the connection of the historical Faust with Wittenberg, see Walz, "An English Faustsplitter," *Modern Language Notes*, XLII (1927), 353 ff.

He was choked to death by the devil in a village in Württemberg, not at Kimlich near Wittenberg, since there is no village by that name. For he was never allowed to return to Wittenberg after he had fled from there to avoid arrest.

* * *

I do not touch upon other trivial, false, and nasty things in the book. I have pointed out these particular things because it has vexed and grieved me greatly, as it has many other honest people, to see the honorable and famous institution together with Luther, Melanchthon, and others of sainted memory so libelled. I myself was a student there, once upon a time. At that time the doings of this magician were still remembered by many there.

* * *

The lewd, devilish fellow Faust stayed for a time in Wittenberg, as I stated before. He came at times to the house of Melanchthon, who gave him a good

Er ist vom teufel erwürget in eim dorffe im land zu Wirtemberg nicht bey Wittenberg zu Kimlich, da kein dorff des namens nirgent ist. Denn nach dem er aussgerissen, dass er nicht gefangen wurde, hat er nie dürffen gen Wittenberg wider kommen.

* * *

Andere eitelkeit lügen vnd teufelsdreck des buchs lasse ich vngereget : diese habe ich darumm angezeigt das michs sehr verdreusst vnd betrübet, wie viele andere ehrliche leute, die wolverdiente hochrhümliche schule, die selige Männer Lutherum Philippum vnd andere dermassen zu schenden : darumm dass ich auch etwan da studiert habe. Welche zeit noch bey vielen da dieses zauberes thun in gedechtnuss war.

* * *

Der vnzüchtige teufelisch bube Faust hielt sich ein weil zu Wittenberg, wie oben gesagt, kam etwan zum Herrn Philippo, der lass jm dann ein guten text, schalt vnd vermanet jn, dass

lecture, rebuked and warned him that he should reform in time, lest he come to an evil end, as finally happened. But he paid no attention to it. Now one day about ten o'clock Melanchthon left his study to go down to eat. With him was Faust, whom he had vigorously rebuked. Faust replied : Sir, you continually rebuke me with abusive words. One of these days, when you go to the table, I will bring it about that all the pots in your kitchen will fly out of the chimney, so that you and your guests will have nothing to eat. To this Melanchthon replied : you had better not. Hang you and your tricks. Nor did Faust carry out his threat : the devil could not rob the kitchen of the saintly man, as he had done to the wedding guests of whom mention was made before.

er von dem ding beyzeit abstünde, es wurde sonst ein böss end nemmen, wie es auch geschahe. Er aber kerete sich nicht daran. Nun wars einmal vmm zehen vhr, dass der Herr Philippus auss seinem studierstüblin herunder gieng zu tisch, war Faust bey jm, den er da hefftig gescholten hatte. Der spricht wider zu jm : Herr Philippe, jr fahret mich allemal mit rauchen worten an, ich wills ein mal machen wann jr zu tische gehet, dass alle häfen in der kuchen zum schornstein hinauss fliegen, dass jr mit ewern gesten nicht zu essen werden haben. Darauff antwortet jm Herr Philippus : Dass soltu wol lassen, ich schiesse dir in deine kunst. Und er liess es auch : Es konte der teufel dem heiligen man seine küche nicht berauben, wie er den hochzeitlichen gesten thete, von denen zuuor gesagt.

XXIV. From the Operae Horarum Subcisivarum of Philipp Camerarius.[72]

We know, moreover, (not to mention Scymus of Tarentum, Philistes of Syracuse, Heraclitus of Mytilene, who as we read were very distinguished and accomplished sorcerers in the time of Alexander the Great) that among the jugglers and magicians who became famous within the memory of our own fathers, John Faust of Kundling, who studied magic at Cracow where it was formerly publicly taught, acquired through his wonderful tricks and diabolical enchantments such a celebrated name that among the common people there can hardly be found anyone who is not able to recount some instance of his art. The same conjurer's tricks are ascribed to him as we have just related of the Bohemian magician.[73] Just as the lives of these magicians were similar, so each ended his life in a

Apud nos[74] adhuc (vt Scymnum Tarentinum Philistidem Syracusium, Heraclitum Mitylenaeum, quos praestigiatores praestantissimos et elegantissimos tempore Alexandri Magni fuisse legimus praetereamus) notum est, inter praestigiatores et magos, qui patrum nostrorum memoria innotuerunt, celebre nomen, propter mirificas imposturas, et fascinationes diabolicas, adeptum fuisse Iohannem Faustum Cundlingensem qui Cracouiae magiam, vbi ea olim publice docebatur, didicerat, adeo vt ex plebe propemodum nullus reperiatur, qui non aliquod documentum eius artis commemorare possit, illique eadem ludibria, quae modo de mago Bohemo diximus, ascribantur. Quemadmodum autem horum praestigiatorum vita similis fuit, ita vterque horrendo modo in viuis esse desiit.

[72] Philipp Camerarius (1537–1624) was the son of the Joachim Camerarius previously mentioned. He was trained in law at Leipzig, Tübingen, Strassburg, Basle, and in Italy. From 1581 to his death he was prorector of the university at Altdorf. His *Opera horarum subcisivarum* was first published in 1591 ff. (enlarged edition 1602–1609). It was translated into French, Italian, English, and German.

[73] The magician referred to is Zyto.

[74] Tille, No. 54.

horrible manner. For Faust, it is said, and this is told by Wier, was found in a village in the Duchy of Württemberg lying dead alongside his bed with his head twisted round. And in the middle of the preceding night the house was shaken. The other, as we mentioned a little while ago, was carried off by his master while he was still alive. These are the fitting rewards of an impious and criminal curiosity. But to come back to Faust. From those in truth, who knew this impostor well, I have heard many things which show him to have been a master of the magic art (if indeed it is an art and not the jugglery of a fool). Among other deeds which he performed there is told one in particular which may seem ridiculous but which is truly diabolical. For from it may be seen how subtly and yet seriously, even in things which seem to us ridiculous, that arch conjurer, the devil, undermines the well being and safety of mankind. . . It is reported that Faust's deception was of this kind. Once upon a time when he was staying with some friends who had heard much about his magician's tricks, they besought him that he should show them some sample of his

Faustus enim, ut fertur, et a Wiero recensetur, in pago ducatus Wirtenbergici inuentus fuit iuxta lectum mortuus, inuersa facie, et domo praecedenti nocte media quassata. Alter autem, vt paulo ante diximus, viuus a suo Magistro raptus est. Haec sunt praemia digna curiositatis impiae et sceleratae. Sed ad Faustum redeamus. Equidem ex iis qui hunc impostorem probe nouerunt, multa audiui, quae declarant ipsum artificem Magicae artis (si modo ars est, non vanissimi cuiusque ludibrium) fuisse. Inter alia autem eius facta, vnvm prae caeteris, licet ridiculum videatur, tamen vere diabolicum narratur. Etenim apparet ex eo, quam subdole et serio, etiam in rebus quae ludicrae nobis videntur, mille artifex ille saluti et incolumitati hominum insidietur. . . Faustinam igitur deceptionem ferunt eiusmodi fuisse. Quum aliquando is apud notos quosdam diuerteret, qui de ipsius praestigiatricibus actionibus multa audiuerant, ij petierunt ab eo, vt aliquod specimen suae

magic. He refused for a long time, but finally, yielding to the importunity of the company, which was by no means sober, he promised to show them whatever they might wish. With one accord therefore they besought him that he should show them a full grown vine with ripe grapes. For they thought that on account of the unsuitable time of the year (for it was toward the end of December) he would by no means be able to accomplish this. Faust assented and promised that they should immediately see on the table what they wished but with this condition : they should all wait without moving and in absolute silence until he should order them to cut the grapes. If they should do otherwise they would be in danger of their lives. When they had promised to do this, then by his tricks he so befuddled the eyes and senses of this drunken crowd that there appeared to them on a beautiful vine as many bunches of grapes of marvellous size and plumpness as there were people present. Made greedy by the novelty of the thing and athirst from too much wine, they took their knives and awaited his orders to cut off the grapes.

magiae exhiberet. Hoc quum diu recusasset, tandem importunitate sodalitij, neutiquam sobrij victus, promisit, se illis exhibiturum quodcunque expeterent. Vnanimi igitur consensu petierunt, vt exhiberet illis vitem plenam vuis maturis. Putabant autem propter alienum anni tempus (erat enim circa brumam) hoc illum praestare nullo modo posse. Assensit Faustus, et promisit iam iam mensa conspectum iri, id quod expeterent : sed hac conditione, vt omnes magno silentio immoti praestolarentur, donec illos iuberet vuas decerpere : si secus facerent, instare illis periculum capitis. Hoc quum se facturos recepissent, mox ludibriis suis, huic ebriae turbae ita oculos et sensus praestrinxit, vt illis tot vuae mirae magnitudinis, et succi plenae, in vite pulcherrima apparerent, quot ipsorum adessent. Rei itaque nouitate cupidi, et ex crapula sitibundi, sumtis suis cultellis expectabant, vt illos iuberet rescindere vuas. Tandem

Finally, when Faust had held these triflers in suspense for some time in their silly error, suddenly the vine with its grapes disappeared in smoke and they were seen, each holding, not the grapes which each thought he had seized, but his own nose with his knife suspended over it so that if anyone had been unmindful of the directions given and had wished to cut the grapes without orders, he would have cut off his own nose. And it would have served them right and they would have deserved other mutilation, since, with intolerable curiosity, they occupied themselves as spectators and participants in the illusions of the devil, which no Christian may be interested in without great danger or rather sin.

quum istos leuiculos aliquandiu suspensos in ipsorum vanissimo errore tenuisset Faustus; subito in fumum abeunte vite vna cum suis vuis, conspecti sunt singuli tenentes loco vuae, quam vnusquisque apprehendisse videbatur suum nasum opposito superne cultello, ita vt si quis immemor praecepti dati, iniussus vuas secare voluisset, se ipsum naso mutilasset. Et recte quidem illis accidisset, dignique fuissent alia mutilatione, qui non ferenda curiositate spectatores et participes satagebant illusionum diabolicarum, quibus sine gravissimo periculo, vel potius piaculo interesse Christiano homini non licet.

IV

THE FAUST BOOKS

THE FAUST BOOKS

CONTEMPORARY evidence of the activities of the historical Faust ceases about the year 1540. The development of the Faust legend begins in all probability not long after that date. Robert Petsch[1] believes that the stories which gradually accumulated around Faust's name were common property in university circles as early as the middle of the century and that a Latin collection of Faust legends existed before 1570, at least in manuscript form. Be that as it may, the earliest tangible evidence of an attempt to gather together the popular tales is in a manuscript notebook written about 1570 by one Christoph Rosshirt,[2] a teacher at the Sebaldus school in Nuremberg.

Of much greater significance is the so-called "Wolfenbüttel manuscript"[3] which was probably written between 1572 and 1587. This manuscript presents in detail a rather prosaic popular account of the career of the notorious magician together with a collection of legendary exploits and adventures, many of which are to be found in earlier tales concerning other magicians.[4] It is a crude piece of compilation of no literary value. The geographical descriptions of the places visited by the arch conjurer, as Milchsack has pointed out, are largely lifted bodily from Hartmann Schedel's *Nürnberger Chronik.* The document is probably an attempt to present a warning to all good Protestants

[1] Cf. *Das Volksbuch vom Dr. Faust,* zweite Auflage, herausgegeben von Robert Petsch. Halle, 1911, pp. XI-XLVI.

[2] Cf. *Nürnberger Faustgeschichten,* von Wilhelm Meyer aus Speyer. No date. Reprint of original which appeared in München, 1895, as Abhandlung d. I. Classe d. K. Akademie d. Wiss. XX. Bd. II Abth.

[3] Cf. *Historia D. Johannis Fausti des Zauberers nach der Wolfenbütteler Handschrift* . . . herausgegeben von Gustav Milchsack. Wolfenbüttel, 1892.

[4] Cf. Petsch, op. cit., p. XII and Anhänge, II. Die wichtigsten Quellen. Many sources and parallels cited in Milchsack.

against imitating Dr. Faust, a warning against inordinate ambition, speculation about the unknowable and any sort of league with evil spirits. Some critics have seen in the book evidence of a more secular character and believe that the demand for the book mentioned in the introduction to the Spies edition was due to the piquancy of some of the stories told rather than to the awful fate of Faust. The importance of the manuscript is that it is the type of manuscript which furnished the form and material for the later printed books.

The first printed book on Faust's life is the famous "Spies Faustbuch" published by Johann Spies in Frankfort on the Main in September, 1587.[5] This Spies text and the Wolfenbüttel text are in large part identical and are undoubtably variants of the same basic version. The book was a great popular success. Spies himself published several editions and pirated editions began to appear before the end of the year 1587. In 1588 a rimed edition made by some students at the University of Tübingen was published by one Hock and brought upon authors and publisher incarceration and a severe reprimand.

In 1588 likewise Balhorn, the blundering book pirate of Lübeck, published an edition in Low German. A new edition of the original story appeared in 1589 containing six new chapters taken from the Faust tradition centering about Erfurt. The Berlin edition of 1590 combines the Spies edition and the enlarged account of 1589. The last "Faustbuch" of the Spies type, the eighteenth edition known, dates from the year 1598.

The popularity of the "Faustbuch" led a Swabian, Georg Rudolff Widman, to elaborate the material into an intolerably long-winded account of Faust's career interspersed with dreary moralizing comments. The

[5] See note (1), page 129.

book was published in Hamburg in 1599 and was, apparently, not reprinted until modern times.[6]

The interest in the "Faustbuch" seems to have died down during the 17th century, owing in part to the "Thirty Years' War," in part to a more rational attitude toward witchcraft, and in part to the spread of the Faust drama. It was not until 1674 that the old story was revived in book form. In that year a Nuremberg physician, Nicolaus Pfitzer, undertook a revision of Widman's book, which was reprinted from time to time down to 1726.[7]

The last of the German Faust books was the so-called *Faustbuch des Christlich Meynenden*, the first shorter account of Faust's career, printed probably sometime during the first two decades of the 1700's. The first dated copy is from 1725. Many subsequent editions are known. Goedeke cites one from 1797 as the last. The book[8] is essentially a condensation of Widman and is important because from it were taken the chapbooks which were sold at the fairs and because it was probably known to Goethe.

The popularity of the Faust book was not confined to Germany. The Spies book or one of its various versions was translated into English, Dutch, and French, before the end of the century. The Dutch translation of Karl Batten dates from the year 1592 and the French translation of Victor Palma Cayet from 1598. The earliest English edition known is dated 1592. In England and Holland the many subsequent editions bear witness to the popular interest in the Faust story. Even during the 17th century, when there is a dearth of Faust books in Germany, new editions of the translations continued to appear, especially in Holland.

[6] Reprinted (nearly complete) in Scheible's *Kloster*, 2. Band, Stuttgart, 1846, pp. 273-804.

[7] Reprinted by Adalbert von Keller, Litt. Verein, Stuttgart, 1880.

[8] Reprinted by Siegfried Szamatólski, Leipzig, 1892. Likewise in Scheible's *Kloster*.

The "Spies Faustbuch" is of importance in tracing the development of the Faust books and of the Faust dramas. It is the direct ancestor of both in all probability. However, for various reasons it has seemed best not to include a reprint of the Spies book in this collection of source material. In the first place the Spies text is readily available in the excellent Braune-Petsch reprint No. 7. 8. 8a/b of the Haller Neudrucke. Then again the 16th century German is an effective stumbling-block to all those who are not experts in the field. And in the third place the English version is the source of Marlowe's *Dr. Faustus,* which opens the series of Faust dramas. The English version, which is more an adaptation than a translation, is still close enough to the Spies text to give the student an adequate notion of the content.

The English Faust Book

The English Faust book is a very free, frequently grossly inaccurate, rendering into English of the Spies edition of 1587 or one of its immediate successors. As a translation it is no better and no worse than other contemporary work, true to the cavalier custom of the Elizabethan translator in using his original. The translator P.F., whose identity is still an unsolved problem of Faust research, omitted some of the uninteresting theological matter in Spies, elaborated or condensed at will, and added a number of descriptions and anecdotes, particularly in that part of the text which deals with Faust's travels.[1] The importance of

[1] The many additions to the account of Faust's travels give an interesting sidelight on the interests and knowledge of P.F.

Logeman believes that P.F. copied his additional descriptive matter from printed sources or depended upon some traveller's relation. Rohde, in his pamphlet on *Das englische Faustbuch und Marlowes Tragödie,* (Halle, 1910), thinks the English Faust book contains material which only an eye witness could have gathered. We have found many of the statements which P.F. added in contemporary documents. They must have been common knowledge. On the other hand P.F. has several descriptions and anecdotes such as the

the book in the development of the Faust legend is twofold; it is undoubtably the source of Marlowe's tragedy and it gives more than one hint of a conception of the titanic elements in Faust's character which Marlowe was to elaborate.

The earliest impression of the English Faust book which has come down to us is the edition of 1592, printed by Thomas Orwin for Edward White. The only known copy is a quarto in the British Museum. Thus far, no earlier impression has been discovered but it is practically certain that an earlier edition was printed. The available evidence points to an earlier edition in the same year.[2] The British Museum text was reprinted in 1900 with notes by Professor H. Logeman as the 24th fascicle in the 'Recueil de Travaux' of the University of Ghent. This edition has long been out of print and has become very difficult to obtain. William Rose modernized and edited the text in his *Doctor John Faustus*, London, 1930. Our text is a copy of the original British Museum text.[3] The notes have been restricted to explanations of rare and obsolete words and phrases. For philological notes the reader should consult Logeman.

detailed description of 'Sandetz' and the folk lore with which he frequently regales us, which point to a personal experience. Rohde's suggestion that John Dee was the translator does not seem to us probable. The style of Dee's *Diary* shows no marked similarity.

[2] See note (1) on page 134.

[3] A photostatic copy has been provided at our request by the Committee on Rotographs of MSS. and Rare Printed Books of the Modern Language Association of America.

The body of the text in the original is in black letter with proper names printed in roman type. Chapter headings are generally in roman type with a very limited use of italics. While we have endeavored to give an accurate reprint, we have not deemed it feasible to attempt anything like a facsimile reproduction. The body of our text is accordingly printed in roman type. Original roman type is reproduced as italic. We have followed the suggestions of McKerrow, *Introduction to Bibliography*, Oxford, 1927, in transcribing from black letter to roman.

THE HISTORIE of the damnable life, and deserued death of *Doctor Iohn Faustus,*

Newly imprinted,[1] and in conueni-
ent places imperfect matter amended:

according to the true Copie printed *at* Franckfort, *and translated into English by* P. F. *Gent.*

Seene and allowed.

[Device]

Jmprinted at London by Thomas Orwin, and are to be solde by Edward White, dwelling at the little North doore of Paules, at the signe of the Gun. 1592.

[1] 'Newly imprinted.' This edition is the oldest extant. It was printed between May and December, 1592. Dr. W. W. Greg in F. S. Boas' edition of Marlowe's *Tragical History of Doctor Faustus,* London, 1932, p. 7-8, believes (on the evidence in the *Records of the Court of the Stationers' Company*) that one Abell Jaffes printed an earlier edition about May, 1592. Our own researches tend to confirm this. From internal evidence, vid. note (70), it appears probable that the manuscript was finished before August, 1590.

A Discourse of the Most Famous Doctor

John Faustus of VVittenberg in Germanie, Coniurer, and Necromancer : wherein is declared many strange things that he himself hath seene, and done in the earth and in the Ayre, with his bringing vp, his trauailes, studies, and last end.

Of his Parentage and Birth. Chap. 1.

IOhn Faustus, borne in the town of *Rhode,*[2] lying in the Prouince of *Weimer* in *Germ*[*anie,*] * his father a poore Husbandman, and not [able] * wel to bring him vp : but hauing an Vncle at *Wittenberg,* a rich man, & without issue, took this *I. Faustus* from his father, & made him his heire, in so much that his father was no more troubled with him, for he remained with his Vncle at *Wittenberg,* where he was kept at yᵉ Vniuersitie in the same citie to study diuinity. But *Faustus* being of a naughty minde & otherwise addicted, applied not his studies, but tooke himselfe to other exercises : the which his Vncle oftentimes hearing, rebuked him for it, as *Eli* oft times rebuked his children for sinning against the Lord : euen so this good man laboured to haue *Faustus* apply his study of Diuinitie, that he might come to the knowledge of God & his lawes. But it is manifest that many vertuous parents haue wicked children, as *Cayn, Ruben, Absolom,* and such like haue béen † to their parents : so this *Faustus* hauing godly parents, and seeing him to be of a toward wit,[3] were very desirous to bring him vp in those vertuous studies, namely, of Diuinitie : but he gaue himself secretly to study Necromancy and Coniuration, in so much that few or none could perceiue his profession.

But to the purpose : *Faustus* continued at study in the Vniuersity, & was by the Rectors and sixteene Masters after-

* Illegible in the British Museum copy (hereafter referred to as B.M.).

† The reason for the accent is not clear. It occurs in the text only where ee is printed as a ligature.

[2] 'Rhode,' modern Roda, about thirty kilometers southeast of Weimar.

[3] an apt or willing mind

wards examined howe he had profited in his studies; and being found by them, that none for his time were able to argue with him in Diuinity, or for the excellency of his wisedome to compare with him, with one consent they made him Doctor of Diuinitie. But Doctor *Faustus* within short time after hee had obtayned his degree, fell into such fantasies and deepe cogitations, that he was marked of many, and of the most part of the Students was called the *Speculator;* and sometime he would throw the Scriptures [Page 2] * from him as though he had no care of his former profession: so that hee began a very vngodly life, as hereafter more at large may appeare; for the olde Prouerb sayth, Who can hold that wil away? so, who can hold *Faustus* from the diuel, that seekes after him with al his indeuour ':† For he accompanied himselfe with diuers that were séene[4] in those diuelish Arts, and that had the *Chaldean, Persian, Hebrew, Arabian,* and *Greeke* tongues, vsing Figures, Characters, Coniurations, Incantations, with many other ceremonies belonging to these infernal Arts as Necromancie, Charmes, South-saying, Witchcraft, Inchantment, being delighted with their bookes, words, and names so well, that he studied day and night therein: in so much that hee could not abide to bee called Doctor of Diuinitie, but waxed a worldly man, and named himselfe an Astrologian, and a Mathematician: & for a shadow[5] sometimes a Phisitian, and did great cures, namely, with hearbs, rootes, waters, drinks, receipts, & clisters.[6] And without doubt he was passing wise, and excellent perfect in the holy scriptures: but hee that knoweth his masters will and doth it not, is worthy to be beaten with many stripes. It is written, no man can serue two masters: and, thou shalt not tempt the Lord thy God: but *Faustus* threw all this in the winde, & made his soule of no estimation, regarding more his worldly pleasure than y[e] ioyes to come: therfore at y[e] day of iudgement there is no hope of his redemptiō.

* The paging of B.M. is indicated in the brackets. There are frequent errors in pagination.

† B.M. uses two types of interrogation point, viz., ': and ?. The difference in significance is not clear. See McKerrow, *Introduction to Bibliography,* Oxford, 1927, p. 316.

[4] versed in

[5] as a blind

[6] enemas

How Doctor Faustus began to practise in his diuelish Arte, and how he coniured the Diuel, making him to appeare and meete him on the morrow at his owne house. Chap. 2.

YOu haue heard before, that all *Faustus* minde was set to study the artes of Necromancie and Coniuration, the which exercise hee followed day and night : and taking to him the wings of an Eagle, thought to flie ouer the whole world, and to know the secrets of heauen and earth ; for his Speculation was so wonderfull, being expert in vsing his *Vocabula,*[7] Figures, Characters, Coniurations, and other Ceremoniall actions, that in all the haste hee put in practise to bring the Diuell before him. And taking his way to a thicke Wood neere to *Wittenberg,* called in the Germane tongue *Spisser Waldt* : that is in English the *Spissers Wood,* (as *Faustus* would oftentimes boast of it among his crue being in his iolitie,) he came into the same wood towards euening into a crosse way, where he made with a wand a Circle in the dust, and within that many more Circles and Characters : and thus he past away the time, vntill it was nine or ten of the clocke [Page 3] in the night, then began Doctor *Faustus* to call for *Mephostophiles* the Spirite, and to charge him in the name of *Beelzebub* to appeare there personally without any long stay : then presently the Diuel began so great a rumor[8] in the Wood, as if heauen and earth would haue come together with winde, the trees bowing their tops to the ground, then fell the Diuell to bleare[9] as if the whole Wood had been full of Lyons, and sodainly about the Circle ranne the Diuell as if a thousand Wagons had been running together on paued stones. After this at the foure corners of the Wood it thundred horribly, with such lightnings as if the whole worlde, to his seeming, had been on fire. *Faustus* all this while halfe amazed at the Diuels so long tarrying, and doubting whether he were best to abide any more such horrible Coniurings, thought to leaue his Circle and depart ; wherevpon the Diuel made him such musick of all sortes, as if the Nimphes themselues had beene in place : whereat *Faustus* was reuiued and stoode stoutly

7 magic words
8 uproar
9 roar

in his Circle aspecting his purpose,[10] and began againe to coniure the spirite *Mephostophiles* in the name of the Prince of Diuels to appeare in his likenesse: where at sodainly ouer his head hanged houering in the ayre a mighty Dragon: then cals *Faustus* againe after his Diuelish maner, at which there was a monstrous crie in the Wood, as if hell had been open, and all the tormented soules crying to God for mercy; presently not three fadome aboue his head fell a flame in manner of a lightning, and changed it selfe into a Globe: yet *Faustus* feared it not, but did perswade himselfe that the Diuell should giue him his request before hee would leaue: Oftentimes after to his companions he would boast, that he had the stoutest head (vnder the cope of heauen) at commandement: whereat they answered, they knew none stouter than the Pope or Emperour: but Doctor *Faustus* said, the head that is my seruant is aboue all on earth, and repeated certain wordes out of Saint *Paul* to the *Ephesians* to make his argument good: The Prince of this world is vpon earth and vnder heauen. Wel, let vs come againe to his Coniuration where we left him at his fiery Globe: *Faustus* vexed at the Spirits so long tarying, vsed his Charmes with full purpose not to depart before he had his intent, and crying on *Mephostophiles* the Spirit; sodainly the Globe opened and sprang vp in height of a man: so burning a time, in the end it conuerted to the shape of a fiery man. This pleasant beast ranne about the circle a great while, and lastly appeared in manner of a gray Frier, asking *Faustus* what was his request. *Faustus* commaunded that the next morning at twelue of the clocke hee should appeare to him at his house; but the diuel would in no wise graunt: [Page 5] *Faustus* began againe to coniure him in the name of *Beelzebub,* that he should fulfil his request: whereupon the Spirit agreed, and so they departed each one his way.

The conference of Doctor Faustus with the Spirit Mephostophiles the morning following at his owne house. Chap. 3.

DOctor *Faustus* hauing commaunded the Spirit to be with him, at his houre appointed he came and appeared in his

[10] keeping in mind his object

chamber, demanding of *Faustus* what his desire was: then began Doctor *Faustus* anew with him to coniure him that he should be obedient vnto him, & to answere him certaine Articles, and to fulfil them in al points.

1 That the Spirit should serue him and be obedient vnto him in all things that he asked of him from y^t^ houre vntil the houre of his death.

2 Farther, any thing that he desired of him he should bring it to him.

3 Also, that in all *Faustus* his demaunds or Interrogations, the spirit should tell him nothing but that which is true.

Hereupon the Spirit answered and laid his case foorth, that he had no such power of himselfe, vntil he had first giuen his Prince (that was ruler ouer him) to vnderstand thereof, and to know if he could obtaine so much of his Lord: therfore speake farther that I may do thy whole desire to my Prince: for it is not in my power to fulfill without his leaue. Shew me the cause why (said *Faustus.*) The Spirit answered: *Faustus,* thou shalt vnderstand, that with vs it is euen as well a kingdome, as with you on earth: yea, we haue our rulers and seruants, as I my selfe am one, and we name our whole number the Legion: for although that *Lucifer* is thrust and fallē out of heauen through his pride and high minde, yet he hath notwithstanding a Legion of Diuels at his commaundement, that we call the *Oriental* Princes; for his power is great and infinite. Also there is an host in *Meridie,*[11] in *Septentrio,* in *Occidente:* and for that *Lucifer* hath his kingdome vnder heauen, wee must change and giue our selues vnto men to serue them at their pleasure. It is also certaine, we haue neuer as yet opened vnto any man the truth of our dwelling, neither of our ruling, neither what our power is, neither haue we giuen any man any gift, or learned him any thing, except he promise to be ours.

Doctor *Faustus* vpon this arose where he sate, & said, I wil haue my request, and yet I wil not be damned. The spirit answered, Then shalt thou want thy desire, & yet art

[11] 'Host' is a mistranslation of the German 'Herrschaft,' kingdom. 'Meridie' is south; 'Septentrio,' north; 'Occidente,' west.

thou mine notwithstanding : if any man would detaine thee it is in vain, for thine infidelity hath confoũded thée.

[Page 4] Hereupon spake *Faustus :* Get thee hence from me, and take Saint *Valentines* farewell & *Crisam* with thee,[12] yet I coniure thee that thou be here at euening, and bethinke thy selfe on that I haue asked thee, and aske thy Princes counsel therein. *Mephostophiles* the Spirit, thus answered, vanished away, leauing *Faustus* in his study, where he sate pondering with himselfe how he might obtaine his request of the diuel without losse of his soule : yet fully he was resolued in himselfe, rather than to want his pleasure, to doe whatsoeuer the Spirit and his Lord should condition vpon.

The second time of the Spirits appearing to Faustus in his house, and of their parley. Chap. 4.

FAustus continuing in his diuelish cogitations, neuer mouing out of the place where the Spirit left him (such was his feruent loue to the diuel) the night approching, this swift flying Spirit appeared to *Faustus,* offering himself with al submissiõ to his seruice, with ful authority from his Prince to doe whatsoeuer he would request, if so be *Faustus* would promise to be his : this answere I bring thee, and an answere must thou make by me againe, yet will I heare what is thy desire, because thou hast sworne me to be here at this time. Doctor *Faustus* gaue him this answere, though faintly (for his soules sake) That his request was none other but to become a Diuel, or at the least a limme of him, and that the Spirit should agree vnto these Articles as followeth.

1 That he might be a Spirite in shape and qualitie.

2 That *Mephostophiles* should be his seruant, and at his commandement.

3 That *Mephostophiles* should bring him any thing, and doo for him whatsoeuer.

4 That at all times he should be in his house, inuisible to all men, except onely to himselfe, and at his commandement to shew himselfe.

5 Lastly, that *Mephostophiles* should at all times appeare

[12] 'Saint Valentines farewell & Crisam with thee' is about equivalent to 'a pest upon you.' Logeman, *English Faustbook of 1592,* p. 137, gives a discussion of the derivation of the phrase.

at his command, in what forme or shape soeuer he would.

Vpon these poynts the Spirit answered Doctor *Faustus,* that all this should be granted him and fulfilled, and more if he would agree vnto him vpon certaine Articles as followeth.

First, that Doctor *Faustus* should giue himselfe to his Lord *Lucifer,* body and soule.

Secondly, for confirmation of the same, he should make him a wri- [Page 6] ting, written with his owne blood.

Thirdly, that he would be an enemie to all Christian people.

Fourthly, that he would denie his Christian beleefe.

Fiftly, that he let not any man change his opinion, if so bee any man should goe about to disswade, or withdraw him from it.

Further, the spirit promised *Faustus* to giue him certaine yeares to liue in health and pleasure, and when such yeares were expired, that then *Faustus* should be fetched away, and if he should holde these Articles and conditions, that then he should haue all whatsoeuer his heart would wish or desire; and that *Faustus* should quickly perceiue himself to be a Spirit in all maner of actions whatsoeuer. Hereupon Doctor *Faustus* his minde was so inflamed, that he forgot his soule, and promised *Mephostophiles* to hold all things as hee had mentioned them: he thought the diuel was not so black as they vse to paynt him, nor hell so hote as the people say, &c.

The third parley between Doctor Faustus and Mephostophiles about a conclusion. Chap. 5.

AFter Doctor *Faustus* had made his promise to the diuell, in the morning betimes he called the Spirit before him and commaunded him that he should alwayes come to him like a Fryer, after the order of Saint *Francis,* with a bell in his hande like Saint *Anthonie,* and to ring it once or twise before he appeared, that he might know of his certaine comming: Then *Faustus* demaunded the Spirit, what was his name? The Spirit answered, my name is as thou sayest, *Mephostophiles,* and I am a prince, but seruant to *Lucifer:* and all the circuit from *Septentrio* to the *Meridian,* I rule vnder him. Euen at these words was this wicked wretch *Faustus* inflamed, to heare himselfe to haue gotten so great a Potentate to be his seruant, forgot the Lord his maker, and Christ his redeemer, became an enemy vnto all man-kinde, yea, worse than the Gyants whom the Poets fayne to climb the hilles to make warre with the Gods : not vnlike that enemy of God and his Christ, that for his pride was cast into hell : so likewise *Faustus* forgot that the high climbers catch the greatest falles, and that the sweetest meate requires the sowrest sawce.

After a while, *Faustus* promised *Mephostophiles* to write and make his Obligation, with full assurance of the Articles in the Chapter before rehearsed. A pitifull case, (Christian Reader,) for certainly this Letter or Obligation was found in his house after his most lamen- [Page 7] table end, with all the rest of his damnable practises vsed in his whole life. Therefore I wish al Christians to take an example by this wicked *Faustus,* and to be comforted in Christ, contenting themselues with that vocation whereunto it hath pleased God to call them, and not to estéeme the vaine delights of this life, as did this vnhappie *Faustus,* in giuing his Soule to the Diuell : & to confirme it the more assuredly, he tooke a small penknife, and prickt a vaine in his left hand, & for certaintie therevpon, were séene on his hand these words written, as if they had béen written with blood, *ô homo fuge :* whereat the Spirit vanished, but *Faustus* continued in his damnable minde, & made his writing as followeth.

How Doctor Faustus set his blood in a saucer on warme ashes, and writ as followeth. Chap. 6.

I *Iohannes Faustus,* Doctor, doe openly acknowledge with mine owne hand, to the greater force and strengthning of this Letter, that siththence I began to studie and speculate the course and order of the Elements, I haue not found through the gift that is giuen mee from aboue, any such learning and wisdome, that can bring mee to my desires : and for that I find, that men are vnable to instruct me any farther in the matter, now haue I Doctor *Iohn Faustus,* vnto the hellish prince of Orient and his messenger *Mephostophiles,* giuen both bodie & soule, vpon such condition, that they shall learne me, and fulfill my desire in all things, as they haue promised and vowed vnto me, with due obedience vnto me, according vnto the Articles mentioned betwéene vs.

Further, I couenant and grant with them by these presents, that at the end of 24. yeares next ensuing the date of this present Letter, they being expired, and I in the meane time, during the said yeares be serued of them at my wil, they accomplishing my desires to the full in al points as we are agréed, that then I giue them full power to doe with mée at their pleasure, to rule, to send, fetch, or carrie me or mine, be it either body, soule, flesh, blood, or goods, into their habitation, be it wheresoeuer : and herevpon, I defie God and his Christ, all the hoast of heauen, and all liuing creatures that beare the shape of God, yea all that liues ; and againe I say it, and it shall be so. And to the more strengthning of this writing, I haue written it with mine owne hand and blood, being in perfect memory, and herevpon I subscribe to it with my name and title, calling all the infernall, middle, and supreme powers to witnesse of this my Letter and subscription.

Iohn Faustus, approued in the Elements,[13]
and the spirituall Doctor.

[Page 8]

How Mephostophiles came for his writing, and in what maner hee appeared, and his sights he shewed him : and how he caused him to keep a copie of his owne writing. Chap. 7.

DOctor *Faustus* sitting pensiue,* hauing but one onely boy with him, sodainely there appeared his Spirite *Mephostophiles,* in likenes of a fierie man, from whome issued most horrible fierie flames, in so much that the boy was afraide, but being hardned by his master, he bad him stand still and he should haue no harme : the Spirit began to blare as in a singing manner. This pretie sport pleased Doctor *Faustus* well, but hee would not call his Spirit into his Counting house, vntill hee had séene more : anon was heard a rushing of armed men, and trampling of horsses : this ceasing, came a kennell of hounds, and they chased a great Hart in the hall, and there the Hart was slaine. *Faustus* tooke heart, came forth, and looked vpon the Hart, but presently before him there was a

* B.M. has 'pensine.'

[13] proved or tested in the elements

Lyon and a Dragon together fighting, so fiercely, that *Faustus* thought they would haue brought downe the house, but the Dragon ouercame the Lyon, and so they vanished.

After this, came in a Peacock, with a Peahen, the cocke brusling of his tayle,[14] and turning to the female, beate her, and so vanished. Afterward followed a furious Bull, that with a full fiercenes ran vpon *Faustus,* but comming neare him, vanished away. Afterward followed a great old Ape, this Ape offered *Faustus* the hand, but he refused : so the Ape ran out of the hal againe. Herevpon fell a mist in the hal, that *Faustus* saw no light, but it lasted not, and so soone as it was gone, there lay before *Faustus* two great sacks, one full of gold, the other full of siluer.

Lastly, was heard by *Faustus* all maner Instruments of musick, as Organs, Clarigolds,[15] Lutes, Viols, Citerns,[16] Waights,[17] Hornepipes, Fluites, Anomes,[18] Harpes, and all maner of other Instruments, the which so rauished his minde, that hee thought hee had been in another world, forgat both body and soule, in so much that he was minded neuer to change his opinion concerning that which he had done. Hereat, came *Mephostophiles* into the Hall to *Faustus,* in apparell like vnto a Frier, to whome *Faustus* spake, thou hast done mee a wonderfull pleasure in shewing mee this pastime, if thou continue as thou hast begun, thou * shalt win my heart and soule, yea and haue it. *Mephostophiles* answered, this is nothing, I will please thee better : yet that thou maist know my power and all, aske what thou wilt request of mee, that shalt thou haue, conditionally hold thy promise, and giue me thy hand-writing : at [page 9] which words, the wretch thrust forth his hand, saying, hold thee, there hast thou my promise : *Mephostophiles* tooke the writing, and willing *Faustus* to take a copie of it, with that the peruerse *Faustus* being resolute in his damnation, wrote a copie thereof, and gaue the Diuell the one, and kept in store

* B.M. has 'thon.'

[14] erecting his tail stiffly

[15] A corruption of clarichord, a spinet-like instrument.

[16] A wire-strung instrument of the guitar type.

[17] oboes

[18] We can find no trace of this instrument. It is possibly a misprint.

the other. Thus the Spirit and *Faustus* were agreed, & dwelt together : no doubt there was a vertuous housekeeping.

The manner how Faustus proceeded with his damnable life, and of the diligent seruice that Mephostophiles vsed towards him. Chap. 8.

DOctor *Faustus* hauing giuen his soule to the diuell, renouncing all the powers of heauen, confirming this lamentable action with his owne blood, and hauing alreadie deliuered his writing not[19] into the diuels hand, the which so puffed vp his heart, that hee had forgot the minde of a man, and thought rather himselfe to bee a spirit. This *Faustus* dwelt in his Vnckles house at *Wirtenberg,* who dyed, and bequethed it in his Testament to his Cousin *Faustus. Faustus* kept a boy with him that was his scholler, an vnhappie wagge, called *Christopher Wagner,* to whome this sporte and life that hee saw his master follow seemed pleasant. *Faustus* loued the boy well, hoping to make him as good or better seene in his diuelish exercise than himselfe ; and hee was fellow with *Mephostophiles :* otherwise *Faustus* had no more companie in his house ; but himselfe, his boy and his Spirit, that euer was diligent at *Faustus* commaund, going about the house, clothed like a Frier, with a little bell in his hand, seene of none but *Faustus.* For his victuall and other necessaries, *Mephostophiles* brought him at his pleasure from the Duke of *Saxon,* the Duke of *Bauaria,* and the Bishop of *Saltzburg :* for they had many times their best wine stolne out of their cellers by *Mephostophiles :* Likewise their prouision for their owne table, such meate as *Faustus* wished for, his spirite brought him in : besides that, *Faustus* himselfe was become so cunning, that when he opened his windowe, what foule soeuer he wished for, it came presently flying into his house, were it neuer so daintie. Moreouer, *Faustus* and his boy went in sumptuous apparrell, the which *Mephostophiles* stole from the Mercers at *Norenberg, Auspurg, Franckeford,* and *Liptzig :* for it was hard for them to find a lock to keep out such a theefe. All their maintenance was but stolne & borrowed ware : and thus

[19] A later undated edition in our possession has 'now.' Logeman suggests 'written note' for 'writing not.'

they liued an odious life in the sight of God, though as yet ye world were vnacquainted with their wickednes. It must be so, for their fruites be none other : as Christ saith through *Iohn,* where hee cals the diuell a theefe, [Page 10] and a murderer : and that found *Faustus,* for hée stole him away both bodie and soule.

How Doctor Faustus would haue married, and how the Diuell had almost killed him for it.
Chap. 9.

DOctor *Faustus* continued thus in his Epicurish life day & night, and beléeued not that there was a God, hell, or diuel : he thought that bodie and soule died together, and had quite forgotten Diuinitie or the immortalitie of his soule, but stoode in his damnable heresie day and night. And bethinking himselfe of a wife, called *Mephostophiles* to counsaile ; which would in no wise agrée : demanding of him if he would breake the couenant made with him, or if hee had forgot it. Hast not thou (quoth *Mephostophiles*) sworne thy selfe an enemy to God and all creatures': To this I answere thée, thou canst not marry ; thou canst not serue two masters, God, and my Prince : for wedlock is a chiefe institution ordained of God, and that hast thou promised to defie, as we doe all, and that hast thou also done : and moreouer thou hast confirmed it with thy blood : perswade thy selfe, that what thou doost in contempt of wedlock, it is all to thine owne delight. Therefore *Faustus,* looke well about thée, and bethinke thy selfe better, and I wish thée to change thy minde : for if thou kéepe not what thou hast promised in thy writing, we wil teare thée in péeces like the dust vnder thy féete. Therefore swéete *Faustus,* thinke with what vnquiet life, anger, strife, & debate thou shalt liue in when thou takest a wife : therefore change thy minde.

Doctor *Faustus* was with these spéeches in despaire : and as all that haue forsaken the Lord, can build vpon no good foundation : so this wreched *Faustus* hauing forsooke the rock, fell in despaire with himself, fearing if he should motion [20] Matrimonie any more, that the diuell would teare him in péeces. For this time (quoth he to *Mephostophiles*)

[20] propose

I am not minded to marry. Then you doe well, answered his spirite. But shortly & that within * two houres after, *Faustus* called his spirit, which came in his old maner like a Frier. Then *Faustus* said vnto him, I am not able to resist nor bridle my fantasie, I must and will haue a wife, and I pray thée giue thy consent to it. Sodainlie vpon these words came such a whirle-winde about the place, that *Faustus* thought the whole house would come down, all the doores in the house flew off the hookes: after all this, his house was full of smoke, and the floore couered ouer with ashes: which when Doctor *Faustus* perceiued, he would haue gone vp the staires: and flying vp, he was taken and throwne into the hall, [Page 11] that he was not able to stir hand nor foote: then round about him ran a monstrous circle of fire, neuer standing still, that *Faustus* fried as hee lay, and thought there to haue béen burned. Then cried hee out to his Spirit *Mephostophiles* for help, promising him hee would liue in all things as he had vowed in his hand-writing. Hereupon appeared vnto him an ougly Diuell, so fearefull and monstrous to beholde, that *Faustus* durst not looke on him. The Diuell said, what wouldst thou haue *Faustus*': how likest thou thy wedding? what minde art thou in now': *Faustus* answered, he had forgot his promise, desiring him of pardon, and he would talke no more of such things. The diuell answered, thou were best so to doe, and so vanished.

After appeared vnto him his Frier *Mephostophiles* with a bel in his hand, and spake to *Faustus*: It is no iesting with vs, holde thou that which thou hast vowed, and wee will performe as wee haue promised: and more than that, thou shalt haue thy hearts desire of what woman soeuer thou wilt, bee shee aliue or dead, and so long as thou wilt, thou shalt kéepe her by thee.

These words pleased *Faustus* wonderfull † well, and repented himselfe that hee was so foolish to wish himselfe married, that might haue any woman in the whole Citie brought to him at his command; the which he practised and perseuered in a long time.

* B.M. has 'wihtin.'

† B. M. has 'wonderfnll.'

Questions put foorth by Doctor Faustus vnto his Spirite Mephostophiles. Chap. 10.

DOctor *Faustus* liuing in all manner of pleasure that his heart could desire, continuing in his amorous drifts, his delicate fare, and costly apparel, called on a time his *Mephostophiles* to him : which being come, brought with him a booke in his hand of all maner of diuelish and inchanted artes, the which he gaue *Faustus,* saying : hold my *Faustus,* worke now thy hearts desire : The copie of this inchanting booke was afterward found by his seruant *Christopher Wagner.* Wel (quoth *Faustus* to his spirit) I haue called thee to know what thou canst doe if I haue néede of thy help. Then answered *Mephostophiles* and said, my Lord *Faustus,* I am a flying spirit : yea, so swift as thought can think, to do whatsoeuer. Here *Faustus* said : but how came thy Lord and master *Lucifer* to haue so great a fal frō heauē': *Mephostophiles* answered : My Lord *Lucifer* was a faire Angell, created of God as immortal, and being placed in the Seraphins, which are aboue the Cherubins,[21] hee would haue presumed vnto the Throne of God, with intent to haue [Page 12] thrust God out of his seate. Vpon this presumption the Lord cast him downe headlong, and where before he was an Angel of light, now dwels hee in darkenes, not able to come neere his first place, without God send for him to appeare before him as *Raphael:*[22] but vnto the lower degree of Angells that haue their conuersation with men hee was come, but not vnto the second degree of Heauens that is kept by the Archangells, namely, *Michael* and *Gabriel,* for these are called Angels of Gods wonders : yet are these farre inferiour places to that from whence my Lord and Master *Lucifer* fell. And thus farre *Faustus,* because thou art one of the beloued children of my Lord *Lucifer,* following and feeding thy minde in maner as he did his, I haue shortly resolued thy request, and more I will doe for thee at thy pleasure. I thanke thee *Mephostophiles* (quoth *Faustus*)

[21] According to the medieval conception, there were nine orders of heavenly beings, of which the Seraphim were the highest and the Cherubim second.

[22] According to Spies, Lucifer, before his fall, was an archangel and was named Raphael.

come let vs now goe rest, for it is night : vpon this they left their communication.

How Doctor Faustus dreamed that hee had seene hell in his sleepe, and how he questioned with his Spirit of matters as concerning hell, with the Spirits answer. Chap. 11.

THe night following, after *Faustus* his communication had with *Mephostophiles,* as concerning the fal of *Lucifer,* Doctor *Faustus* dreamed that he had seene a part of hell : but in what maner it was, or in what place he knew not : whereupon he was greatly troubled in minde, and called vnto him *Mephostophiles* his spirit, saying to him, my *Mephostophiles,* I pray thee resolue me in this doubt : what is hell, what substance is it of, in what place stands it, and when was it made': *Mephostophiles* answered : my *Faustus,* thou shalt knowe, that before the fall of my Lord *Lucifer* there was no hell, but euen then was hell ordained : it is of no substance, but a confused thing : for I tell thee, that before al Elements were made, and the earth seene, the Spirit of God moued on the waters, and darkenes was ouer all : but when God said, let it bee light, it was so at his word, and the light was on Gods right hand, and God praised the light. Iudge thou further : God stood in the middle, the darkenes was on his left hand, in the which my Lorde was bound in chaines vntill the day of iudgement : in this confused hell is nought to finde but a filthie, Sulphurish, firie, stinking mist or fog. Further wee Diuels know not what substance it is of, but a confused thing. For as a bubble of water flieth before the wind, so doth hell before the breath of God. Further, we Diuels know not how God hath [Page 13] laid the foundation of our hell, nor whereof it is : but to bee short with thee *Faustus,* we know that hell hath neither bottome nor end.

The second question put foorth by Doctor Faustus to his Spirite, what Kingdomes there were in hell, how many, and what were their rulers names. Chap. 12.

Faustus spake againe to *Mephostophiles,* saying : thou speakest of wonderfull things, I pray thee now tell mee what

Kingdomes is there in your hell, how many are there, what are they called, and who rules them : the Spirite answered him : my *Faustus,* knowe that hell is as thou wouldst thinke with thy selfe another world, in the which wee haue our being, vnder the earth, and aboue the earth, euen to the Heauens ; within the circumference whereof are contained ten Kingdomes, namely :

1	*Lacus mortis.*	6	*Gehenna.*
2	*Stagnum ignis.*	7	*Herebus.*
3	*Terra tenebrosa.*	8	*Barathrum.*
4	*Tartarus.*	9	*Styx.*
5	*Terra obliuionis.*	10	*Acheron.*

The which Kingdomes are gouerned by fiue kings, that is, *Lucifer* in the *Orient, Beelzebub* in *Septentrio, Belial* in *Meridie, Astaroth* in *Occidente,* and *Phlegeton*[23] in the middest of them all : whose rule and dominions haue none end vntill the day of Dome. And thus farre *Faustus,* hast thou heard of our rule and kingdomes.

Another question put foorth by Doctor Faustus to his Spirite concerning his Lorde Lucifer, with the sorrow that Faustus fell afterwards into. Chap. 13.

DOctor *Faustus* began againe to reason with *Mephostophiles,* requiring him to tell him in what forme and shape, & in what estimation his Lord *Lucifer* was when he was in fauour with God. Whereupon his spirit required him of three daies respite, which *Faustus* granted. The 3. daies being expired, *Mephostophiles* gaue him this answer : *Faustus,* my Lord *Lucifer,* (so called now, for that he was banished out of the cleare light of Heauen) was at the first an Angell of God, he sate on[24] the Cherubins, and sawe all the wonderfull works of God, yea he was so of God ordained, for shape, pompe, authority, worthines, & dwelling, that he far

[23] 'Phlegeton,' used here as the name of a king, is usually the name of a mythical river in the underworld.

[24] Probably, 'had a place above.' According to N. E. D. a frequent expression for the Divine Being was : he sitteth or dwelleth between (or on) the Cherubim.

exceeded all other the creatures of God, [Page 14] yea our gold and precious stones : and so illuminated, that he farre surpassed the brightnes of the Sunne and all other Starres : wherefore God placed him on the Cherubins, where he had a kinglie office, and was alwaies before Gods seate, to the end hee might bee the more perfect in all his beings: but when hee began to be high minded, proude, and so presumptuous that hee would vsurpe the seate of his Maiestie, then was he banished out from amongst the heauenly powers, separated from their abiding into the manner of a fierie stone, that no water is able to quench, but continually burneth vntill the ende of the world.

Doctor *Faustus,* when he had heard the words of his spirit, began to consider with himselfe, hauing diuerse and sundrie opinions in his head : and very pensiuely (saying nothing) * vnto his Spirit, hee went into his chamber, and laid him on his bed, recording the words of *Mephostophiles;* which so pearced his heart, that hee fell into sighing and great lamentation, crying out : alas, ah, wo is me ! what haue I done': Euen so shall it come to passe with me : am not I also a creature of Gods making, bearing his owne Image and similitude, into whom he hath breathed the Spirite of life and immortalitie, vnto whome hee hath made all things liuing subiect : but woe is me, mine hautie minde, proud aspyring stomack, and filthie flesh, hath brought my soule into perpetuall damnation ; yea, pride hath abused my vnderstanding, in so much that I haue forgot my maker, the Spirit of God is departed from mee. I haue promised the Diuell my Soule : and therefore it is but a folly for me to hope for grace, but it must bee euen with mee as with *Lucifer,* throwne into perpetuall burning fire : ah, woe is mée that euer I was borne. In this perplexitie lay this miserable Doctor *Faustus,* hauing quite forgot his faith in Christ, neuer falling to repentance truly, thereby to attaine the grace & holy Spirit of God againe, the which would haue béen able to haue resisted the strong assaults of Sathan : For although hee had made him a promise, yet hee might haue remembred throught true repentance sinners come againe into the fauour of God ; which faith the faithfull firmely holde, knowing they that kill the bodie, are

* This second parenthesis mark evidently should come after 'Spirit.'

not able to hurt the soule : but he was in all his opinions doubtfull, without faith or hope, and so he continued.

Another disputation betwixt Doctor Faustus and his Spirite, of the power of the Diuell, and of his enuie to mankinde. Chap. 14.

AFter Doctor *Faustus* had a while pondered and sorrowed with himselfe of his wretched estate, hee called againe *Mephostophiles* [Page 15] vnto him, commaunding him to tell him the iudgement, rule, power, attempts, tyranny and temptation of the Diuell, & why he was moued to such kinde of liuing : whereupon the spirit answered, this question that thou demandest of me, will turne thee to no small discontentment : therefore thou shouldst not haue desired me of such matters, for it toucheth the secrets of our kingdome, although I cannot denie to resolue thy request. Therefore know thou *Faustus,* that so soone as my Lorde *Lucifer* fell from heauen, he became a mortall enemie both to God and man, and hath vsed (as now he doth) all manner of tyranny to the destruction of man, as is manifest by diuers examples, one falling sodainly dead, another hangs himselfe, another drownes himselfe, others stabbe themselues, others vnfaithfully despayre, and so come to vtter confusion : the first man *Adam* that was made perfect to the similitude of God, was by my Lord his pollicie, the whole decay of man : yea, *Faustus,* in him was the beginning and first tyranny of my Lord *Lucifer* vsed to man : the like did he with *Cain,* the same with the children of *Israel,* when they worshipped strange Gods, and fell to whoredome with strange women : the like with *Saul :* so did he by the seuen husbands of her that after was the wife of *Tobias :* likewise *Dagon* our fellow brought to destruction 30000. men, whereupon the Arke of God was stolen : and *Belial* made *Dauid* to number his men, whereupon were slaine 60000 also hee deceiued King *Salomon* that worshipped the Gods of the heathen : and there are such Spirits innumerable* that can come by men and tempt them, driue them to sinne, weaken their beliefe : for we rule the hearts of Kings and Princes, stirring them vp to warre and blood-shed ; and to this intent doe wee spread our selues

* B.M. has 'innmerable.'

throughout all the world, as the vtter enemies of God, and his Son[n]e Christ, yea & all those that worship them : and that thou knowest by thy selfe *Faustus,* how we haue dealt with thee. To this answered Faustus, why then thou didst also beguile me. Yea (quoth *Mephostophiles*) why should not we help thee forwards : for so soone as we saw thy heart, how thou didst despise thy degree taken in Diuinitie, and didst study to search and know the secrets of our kingdome ; euen then did we enter into thee, giuing thee diuers foule and filthy cogitations, pricking thee forward in thine intent, and perswading thee that thou couldst neuer attaine to thy desire, vntill thou hast the help of some diuell : and when thou wast delighted with this, then tooke we roote in thee ; & so firmely, that thou gauest thy selfe vnto vs, both body and soule the which thou (*Faustus*) canst not denie. Hereat answered *Faustus,* Thou sayest true *Mephostophiles,* [Page 18] I cannot denie it : Ah, woe is me miserable *Faustus ;* how haue I beene deceiued': had not I desired to know so much, I had not been in this case : for hauing studied the liues of the holy Saints and Prophets, & therby thought my self to vnderstand sufficient in heauenly matters, I thought my self not worthy to be called doctor *Faustus,* if I should not also know the secrets of hell, & be associated with the furious Fiend thereof ; now therefore must I be rewarded accordingly. Which speeches being vttered, *Faustus* went very sorrowfully away from *Mephostophiles.*

How Doctor Faustus desired againe of his Spirit to know the secrets and paines of hell ; and whether those damned Diuels and their company might euer come into the fauour of God againe or not? Chap. 15.

DOctor *Faustus* was euer pondering with himselfe how he might get loose from so damnable an end as he had giuen himself vnto, both of body and soule : but his repentance was like to that of *Cain* and *Iudas,* he thought his sinnes greater then God could forgiue, hereupon rested his minde : he looked vp to heauen, but sawe nothing therein ; for his heart was so possessed with the Diuel, that hee could thinke of nought els but of hell, and the paynes thereof. Wherefore in all the hast he calleth vnto him his Spirit *Mephostophiles,* desiring him to tell him some more of the secrets of hell, what paines the damned were in, and how they were tormented, and whether the damned soules might get againe the fauour of God, and so bee released out of their torments or not: whereupon the Spirit answered, my *Faustus,* thou mayst wel leaue to question any more of such matters, for they wil but disquiet thy mind, I pray thee what meanest thou': thinkest thou through these thy fantasies to escape vs? No, for if thou shouldest climb vp to heauen, there to hide thy selfe, yet would I thrust thee downe agayne; for thou art mine, and thou belongest vnto our society: therefore sweete *Faustus,* thou wilt repent this thy foolish demaund, except thou be content that I shall tell thee nothing. Quoth *Faustus* ragingly, I will know, or I will not liue, wherefore dispatch and tell me: to whom *Mephostophiles* answered, *Faustus,* it is no trouble vnto mee at all to tell thee, and therefore sith thou forcest mee thereto, I will tell thee things to the terror of thy soule, if thou wilt abide the hearing. Thou wilt haue me tel thee of the secrets of hell, and of the paynes thereof: know *Faustus,* that hell hath many figures, semblances, and names, but it cannot be named nor figured in such sort vnto the liuing that are damned, as it is vnto those that are dead, and doe both see and feele the [Page 19] torments thereof: for hell is sayd to bee deadly, out of the which came neuer any to life agayne but one, but he is as nothing for thee to reckon vpon, hell is blood-thirstie, and is neuer satisfied: hell is a valley, into the which the damned soules fal: for so soon as the soule is out of mans body, it would gladly goe to the place from whence it came, and climbeth vp aboue the highest hils, euen to the heauens; where being by the Angels of the first *Mobile*[25] denied entertainement* (in consideration of their euill life spent on the earth) they fall into the deepest pit or valley which hath no bottome, into a perpetuall fire, which shall neuer bee quenched: for like

* B.M. has 'eutertainement.'

25 'the first Mobile,' the outermost of the nine or ten spheres, which, according to the Ptolemaic system, were supposed to revolve around the earth from east to west, accounting for the diurnal revolution of the heavens. Here used in the Aristotelian sense, i.e., the physical system next to God, the unmoved mover.

as the Flint throwne into the water, looseth not his vertue, neither is his fire extinguished; euen so the hellish fire is vnquenchable: and euen as the Flint stone in the fire being burned is red hot, and yet consumeth not: so likewise the damned soules in our hellish fire are euer burning, but their paines neuer dimin[i]shing. Therefore is hel called the euerlasting pain, in which is neither hope nor mercy: So is it called vtter darknesse, in which we see neither the light of Sunne, Moone, nor Starre: and were our darkenesse like the darknes of the night, yet were there hope of mercie, but ours is perpetuall darkenesse, cleane exempt from the face of God. Hell hath also a place within it called *Chasma,* out of the which issueth all manner of thunders, lightnings, with such horrible shrikings and waylings, that ofttimes the very diuels themselues stand in feare thereof: for one while it sendeth foorth windes with exceeding snow, hayle, and raine congealing the water into yce; with the which the damned are frozen, gnash their teeth, howle and cry, and yet cannot die. Otherwhiles, it sendeth foorth most horrible hote mists or fogges, with flashing flames of fire and brimstone, wherein the sorrowfull soules of the damned lie broyling in their reiterated torments: yea *Faustus,* hell is called a prison wherein the damned lie continually bound; it is also called *Pernicies,* and *Exitium,* death, destruction, hurtfulnesse, mischiefe, a mischance, a pitifull and an euill thing worlde without end. We haue also with vs in hell a ladder, reaching of an exceeding height, as though it would touch the heauens, on which the damned ascend to seeke the blessing of God; but through their infidelitie, when they are at the very highest degree, they fall downe againe into their former miseries, complayning of the heate of that vnquenchable fire: yea sweete *Faustus,* so must thou vnderstand of hell, the while thou art so desirous to know the secrets of our kingdome. And marke *Faustus,* hell is the nurse of death, the heate of all fire, the shadow of heauen and earth, the obliuion of all goodnes, the paynes vnspeakeable, the griefes vnremoueable, the dwelling of [Page 18] Diuels, Dragons, Serpents, Adders, Toades, Crocodils, and all maner of venymous creatures, the puddle of sinne, the stinking fogge ascending from the Stigian lake, Brimstone, Pitch, and all maner of vncleane mettals, the perpetual and vnquenchable fire, the end of whose miseries was neuer purposed by God : yea, yea *Faustus,* thou sayst, I shall, I must, nay I will tell thee the secrets of our kingdome, for thou buyest it dearely, and thou must * and shalt be partaker of our torments, that (as the Lord God sayd) neuer shall cease : for hell, the womans belly, and the earth are neuer satisfied ; there shalt thou abide horrible torments, trembling, gnashing of teeth, howling, crying, burning, freezing, melting, swimming in a labyrinth of miseries, scalding, burning, smoking in thine eyes, stinking in thy nose, horsenes of thy speech, deaffenesse of thine eares, trembling of thy handes, biting thine owne tongue with payne, thy hart crushed as in a presse, thy bones broken, the diuels tossing fire brands vpon thee, yea thy whole carkasse tossed vpon muckforkes from one diuel to another, yea *Faustus,* then wilt thou wish for death, and he will flie from thee, thine vnspeakable torments shall be euery day augmented more and more, for the greater the sinne, the greater is the punishment : howe likest thou this, my *Faustus,* a resolution answerable to thy request ?

Lastly, thou wilt haue mee tell thee that which belongeth onely to God, which is, if it be possible for the damned to come againe into the fauour of God, or not : why *Faustus,* thou knowest that this is agaynst thy promise, for what shouldst thou desire to know that, hauing alreadie giuen thy soule to the Diuell to haue the pleasure of this worlde, and to know the secrets of hell : therefore art thou damned, and howe canst thou then come agayne to the fauour of God ? Wherefore I directly answere, no ; for whomsoeuer God hath forsaken and throwne into hell, must there abide his wrath and indignation in that vnquenchable fire, where is no hope nor mercy to bee looked for, but abiding in perpetuall paines world without end : for euen as much it auaileth thee *Faustus,* to hope for the fauour of GOD agayne, as *Lucifer* himselfe, who indeede although he and we all haue a hope, yet is it to small auaile, and taketh none effect, for out of that place GOD will neither heare crying nor sighing ; if he doe, thou shalt haue as little remorse, as *Diues, Cain,* or *Iudas* had : what helpeth the Emperour, King, Prince, Duke, Earle, Baron, Lord, Knight, Squire or Gentleman, to crie for mercy

* B.M. has 'mnst.'

being there': Nothing: for if on the earth they would not be Tyrants, and selfe-willed, rich with couetousnesse; proud with pomp, gluttons, drunkards, whoremongers, backbiters, robbers, [Page 19] murderers, blasphemers, and such like, then were there some hope to be looked for: therefore my *Faustus,* as thou commest to hell with these qualities, thou must say with *Cain,* My sinnes are greater then can be forgiuen, goe hang thy selfe with *Iudas:* and lastly, bee content to suffer torments with *Diues.* Therefore know *Faustus,* that the damned haue neither ende nor time appoynted in the which they may hope to bee released, for if there were any such hope, that they but by throwing one drop of water out of the Sea in a day, vntill it were all drie: or if there were an heape of sand as high as from the earth to the heauens, that a bird carying away but one corne in a day, at the end of this so long labour; that yet they might hope at the last, God would haue mercy on them, they would be comforted: but now there is no hope that God once thinkes vpon them, or that their howlings shall neuer bee heard; yea, so vnpossible, as it is for thee to hide thy self from God, or vnpossible for thee to remoue the mountaines, or to emptie the sea, or to tell the number of the drops of raine that haue falne from Heauen vntill this day, or to tell what there is most of in the worlde, yea and for a Camel to goe thorough the eye of a néedle: euen so vnpossible it is for thee *Faustus,* and the rest of the damned, to come againe into the fauour of God. And thus *Faustus* hast thou heard my last sentence, & I pray thee how doest thou like it': But know this, that I counsell thee to let me be vnmolested hereafter with such disputations, or els I will vexe thee euery limme, to thy small contentment. Doctor *Faustus* departed from his Spirit very pensiue and sorrowful, layd him on his bed, altogether doubtful of the grace and fauour of God, wherfore he fell into f[a]ntasticall cogitations: faine he would haue had his soule at liberty again, but the diuel had so blinded him, & taken such deepe roote in his heart, that he could neuer think to craue Gods mercy, or if by chance hee had any good motion,[26] straightwaies the diuel would thrust him a fayre Lady into his chamber, which fell to kissing and dalliance with him,

[26] impulse

through which meanes, he threw his godly motions in the wind, going forward stil in his wicked practises, to the vtter ruine both of his body and soule.

Another question put foorth by Doctor Faustus to his Spirite Mephostophiles of his owne estate.
Chap. 16.

DOctor *Faustus,* beeing yet desirous to heare more straunge things, called his Spirit vnto him, saying : My *Mephostophiles,* I haue yet another suite vnto thee, which I pray thee denie not to resolue me of, *Faustus* (quoth the Spirite) I am loth to [Page 22] reason with thee any further, for thou art neuer satisfied in thy minde, but alwayes bringest me a new. Yet I pray thee this once (quoth *Faustus*) doe me so much fauour, as to tell me the truth in this matter, and hereafter I will be no more so earnest with thee. The Spirit was altogether against it, but yet once more he would abide him : well, (said the Spirit to *Faustus*) what demaundest thou of mee ? *Faustus* said, I would gladly know of thee, if thou wert a man in manner and forme as I am ; what wouldest thou doe to please both God and man': Whereat the Spirit smiled saying : my *Faustus,* if I were a man as thou art, and that God had adorned me with those gifts of nature as thou once haddest ; euen so long as the breath of God were by, & within me, would I humble my selfe vnto his Maiestie, indeuouring in all that I could to keepe his Commaundements, prayse him, glorifie him, that I might continue in his fauour, so were I sure to enioy the eternall ioy and felicity of his kingdome. *Faustus* said, but that haue not I done. No, thou sayest true (quoth *Mephostophiles*) thou hast not done it, but thou hast denied thy Lord and maker, which gaue thee the breath of life, speech, hearing, sight, and all other thy reasonable senses that thou mightest vnderstand his will and pleasure, to liue to the glory and honour of his name, and to the aduancement of thy body and soule, him I say being thy maker hast thou denied and defied, yea wickedly thou hast applyed that excellent gift of thine vnderstanding, and giuen thy soule to the Diuell : therefore giue none the blame but thine owne selfe-will, thy proude and aspiring minde, which hath brought thee into the wrath of God and vtter damnation. This is most true (quoth *Faustus*) but tell me *Mephostophiles,* wouldst thou be in my case as I am nowe′: Yea, saith the Spirite (and with that fetcht a great sigh) for yet would I so humble my selfe, that I would winne the fauour of God. Then (said Doctor *Faustus*) it were time enough for me if I amended. True (said *Mephostophiles*) if it were not for thy great sinnes, which are so odious and detestable in the sight of God, that it is too late for thee, for the wrath of God resteth vpon thee. Leaue off (quoth *Faustus*) and tell me my question to my greater comfort.

Here followeth the second part of Doctor Faustus his life, and practises, vntill his end. Chap. 17.

DOctor *Faustus* hauing receiued deniall of his Spirit, to be resolued any more in such like questions propounded; forgot all good workes, and fell to be a Kalender maker by helpe of his [Page 23] Spirit; and also in short time to be a good Astronomer or Astrologian: he had learned so perfectly of his Spirite the course of the Sunne, Moone, and Starres, that he had the most famous name of all the Mathematicks that liued in his time; as may well appeare by his workes dedicated vnto sundry Dukes and Lords: for he did nothing without the aduice of his Spirit, which learned him to presage of matters to come, which haue come to passe since his death. The like prayse wonne he with his Kalenders, and Almanacks making, for when he presaged vpon any change, Operation, or alteration of the weather, or Elements; as winde, raine, fogges, snow, hayle, moyst, dry, warme, colde, thunder, lightening: it fell so duely out, as if an Angel of heauen had forewarned it. He did not like the vnskilfull Astronomers of our time, that set in Winter cold, moyst, ayrie, frostie; and in the Dogge-dayes, hote, dry, thunder, fire, and such like: but he set in all his works, day and houre, when, where, and how it should happen. If any thing wonderful were at hand, as death, famin, plague, or warres, he would set the time and place in true and iust order, when it should come to passe.

A question put foorth by Doctor Faustus to his Spirit concerning Astronomie. Chap. 18.

DOctor *Faustus* falling to practise, and making his Prognostications, he was doubtfull in many poynts: wherefore hee called vnto him *Mephostophiles* his spirit, saying: I finde the ground of this science very difficult to attaine vnto: for that when I conferre[27] *Astronomia* and *Astrologia,* as the Mathematicians and auncient writers haue left in memory, I finde them to vary and very much to disagree: wherefore I pray thee to teach me the truth in this matter. To whome his Spirit answered, *Faustus,* thou shalt know that the practioners or speculators, or at least the first inuentors of these Artes, haue done nothing of themselues certaine, whereupon thou mayst attaine to the true prognosticating or presaging of things concerning the heauẽs, or of the influence of the Planets: for if by chance some one Mathematician or Astronomer hath left behinde him any thing worthy of memorie: they haue so blinded it with *Ænigmaticall* wordes, blinde Characters, and such obscure figures; that it is vnpossible for an earthly man to attaine vnto the knowledge therof, without the ayde of some Spirit, or els the special gift of God; for such are the hidden works of God from men: yet doe we Spirits that flie and fleete in all Elements, knowe such, & there is nothing to be done, or by the Heauens pretended, but we [Page 22] know it, except onely the day of Dome. Wherefore (*Faustus*) learne of me, I will teach thee the course and recourse of ♄. ♃ ♂. ☉. ♀. ☿. and ☾.[28] the cause of winter and summer, the exaltation and declination of the Sunne, the eclipse of the Moone, the distance and height of the Poles, and euery fixed Starre, the nature and operation of the elements, fire, ayre, water, and earth, and all that is contained in them, yea herein there is nothing hidden from me, but onely the fift essence,[29] which once thou hadst *Faustus* at liberty, but now *Faustus* thou hast lost it past recouery: wherfore leauing that which

[27] compare

[28] These are the common symbols for Saturn, Jupiter, Mars, Sun, Venus, Mercury, and the Moon, in the order named.

[29] 'the fift essence.' In ancient or medieval philosophy the substance of which heavenly bodies were composed. It was supposed to be latent in all things. Here it seems to imply a divine element which Faust lost. Compare 'quintessence.'

wil not be againe had, learne now of me to make thunder, lightening, hayle, snow, and raine : the cloudes to rent, the earth and craggie rockes to shake and split in sunder, the Seas to swell, and rore, and ouer-run * their markes. Knowest not thou that the deeper the Sunne shines, the hotter he pearces': so, the more thy Arte is famous whilest thou art here, the greater shall be thy name when thou art gone. Knowest not thou that the earth is frozen cold and dry ; the water running, colde and moyst ; the ayre flying, hote and moist ; the fire consuming, hote and drie ? Yea *Faustus,* so must thy heart bee enflamed lik the fire to mount on high : learne, *Faustus,* to flie like my selfe, as swift as thought from one kingdome to another, to sit at princes tables, to eate their daintiest fare, to haue thy pleasure of their fayre Ladies, wiues, and concubines, to vse their iewels, and costly robes as things belonging to thee, and not vnto them : learne of mee, *Faustus,* to runne through wals, doores, and gates of stone and yron, to creepe into the earth like a worme, to swimme in the water like a fish, to flie in the ayre like a bird, and to liue and nourish thy selfe in the fire like a Salamander ; so shalt thou be famous, renowmed, far-spoken of, and extolled for thy skill : going on kniues, not hurting thy feete ; carying fire in thy bosome, and not burning thy shirt ; seeing through the heauens as through a Christall, wherein is placed the Planets, with all the rest of the presaging Comets, the whole circuite of the worlde from the East to the West, North and South : there shalt thou know, *Faustus,* wherefore the fiery spheare aboue ♄ and the signes of the Zodiack doth not burne & consume the whole face of the earth, being hindered by placing the two moyst elements between them, the ayrie cloudes and the wauering waues of water : yea, *Faustus,* I will learne thee the secrets of na[t]ure, what the causes that the Sun in summer being at the highest, giueth all his heate downewards on the earth ; and being in winter at the lowest, giueth all his heate vpward into the heauens : that the snow should be of so great vertue, as the honie ; and the Lady *Saturnia* ♓ in *Occulto,*[30] more hotter

* B.M. has 'ouer-rnn.'

30 This whole phrase is obscure. The symbol given is the sign of Pisces in the twelve signs of the zodiac. Its application here is not clear to us. 'In Occulto' and 'in Manifesto' mean respectively 'hidden' or 'eclipsed' and 'not hidden.'

then the Sun in *Manifesto*. Come [Page 23] on my *Faustus*, I will make thée as perfect in these things as myselfe, I will learne thee to goe inuisible, to finde out the mines of golde and siluer, the fodines[31] of precious stones, as the Carbuncle, the Diamond, Saphir, Emerald, Rubie, Topas, Iacinct,[32] Granat,[33] Iaspis,[34] Amathist, vse all these at thy pleasure, take thy hearts desire : thy time *Faustus* weareth away, then why wilt thou not take thy pleasure of the worlde': Come vp, we wil goe visite Kings at their owne courtes, and at their most sumptuous banquets be their guests, if willingly they inuite vs not, then perforce wee will serue our owne turne with their best meate and daintiest wine : Agreed quoth *Faustus* ; but let mee pause a while vpon this thou hast euen now declared vnto me.

How Doctor Faustus fell into despaire with himselfe : for hauing put foorth a question vnto his Spirit, they fell at variance, whereupon the whole route of diuels appeared vnto him, threatning him sharply. Chap. 19.

DOctor *Faustus* reuoluing with himselfe the spéeches of his Spirit, he became so wofull and sorrowfull in his cogitations, that he thought himselfe already frying in the hottest flames of hell, and lying in his muse, sodainely there appeared vnto him his Spirit, demaunding what things so griued and troubled his conscience, whereat Doctor *Faustus* gaue no answere : yet the Spirite very earnestly lay vpon him to know the cause ; and if it were possible, he would finde remedie for his griefe, and ease him of his sorrowes. To whome *Faustus* answered, I haue taken thée vnto mée as a seruant to doe mee seruice, and thy seruice will be very deare vnto me ; yet I cannot haue any diligence of thee farther than thou list thy selfe, neither doost thou in any thing as it becommeth thée. The spirit replied, my *Faustus*, thou knowest that I was neuer against thy commaundements as yet, but readie to serue and resolue thy questions, although I am not bound vnto thee in such re-

[31] mines

[32] Hyacinth. Among the ancients a blue gem, possibly the sapphire. In modern usage a reddish-orange gem.

[33] garnet

[34] jasper

spects as concerne the hurt of our kingdome, yet was I alwaies willing to answere thée, and so I am still: therefore my *Faustus* say on boldly, what is thy will and pleasure': At which words, the spirit stole away the heart of *Faustus,* who spake in this sorte, *Mephostophiles,* tell me how and after what sorte God made the world, and all the creatures in them, and why man was made after the Image of God': The spirit hearing this, answered, *Faustus* thou knowest that all this is in vaine for thee to aske, I knowe that thou art sory for that thou hast done, but it auaileth thee not, for I will teare thee in thousands of pee-[Page 24]ces, if thou change not thine opinions, and hereat hee vanished away. Whereat *Faustus* al sorrowful for that he had put forth such a question, fel to weeping and to how[l]ing bitterly, not for his sinnes towards God, but for that the Diuel was departed from him so sodainely, and in such a rage. And being in this perplexitie, hee was sodainely taken in such an extreame cold, as if he should haue frozen in the place where he sate, in which, the greatest Diuel in hell appeared vnto him, with certaine of his hideous and infernal companie in the most ougliest shapes that it was possible to think vpon, and trauersing the chamber round about where *Faustus* sate, *Faustus* thought to himselfe, now are they come for me though my time bee not come, and that because I haue asked such questions of my seruant *Mephostophiles:* at whose cogitations, the chiefest Diuel which was his Lord, vnto whom he gaue his soule, that was *Lucifer,* spake in this sorte: *Faustus,* I haue seene thy thoughtes, which are not as thou hast vowed vnto me, by vertue of this letter, and shewed him the Obligation that hee had written with his owne blood, wherefore I am come to visite thee and to shewe thee some of our hellish pastimes, in hope that will drawe and confirme thy minde a little more stedfast vnto vs. Content quoth *Faustus,* goe too, let mee see what pastime you can make. At which words, the great Diuell in his likenes sate him downe by *Faustus,* commanding the rest of the Diuels to appeare in their forme, as if they were in hel: first entred *Belial* in forme of a Beare, with curled black haire to the ground, his eares standing vpright: within the eare was as red as blood, out of which issued flames of fire, his teeth were a foote at least long, as white as snowe, with a tayle three elles long (at the least) hauing two wings, one behinde each arme, and thus one after another they appeared to *Faustus* in forme as they were in hell. *Lucifer* himselfe sate in manner of a man, all hairie, but of a browne colour like a Squirrell, curled, and his tayle turning vpwards on his back as the Squirrels vse, I thinke hee could cracke nuts too like a Squirrel. After him came *Beelzebub* in curled hayre of hors flesh colour, his head like the head of a Bull, with a mightie payre of hornes, and two long eares downe to the grounde, and two winges on his backe, with pricking stinges like thornes: out of his wings issued flames of fire, his tayle was like a Cowe. Then came *Astaroth* in forme of a worme, going vpright on his taile; he had no feete, but a tayle like a slowe-worme: vnder his chappes[35] grew two shorte hands, and his back was cole blacke, his belly thick in the middle, and yellow like golde, hauing many bristles on his backe like a Hedgehog. After him came *Chamagosta,* being white and gray mixed, ex-[Page 25] ceeding curled and hayrie: hee had a head like the head of an Asse, the tayle like a Cat, and Cleaes[36] like an Oxe, lacking nothing of an ell broade. Then came *Anobis;* this Diuell had a head like a Dog, white and black hayre in shape of a Hogge, sauing that he had but two feete, one vnder his throate, the other at his tayle: he was foure elles long, with hanging eares like a Blood-hound. After him came *Dythycan,* he was a short theefe in forme of a Feasant, with shining feathers, and foure feete: his neck was greene, his bodie red, and his feete blacke. The last was called *Brachus,* with foure shorte feete like an Hedgehog, yellow and greene: the vpper side of his bodie was browne, and the bellie like blewe flames of fire; the tayle redde, like the tayle of a Monkey. The rest of the Diuels were in forme of vnsensible beasts, as Swine, Harts, Beares, Woolues, Apes, Buffes, Goates, Antelopes, Elephants, Dragons, Horsses, Asses, Lions, Cats, Snakes, Toades, and all manner of vgly odious Serpents and Wormes: yet came in such sorte, that euery one at his entrie into the Hall, made their reuerence vnto *Lucifer,* and so tooke their places, standing in order as they came, vntill they had filled the whole Hall: wherewith sodainely fell a most horrible thunder-clap,

[35] jaws
[36] claws

that the house shooke as though it would haue fallen to the ground, vpon which euerie monster had a muck-fork in his hande, holding them towards *Faustus* as though they would haue runne a tilt at him : which when *Faustus* perceiued, hee thought vpon the words of *Mephostophiles,* when he tolde him how the soules in hell were tormented, being cast from Diuel to Diuel vpon muck-forkes, he thought verely to haue been tormented there of them in like sort. But *Lucifer* perceiuing his thought, spake to him, my *Faustus,* how likest thow this crewe of mine': Quoth *Faustus,* why came you not in another manner of shape ? *Lucifer* replied, wee cannot chaunge our hellish forme, we haue shewed our selues heere, as we are there ; yet can we blind mens eyes in such sort, that when we will repayre vnto them, as if we were men or Angels of light, although our dwelling bee in darknesse. Then said *Faustus,* I like not so many of you together, whereupon *Lucifer* commaunded them to depart, except seauen of the principall, forthwith they presently vanished, which *Faustus* perceiuing, hee was somewhat better comforted, and spake to *Lucifer,* where is my seruant *Mephostophiles,* let me see if hee can doe the like, wherevpon came a fierce Dragon, flying and spitting fire round about the house, and comming towards *Lucifer,* made reuerence, and then changed himself to ye forme of a Frier, saying, *Faustus,* what wilt thou': Saith *Faustus,* I will that thou teach me to transforme my selfe in like [Page 26] sort as thou and the rest haue done : then *Lucifer* put forth his Pawe, and gaue *Faustus* a booke, saying holde, doe what thou wilt, which hee looking vpon, straight waies changed himselfe into a Hog, then into a Worme, then into a Dragon, and finding this for his purpose, it liked him well. Quoth he to *Lucifer,* and how commeth it that all these filthy formes are in the world ? *Lucifer* answered, they are ordained of God as plagues vnto men, and so shalt thou be plagued (quoth he) whereupon, came Scorpions, Waspes, Emits, Bees, and Gnattes, which fell to stinging and biting him, and all the whole house was filled with a most horrible stinking fogge, in so much, that *Faustus* sawe nothing, but still was tormented ; wherefore hee cried for helpe saying, *Mephostophiles* my faithfull seruant where art thou, helpe, helpe I pray thee : hereat his Spirite answered nothing, but *Lucifer* himself said, ho ho ho *Faustus,* how likest thou the creation of the worlde, and in continent[37] it was cleare againe, and the Diuels and all the filthy Cattell were vanished, onely *Faustus* was left alone; seeing nothing, but hearing the sweetest musick that euer he heard before, at which he was so rauished with delight, that he forgat the feares hee was in before: and it repented him that he had seene no more of their pastime.

How Doctor Faustus desired to see hell, and of the maner how hee was vsed therein. Chap. 20.

DOctor *Faustus* bethinking how his time went away, and how he had spent eight yeares thereof, he ment to spend the rest to his better contentment, intending quite to forget any such motions as might offend the Diuell any more: wherefore on a time he called his spirit *Mephostophiles,* and said vnto him, bring thou hither vnto mee thy Lord *Lucifer,* or *Belial:* he brought him (notwithstanding) one that was called *Beelzebub,* the which asked *Faustus* his pleasure. Quoth *Faustus,* I would knowe of thee if I may see Hell and take a view thereof': That thou shalt (said the diuell) and at midnight I will fetch thee. Well, night being come, Doctor *Faustus* awaited very diligently for the comming of the Diuell to fetch him, and thinking that hee tarried all too long, he went to the window, where hee pulled open a cazement, and looking into the Element, hee sawe a cloude in the North more black, darke and obscure, than all the rest of the Sky, from whence the winde blew most horrible right into *Faustus* his chamber, filled the whole house with smoake, that *Faustus* was almost smothered: hereat fell an exceeding thunderclap, and withall came a great rugged black [Page 27] Beare, all curled, & vpon his backe a chayre of beaten golde, and spake to *Faustus,* saying, sit vp and away with me: and Doctor *Faustus* that had so long abode the smoake, wisht rather to be in hell than there, got on the Diuell, and so they went together. But marke how the Diuell blinded him, and made him beleeue that he carried him into hell, for he caried him into the ayre, where *Faustus* fell into a sound sleepe, as if hee had sate in a warme water or bath: at last they came to a place which burneth continually with flashing flames of fire and brimstone,

[37] i.e. incontinent, forthwith.

whereout issued an exceeding mighty clap of thunder, with so horrible a noyse, that *Faustus* awaked, but the Diuell went forth on his way and caried *Faustus* therinto, yet notwithstanding, howsoeuer it burnt, Doctor *Faustus* felt no more heate, than as it were the glimps of the Sunne in May : there heard he all manner of musicke to welcome him, but sawe none playing on them ; it pleased him well, but he durst not aske, for hee was forbidden it before. To meet the Diuel & the guest that came with him, came three other ougly Diuels, the which ran back againe before the Beare to make them way, against whome there came running an exceeding great Hart, which would haue thrust *Faustus* out of his chayre, but being defended by the other three Diuels, the Hart was put to the repulse : thence going on their way *Faustus* looked, and beholde there was nothing but Snakes, and all manner of venemous beastes about him, which were exceeding great, vnto the which Snakes came many Storks, and swallowed vp all the whole multitude of Snakes, that they left not one : which when *Faustus* sawe, he marueiled greatly : but proceeding further on their hellish voyage, there came forth of a hollow cliffe an exceeding great flying Bull, the which with such a force hit *Faustus* his chayre with his head and hornes, that he turned *Faustus* and his Beare ouer and ouer, so that the Beare vanished away, whereat *Faustus* began to crie : oh, woe is mee that euer I came here : for hee thought there to haue been beguiled of the Diuel, and to make his ende before his time appointed or conditioned of the Diuel : but shortly came v[n]to him a monstrous Ape, bidding *Faustus* bee of good cheare, and said, get vpon me ; all the fire in hel seemed to *Faustus* to haue been put out, wherevpon followed a monstrous thick fogge, that hee sawe nothing, but shortly it seemed to him to waxe cleare, where he saw two great Dragons fastned to a waggon, into the which the Ape ascended and set *Faustus* therein ; foorth flewe the Dragons into an exceeding darke cloude, where *Faustus* saw neither Dragon nor Chariot wherein he sat, and such were the cries of tormented soules, with mightie thunder-claps and flashing light-[Page 28]nings about his eares, that poore *Faustus* shooke for feare. Vpon this came they to a water, stinking and filthie, thick like mudde, into the which ran the Dragons, sinking vnder with waggon and all; but *Faustus* felt no water but as it were a small mist, sauing that the waues beate so sore vpon him, that hee saw nothing vnder and ouer him but only water, in the which he lost his Dragons, Ape, and waggon; and sinking yet deeper and deeper, hee came at last as it were vpon an high Rock, where the waters parted and left him thereon: but when the water was gone, it seemed to him hee should there haue ended his life, for he saw no way but death: the Rocke was as high from the bottome as Heauen is from the earth: there sate he, seeing nor hearing any man, and looked euer vpon the Rocke; at length hee saw a little hole, out of the which issued fire; thought he, how shall I now doe': I am forsaken of the Diuels, and they that brought mee hither, here must I either fall to the bottome, or burne in the fire, or sit still in despaire: with that in his madnesse he gaue a leape into the fierie hole, saying: holde you infernall Hagges, take here this sacrifice as my last ende; the which I iustly haue deserued: vpon this he was entred, and finding himselfe as yet vnburned or touched of the fire, he was the better appayed,[38] but there was so great a noyse as he neuer heard the like before, it passed all the thunder that euer he had heard; & cōming down further to the bottome of the Rocke, he sawe a fire, wherein were many worthie and noble personages, as Emperours, Kings, Dukes and Lords, and many thousands more of tormented soules, at the edge of which fire ran a most pleasant, cleare, and coole water to beholde, into the which many tormented soules sprang out of the fire to coole themselues; but b[e]ing so freezing cold, they were constrained to returne againe into the fire, and thus wearied themselues and spent their endles torments out of one labyrinth into another, one while in heate, another while in colde: but *Faustus* standing thus all this while gazing on them that were thus tormented, hee sawe one leaping out of the fire and scriching horriblie, whome he thought to haue knowne, wherefore he would faine haue spoken vnto him, but remembring that hee was forbidden, hee refrained speaking. Then this Diuel that brought him in, came to him againe in likenes of a Beare, with the chayre on his back, and bad him sit vp, for it was time to depart: so *Faustus* got vp, and the Diuel caried him out into the ayre,

[38] contented

where he had so sweete musick that hee fell asleepe by the way. His boy *Christopher* being all this while at home, and missing his master so long, thought his master would haue taried and dwelt with the Diuell for euer : but whilest his boy was in these co-[Page 29]gitations, his master came home, for the Diuel brought him home fast a sleepe as he sate in his chayre, and so he threw him on his bed, where (being thus left of the Diuel) he lay vntil day. When hee awaked, hee was amazed, like a man that had been in a darke dungeon ; musing with himselfe* if it were true or false that he had seene hel, or whether he was blinded or not : but he rather perswaded himself that he had been there than otherwise, because he had seene such wonderful things : wherefore he most carefully tooke pen and incke, and wrote those thinges in order as hee had seene : the which writing was afterwards found by his boy in his studie ; which afterwards was published to the whole citie of *Wittenberg* in open print, for example to all Christians.

How Doctor Faustus was carried through the ayre vp to the heauens to see the world, and how the Skie and Planets ruled : after the which he wrote one letter to his friend of the same to Liptzig, how he went about the world in eight daies. Chap. 21.

THis letter was found by a freeman and Citizen of *Wittenberg,* written with his own hande, and sent to his friend at *Liptzig* a Phisition, named *Ioue Victori,* the contents of which were as followeth.

Amongst other things (my louing friend and brother) I remember yet the former friendship had together, when wee were schoolefellowes and students in the Vniuersitie at *Wittenberg,* whereas you first studied Phisicke, Astronomie, Astrologie, Geometrie, and Cosmographie ; I to the contrarie (you know) studied Diuinitie : notwithstanding now in any of your owne studies I am seene (I am perswaded) further then your selfe : for sithence I began I haue neuer erred, for (might I speake it without affecting my owne praise) my Kalendars and other practises haue not onely the commenda-

* B.M. has 'himfelfe.'

tions of the common sorte, but also of the chiefest Lordes and Nobles of this our Dutch Nation : because (which is chiefly to be noted) I write and presaged of matters to come, which all accorde and fall out so right, as if they had been alreadie seene before. And for that (my beloued *Victori*) you write to know my voyage which I made into the Heauens, the which (as you certifie me you haue had some suspition of, although you partly perswaded your selfe, that it is a thing vnpossible) no matter for that, it is as it is, and let it be as it will, once it was done, in such maner as now according vnto your request I giue you here to vnderstand.

I being once laide on my bed, and could not sleepe for thinking on [Page 30] my Kalender and practise, I marueiled with my selfe how it were possible that the Firmament should bee knowne and so largely written of men, or whether they write true or false, by their owne opinions, or supposition, or by due obseruations and true course of the heauens. Beholde, being in these my muses, sodainly I heard a great noyse, in so much that I thought my house would haue been blowne downe, so that all my doores and chestes flewe open, whereat I was not a little astonied, for withall I heard a groning voyce which said, get vp, the desire of thy heart, minde, and thought shalt thou see : at the which I answered, what my heart desireth, that would I faine see, and to make proofe, if I shall see I will away with thee. Why then (quoth he) looke out at thy windowe, there commeth a messenger for thee, that did I, and beholde, there stoode a Waggon, with two Dragons before it to drawe the same, and all the Waggon was of a light burning fire, and for that the Moone shone, I was the willinger at that time to depart : but the voyce spake againe, sit vp and let vs away : I will, said I, goe with thee, but vppon this condition, that I may aske after all things that I see, heare, or thinke on : the voyce answered, I am content for this time. Hereupon I got me into the Waggon, so that the Dragons caried me vpright into ye ayre. The Waggon had also foure wheels the which ratled so, and made such a noyse as if we had been all this while running on the stones : and round about vs flew out flames of fier, and the higher that I came, the more the earth seemed to be darkened, so that me thought I came out of a dungeon, and looking downe from Heauen, beholde, *Mephostophiles* my Spirit and seruant was behinde me, and when he perceiued that I saw him, he came and sate by mee, to whome I said, I pray thee *Mephostophiles* whether shall I goe now? Let not that trouble thy minde, said hee, and yet they caried vs higher vp. And now will I tell thee good friend and schoole-fellow, what things I haue seene and prooued; for on the Tewsday went I out, and on Tewsday seuen-nights following I came home againe, that is, eight dayes, in which time I slept not, no not one winke came in mine eyes, and we went inuisible of any man: and as the daye began to appeare, after our first nights iorney, I saide to my Spirite *Mephostophiles,* I pray thee how farre haue wee now ridden, I am sure thou knowest: for me thinkes that we are ridden exceeding farre, the Worlde seemeth so little: *Mephostophiles* answered mee, my *Faustus* beleeue mee, that from the place from whence thou camst, vnto this place where wee are now, is already 47. leagues right in height, and as the day increased, I looked downe vpon the Worlde, [Page 31] there saw I many kingdomes and prouinces, likewise the whole world, *Asia, Europa,* and *Africa,* I had a sight of: and being so high, quoth I to my Spirit, tell me now how these kingdomes lye, and what they are called, the which he denied not, saying, see this on our left hand is *Hungaria,* this is also *Prussia* on our left hand, and *Poland, Muscouia, Tartascelesia,*[39] *Bohemia, Saxony:* and here on our right hand, *Spaine, Portugal, France, England,* and *Scotland:* then right out before vs lie the kingdoms of *Persia, India, Arabia,* the king of *Alchar,*[40] and the great *Cham:*[41] nowe are we come to *Wittenberg,* and are right ouer the towne of *Weim*[42] in *Austria,* and ere long will we be at *Constantinople, Tripolie,* and *Ierusalem,* and after will we pearce the frozen Zone, and shortly touch the Horizon, and the Zenith of *Wittenberg.* There looked I on the *Ocean* Sea, and beheld a great many of ships & Gallies ready to the battaile, one against another: and thus I spent my iourney, now cast I my eies here, now there, toward South, North, East, and West, I haue béen in one place where it rained and hailed, and in another where the Sun shone ex-

39 'Tartascelesia' looks like a combination of Tartary and Silesia.
40 Cairo
41 Khan, the ruler of Tartary.
42 Probably 'Wien,' Vienna.

cellent fayre, and so I thinke that I saw the most things in and about the world, with great admiration that in one place it rained, and in an other hayle and snow, on this side the Sunne shone bright, some hils couered with snow neuer consuming, other were so hot that grasse and trees were burned and consumed therewith. Then looked I vp to the heauens, and behold, they went so swift, that I thought they would haue sprong in thousands. Likewise it was so cleare and so hot, that I could not long gaze into it, it so dimmed my sight: & had not my Spirit *Mephostophiles* couered me as it were with a shadowing cloude, I had been burnt with the extreame heat thereof, for the Skie the which we beholde here when we looke vp from the earth, is so fast and thicke as a wal, cleare and shining bright as a Christal, in the which is placed the Sunne, which casteth foorth his rayes or beames ouer the vniuersall worlde, to the vttermost confines of the earth. But we thinke that the Sun is very little: no, it is altogether as big as the world. Indeed the body substantiall is but little in compasse, but the rayes or streame that it casteth forth, by reason of the thing wherein it is placed, maketh him to extend and shew himselfe ouer the whole world: and we thinke that the Sunne runneth his course, and that the heauens stand still: no, it is the heauens that moue his course, and the Sun abideth perpetually in his place, he is permanent, & fixed in his place, & although we see him beginning to ascend in the Orient or East, at the highest in the Meridian or South, setting in the Occident or West, yet is hee at [Page 32] the lowest in Septentrio or North, and yet he moueth not. It is the axle of the heauens that moueth the whole firmamēt, being a Chaos or confused thing, and for that proofe, I will shew thee this example, like as thou seest a bubble made of water and sope blowne forth of a quill, is in forme of a confused masse or Chaos, & being in this forme, is moued at pleasure of the wind, which runneth round about that Chaos, & moueth him also round: euen so is the whole firmament or Chaos, wherein are placed the sun, and the rest of the Planets turned and caried at the pleasure of the Spirit of God, which is wind. Yea Christian Reader,[43] to the glory of God, and for the

[43] The long address to the 'Christian Reader' is, of course, an interpolation of the English translator.

profite of thy soule, I wil open vnto thee the diuine opinion touching the ruling of this confused Chaos, farre more than any rude Germane Author, being possessed with the diuell, was able to vtter; and to prooue some of my sentence before to be true, looke into *Genesis* vnto the workes of God, at the creation of the world, there shalt thou finde, that the Spirit of God moued vpon the waters before heauen and earth were made. Marke how he made it, and howe by his word euery element tooke his place: these were not his workes, but his words; for all the words he vsed before, he concluded afterwards in one worke, which was in making man: marke reader with patience for thy soules health, see into all that was done by the word and worke of God, light and darkenes was, the firmament stoode, and their great ☉ & little light ☽ in it: the moyst waters were in one place, the earth was dry, & euery element brought foorth according to the word of God: now followeth his workes he made man like his owne image, how′: out of the earth′: The earth wil shape no image without water, there was one of the elements. But all this while where was winde? all elements were at the word of God, man was made, and in a forme by the worke of God, yet moued not that worke, before God breathed the Spirit of life into his nostrils, and made him a liuing soule, here was the first wind and Spirit of God out of his owne mouth, which wee haue likewise from the same seede which was onely planted by God in *Adam*, which winde, breath, or spirit, when he had receiued, hee was liuing & moouing on earth, for it was ordayned of God for his habitation, but the heauens are the habita[t]ion of the Lord: and like as I shewed before of the bubble or confused Chaos made of water and sope, through the wind and breath of man is turned round, and carried with euery wind; euen so the firmament wherein the Sun and the rest of the Planets are fixed, moued, turned, and carried with the winde, breath, or Spirit of God, for the heauens and firmament are moueable as the Chaos, but the sun is fixed in the firmament. And farther my good [Page 33] schoolefellow, I was thus nigh the heauens, where me thought euery Planet was but as halfe the earth, and vnder the firmament ruled the Spirits in the ayre, and as I came downe I looked vpon the worlde & the heauens, and me thought that the earth was inclosed in comparison within the firmament, as the yolke of an egge within the white, and me thought that the whole length of the earth was not a span long, and the water was as if it had been twise as broad and long as the earth, euen thus at the eight dayes end came I home againe, & fell a sleepe, and so I continued sleeping * three dayes and three nights together : & the first houre that I waked, I fell fresh againe to my Kalender, and haue made them in right ample maner as you know, and to satisfie your request, for that you writ vnto me, I haue in consideration of our olde friendship had at the Vniuersitie of *Wittenberg,* declared vnto you my heauenly voyage, wishing no worse vnto you, than vnto my selfe, that is, that your minde were as mine in all respects. *Dixi.*

Doctor Faustus the Astrologian.

How Doctor Faustus made his iourney thorough the principal and most famous lands in the world.
Chap. 22.

DOctor *Faustus* hauing ouer-runne † fiftéen yeers of his appointed time, he tooke vpon him a iourney, with ful pretence to see the whole world : and calling his spirit *Mephostophiles* vnto him, he sayd : thou knowest that thou art bound vnto me vpon conditions, to performe and fulfill my desire in all thengs, wherfore my pretence is to visite the whole face of the earth visible & inuisible when it pleaseth me : wherfore, I enioyne and command thée to the same. Whereupon *Mephostophiles* answered, I am ready my Lord at thy command & foorthwith the Spirit changed himselfe into the likenes of a flying horse, saying, *Faustus* sit vp, I am ready. Doctor *Faustus* loftily sate vpon him, & forward they went : *Faustus* came thorough many a land & Prouince ; as *Pannonia,*[44] *Austria, Germania, Bohemia, Slesia, Saxony, Missene,*[45] *During,*[46] *Francklandt,*[47] *Shawblandt,*[48] *Beyerlandt,*[49] *Stiria, Ca-*

* B.M. has 'sleepiug.'

† B.M. has 'runue.'

44 The region of Hungary.

45 Meissen

46 Thuringia

47 Franconia

48 Suabia

49 Bavaria

rinthia, Poland, Litaw,[50] *Liefland,*[51] *Prussia, Denmarke, Muscouia, Tartaria, Turkie, Persia, Cathai, Alexandria, Barbaria, Ginnie, Peru,* the strayghts of *Magelanes, India,* all about the frozen *Zone,* and *Terra Incognita,*[52] *Noua Hispaniola,*[53] the Isles of *Terzera,*[54] *Mederi,*[55] *S. Michaels,*[56] the *Canaries,* and the *Tenorrifocie,*[57] into *Spaine,* the *Mayne Land,*[58] *Portugall, Italie, Campania,* the Kingdome of *Naples,* the Isles of *Sicilia, Malta, Maioria,*[59] *Minoria,*[60] to the Knights of the *Rhodes, Candie,* or [Page 34] *Creete, Ciprus, Corinth, Switzerland, France, Freesland, Westphalia, Zeland, Holland, Brabant,* and all the 17. Prouinces in *Netherland, England, Scotland, Ireland,* all *America,* and *Island,*[61] the out Isles of *Scotland,* the *Orchades, Norway,* the Bishoprick of *Breame,*[62] and so home agayne : all these Kingdomes, Prouinces and Countries he passed in 25. dayes, in which time he saw very little that delighted his minde : wherefore he tooke a little rest at home, and burning in desire to see more at large, and to beholde the secrets of each kingdome, he set forward again on his iourney vpon his swift horse *Mephostophiles,* and came to *Treir,*[63] for that he chiefly desired to see this towne, and the monuments thereof ; but there he saw not many wonders, except one fayre Pallace that belonged vnto the Bishop, and also a mighty large Castle that was built of bricke, with three walles and three great trenches, so strong, that it was impossible for any princes power to win it ; then he saw a Church, wherein was buried *Simeon,* and the Bishop *Popo :* their Tombes are of most sumptuous large Marble stone, closed and ioyned together with great bars of yron : from whence he departed to *Paris,* where hee liked well the Academie ; and what place or Kingdome soeuer fell in his minde, the same

[50] Lithuania
[51] Livonia
[52] Probably the unknown regions near the poles.
[53] Mexico
[54] One of the Azores.
[55] Probably Madeira.
[56] One of the Azores.
[57] Probably Teneriffe.
[58] Perhaps the old province of Maine in France.
[59] Majorca
[60] Minorca
[61] Iceland
[62] Bremen
[63] Trèves, German Trier.

he visited. He came from *Paris* to *Mentz,*[64] where the riuer of *Mayne* fals into the *Rhine;* notwithstanding he taried not long there, but went to *Campania* in the Kingdome of *Neapolis,* in which he saw an innumerable * sort of Cloysters, Nunneries, and Churches, great and high houses of stone, the streetes fayre and large, and straight foorth from one end of the towne to the other as a line, and al the pauement of the Citie was of brick, and the more it rayned in the towne, the fayrer the streetes were; there saw he the Tombe of *Virgil;* & the high way that hee cutte through that mighty hill of stone in one night, the whole length of an English mile: then he saw the number of Gallies, and Argozies that lay there at the Citie head, the Windmil that stood in the water, the Castle in the water, and the houses aboue the water where vnder the Gallies might ride most safely from raine or winde; then he saw the Castle on the hil ouer the towne, and many monuments within: also the hil called *Vesuvius,* whereon groweth all the Greekish wine, and most pleasant sweet Oliues. From thence he came to *Venice,* whereas he wondered not a little to see a Citie so famously built standing in the Sea: where, through euery streete the water ranne in such largenes, that great Ships and Barks might passe from one streete to another, hauing yet a way on both sides the water, whereon men and horse might passe; he maruailed also howe it was possible for so much victual to be found in the towne and so good cheape, considering [Page 35] that for a whole league off nothing grew neere the same. He wondred not a little at the fayrenes of Saint *Markes* place, and the sumptuous Church standing therein called Saint *Markes;* how all the pauement was set with coloured stones, and all the Roode or loft[65] of the Church double gilded ouer. Leauing this, he came to *Padoa,* beholding the maner of their Academie, which is called the mother or nurse of Christendome, there he heard the Doctors, and saw the most monuments in the towne, entred his name into the Vniuersitie of the Germane nation, and wrote himselfe Doctor *Faustus* the vnsatiable Speculator: then saw he the worthiest monument in the world for a Church, named S.

* B.M. has 'innmerable.'

64 Mayence

65 Possibly the 'roodloft.' Logeman also suggests a second possibility, i.e. that 'roode' is a misprint for 'roofe.'

Anthonies Cloyster, which for the pinacles thereof, and the contriuing of the Church, hath not the like in Christendome. This towne is fenced about with three mighty walles of stone and earth, betwixt the which runneth goodly ditches of water : twise euery 24. houres passeth boates betwixt *Padoa* and *Venice* with passengers, as they doe here betwixt *London* and *Grauesend,* and euen so far they differ in distance : *Faustus* beheld likewise the Counsaile house & the Castle with no small wonder. Well, forward he went to *Rome,* which lay, & doth yet lie, on the riuer *Tybris,* the which deuideth the Citie in two parts : ouer the riuer are foure great stone bridges, and vpon the one bridge called *Ponte* S. *Angelo* is the castle of S. *Angelo,* wherein are so many great cast peeces as there are dayes in a yeare, & such Pieces that will shoote seuen bullets off with one fire, to this Castle commeth a priuie vault from the Church and Pallace of Saint *Peter,* through the which the Pope (if any danger be) passeth from his Pallace to the Castle for safegard ; the Citie hath eleuen gates, and a hill called *Vaticinium,*[66] whereon S. *Peters* Church is built : in that Church the holie Fathers will heare no confession, without the penitent bring mony in his hand. Adioyning to this Church, is the *Campo Santo,* the which *Carolus Magnus* * built,[67] where euery day thirteen Pilgrims haue their dinners serued of the best : that is to say, Christ and his twelue Apostles. Hard by this he visited the Church yard of S. *Peters,* where he saw the *Pyramide*[68] that *Iulius Cæsar*[69] brought out of *Africa;* it stood in *Faustus* his time leaning against the Church wall of Saint *Peters,* but now *Papa Sixtus* hath erected it[70] in the middle of S. *Peters* Church yard ; it is 24. fathom long and at the lower end sixe fathom foure square, and so forth

* B.M. has 'Maguus.'

66 'Vaticinium' should of course be Vaticanum.

67 'Campo Santo' is the usual Italian term for cemetery. We can find no connection between Charlemagne and this 'Campo Santo.' The reference to the 'thirteen Pilgrims' seems to have something to do with the mandatum ceremony.

68 A common term for obelisk in the sixteenth century.

69 The obelisk was brought from Egypt by Caligula and placed in the center of the Gaianum, the circus of Caligula, the north side of which was used as a foundation for the south half of St. Peter's. For centuries it was considered the tomb of Julius Caesar.

70 This phrase may furnish a hint as to the date of the translation. The tense used seems to indicate that Pope Sixtus was still alive at the time of writing. He died August 27, 1590. The obelisk was erected on its present site in the summer of 1586.

smaller vpwards, on the top is a Crucifixe of beaten golde, the stone standeth on foure Lyons of brasse. Then he visited the seuen Churches of *Rome,* that were S. *Peters,* S. *Pauls,* S. *Sebastians,* S. *Iohn Lateran,* S. *Laurence,* S. *Mary Magdalen,* and S. *Marie maiora:* then went he [Page 36] without the towne, where he saw the conduits of water that runne leuell through hill and dale, bringing water into the town fifteen Italian miles off: other monuments he saw, too many to recite, but amongst the rest he was desirous to see the Popes Pallace, and his maner of seruice at his table, wherefore he and his Spirit made themselues inuisible, and came into the Popes Court, and priuie chamber where he was, there saw he many seruants attendant on his holines, with many a flattering Sycophant carrying of his meate, and there hee marked the Pope and the manner of his seruice, which hee seeing to bee so vnmeasurable and sumptuous; fie (quoth *Faustus*) why had not the Diuel made a Pope of me? *Faustus* saw notwithstanding in that place those that were like to himselfe, proud, stout, wilfull, gluttons, drunkards, whoremongers, breakers of wedlocke, and followers of all manner of vngodly exercises: wherefore he said to his Spirit, I thought that I had been alone a hogge, or porke of the diuels, but he must beare with me yet a little longer, for these hogs of *Rome* are already fatned, and fitted to make his roste-meate, the Diuel might doe well nowe to spit them all and haue them to the fire, and let* him summon the Nunnes to turne the spits: for as none must confesse the Nunne but the Frier, so none should turne the rosting Frier but the Nunne. Thus continued *Faustus* three dayes in the Popes Pallace, and yet had no lust to his meate, but stood still in the Popes chamber, and saw euery thing whatsoeuer it was: on a time the Pope would haue a feast prepared for the Cardinall of *Pauia,* and for his first welcome the Cardinall was bidden to dinner: and as he sate at meate, the Pope would euer be blessing and crossing ouer his mouth; *Faustus* could suffer it no longer, but vp with his fist and smote the Pope on the face, and withall he laughed that the whole house might heare him, yet none of them sawe him nor knew where he was: the Pope perswaded his company that it was a damned soule, commanding a Masse presently to be said for his de-

* B.M. has the e in 'let' upside down.

liuerie out of Purgatory, which was done : the Pope sate still at meate, but when the latter messe came in to the Popes boord, Doctor *Faustus* laid hands thereon saying ; this is mine : & so he took both dish & meate & fled vnto the Capital or Campadolia,[71] calling his spirit vnto him and said : come let vs be merry, for thou must fetch me some wine, & the cup that the Pope drinkes of, & here vpon *monte caual*[72] will wee make good cheare in spight of the Pope & al his fat abbie lubbers. His spirit hearing this, departed towards the Popes chamber, where he found thē yet sitting and quaffing : wherefore he tooke from before the Pope the fairest peece of plate or drinking goblet, & a flaggon of wine, & brought [Page 37] it to *Faustus ;* but when the Pope and the rest of his crue perceiued they were robbed, and knew not after what sort, they perswaded themselues that it was the damned soule that before had vexed the Pope so, & that smote him on the face, wherefore he sent commandement through al the whole Citie of *Rome,* that they should say Masse in euery Church, and ring al the bels for to lay the walking Spirit, & to curse him with Bel, Booke, and Candle, that so inuisiblie had misused the Popes holinesse, with the Cardinall of *Pauia,* and the rest of their company : but *Faustus* notwithstanding made good cheare with y^t^ which he had beguiled ye pope of, and in the middest of the order of Saint *Barnards* bare footed Friers, as they were going on Procession through the market place, called *Campa de fiore,* he let fall his plate dishes and cup, and withall for a farwell he made such a thunder-clap and a storme of raine, as though Heauen and earth should haue met together, and so he left *Rome,* and came to *Millain* in *Italie,* neere the Alpes or borders of *Switzerland,* where hee praysed much to his Spirit the pleasantnesse of the place, the Citie being founded in so braue a plaine, by the which ranne most pleasant riuers on euery side of the same, hauing besides within the compasse or circuit of seuen miles, seuen small Seas : he sawe also therein many fayre Pallaces & goodly buildings, the Dukes Pallace, and the mighty strong Castle, which is in maner halfe the bignes of the towne. Moreouer, it liked him well to see the Hospitall of Saint *Maryes,* with diuers other things. He did

[71] Probably Campidoglio. It was on the Capitoline hill.

[72] Monte Cavallo, the Quirinal, upon which Pope Sixtus V had built his palace. P.F. confuses the Quirinal and the Capitoline.

nothing there worthy of memorie, but hee departed backe agayne towards *Bolognia,* and from thence to *Florence,* where hee was well pleased to see the pleas[a]nt walke of Merchants, the goodly vaults of the citie, for that almost the whole City is vaulted, & the houses themselues are built outwardly, in such sort that the people may go vnder them as vnder a vault : then hee perused the sumptuous Church in the Dukes Castle called *Nostra Donna,* our Ladies Church, in which he saw many monuments, as a Marble doore most huge to looke vpon : the gate of the Castle was Bell mettall, wherein are grauen the holy Patriarkes, with Christ and his twelue Apostles, and diuers other histories out of the olde and new Testament. Then went he to *Sena,* where he highly praysed the church and Hospital of *Santa Maria formosa,* with the goodly buildings,* and especially the fayrenesse and greatnesse of the Citie, and beautifull women. Then came he to *Lyons* in *France,* where hee marked the scituation of the Citie, which lay betweene two hilles, inuironed with two waters : one worthy monument in the citie pleased him wel, that was the great Church with the Image therin ; he cōmended y^{e} [Page 38] Citie highly for the great resort that it had vnto it of strangers. From thence he went to *Cullin,*[73] which lieth vpon the Riuer of *Rhine,* wherein he saw one of the auncientest monuments of the worlde, the which was the Tombe of the three Kings that came by the Angel of God, & their knowledge they had in the starre, to worship Christ : which when *Faustus* saw, he spake in this manner. Ah, alas good men how haue you erred and lost your way, you should haue gone to *Palestina* and *Bethelem* in *Iudea,* how came you hither': or belike after your death you were throwne into *Mare Mediterraneum* about *Tripolis* in *Syria ;* and so you fleeted,[74] out of the Straights of *Giblaterra* into the Ocean Sea, and so into the bay of *Portugal ;* & not finding any rest you were driuen alongst the coast of *Galicia, Biskay,* and *France,* and into the narrow Seas, then from thence into *Mare Germanicum,* and so I think taken vp about the towne of *Dort* in *Holland,* you were brought to *Cullin* to bee buried : or else I think you came more easily with a whirle-wind ouer the Alpes, and being

* B.M. has 'buidings.'

[73] Cologne

[74] floated

throwne into the Riuer of *Rhine,* it conuayed you to this place, where you are kept as a monument? There sawe he the Church of S. *Vrsula,* where remaines a monument of the 1000. Virgins: it pleased him also to see the beauty of the women. Not farre from *Cullin* lyeth the towne of *Ach,*[75] where he saw the gorgeous Temple that the Emperour *Carolus quartus* built of Marble stone for a remembrance of him, to the end that all his successors should there be crowned. From *Cullin* and *Ach,* he went to *Genf,** a Citie in *Sauoy,* lying neere *Switzerland:* it is a towne of great trafficke, the Lorde thereof is a Bishop, whose Wine-celler *Faustus,* and his Spirit visited for the loue of his good wine. From thence he went to *Strasburg,* where he beheld the fayrest steeple that euer he had seene in his life before, for on each side therof he might see through it, euen from the couering of the Minister to the top of the Pinacle, and it is named one of the wonders of the worlde: wherefore he demaunded why it was called *Strasburg:* his Spirit answered, because it hath so many high wayes comming to it on euery side, for *Stras* in Dutch is a high way, and hereof came the name, yea (sayd *Mephostophiles*) the Church which thou so wonderest at, hath more reuenues belonging to it, then the twelue Dukes of *Slesia* are worth, for there pertaine vnto this Church 55. Townes, and 463. Villages besides many houses in the Towne. From hence went *Faustus* to *Basile* in *Switzerland,* whereas the Riuer of *Rhine* runneth thorough the towne, parting the same as the Riuer of *Thames* doth *London:* in this towne of *Basile* he saw many rich Monuments, the towne walled with brick, and round about without it goeth a great trench: [Page 39] no Church pleased him but the Iesuites Church, which was so sumptuouslie builded, and beset full of Alabaster pillers. *Faustus* demanded of his Spirite, how it tooke the name of *Basyl:* his Spirite made answere and saide, that before this Citie was founded, there vsed a *Basiliscus,* a kinde of Serpent, this Serpent killed as many men, women, and children, as it tooke a sight of: but there was a Knight that made himselfe a couer of Christall to come ouer his head, and so downe to the ground, and being first couered with a

* B.M. has 'Geuf.'

[75] Aix-la-Chapelle

blacke cloth, ouer that he put the Christall, and so boldlie went to see the *Basiliscus,* and finding the place where he haunted, he expected his cōming, euen before the mouth of her caue : where standing a while, the *Basylike* came forth, who, when shee sawe her owne venemous shadowe in the Christall, shee split in a thousand peeces; wherefore the Knight was richlie rewarded of the Emperour : after the which the Knight founded this Towne vpon the place where he had slaine the Serpent, and gaue it the name of *Basyl,* in remembrance of his deede.

From *Basyl Faustus* went to *Costuitz*[76] in *Sweitz,* at the head of the *Rhine,* where is a most sumptuous Bridge, that goeth ouer the *Rhine,* euen from the gates of the Towne vnto the other side of the streame : at the head of the Riuer of *Rhine,* is a small Sea, called of the *Switzers* the black Sea, twentie thousand paces long, and fiftie hundred paces broad. The towne *Costuitz* tooke the name of this, the Emperour gaue it to a Clowne for expounding of his riddle, wherefore the Clowne named the Towne *Costuitz,* that is in English, cost nothing. From *Costuitz* hee came to *Vlme,* where hee sawe the sumptuous Towne-house built by two and fiftie of the ancient Senators of the Citie, it tooke the name of *Vlma,* for that the whole land thereabout are full of Elmes : but *Faustus* minding to depart from thence, his Spirite saide vnto him : *Faustus* thinke on the towne as thou wilt, it hath three Dukedomes belonging to it, the which they haue bought with readie mon[i]e. From *Vlme,* he came to *Wartzburg*[77] the chiefest towne in *Frankelandt,* wherein the Bishop altogether keepeth his Court, through the which Towne passeth the Riuer of *Mayne* that runnes into the *Rhine :* thereabout groweth strong and pleasant wine, the which *Faustus* wel prooued. The Castle standeth on a hill on the North side of the Towne, at the foote whereof runneth the Riuer : this Towne is full of beggerlie Fryers, Nunnes, Priestes, and Iesuites : for there are fiue sortes of begging Friers, besides three Cloysters of Nunnes. At the foote of the Castle stands a Church, in the which there is an Alter, where are ingrauen all the foure Elements, and all the orders and degrees in Heauen, that any

[76] Constance. The old name was Kostnitz. The 'u' is evidently a printer's error.

[77] Würzburg

[Page 40] man of vnderstanding whosoeuer that hath a sight thereof, will say that it is the artificiallest thing that euer he beheld. From thence he went to *Norenberg,* whither as he went by the waie, his Spirite enformed him that the Towne was named of *Claudius Tiberius* the Sonne of *Nero* the Tyrant. In the Towne are two famous Cathedrall Churches, the one called Saint *Sabolt,* the other Saint *Laurence ;* in which Church hangeth al the reliques of *Carolus Magnus,* that is his cloake, his hose and doublet, his sworde and Crowne, his Scepter, and his Apple. It hath a very gorgious gilden Conduit[78] in the market of Saint *Laurence,* in which Conduit, is the speare that thrust our Sauiour into the side, and a peece of the holy Crosse; the wall is called the fayre wall of *Norenberg,* and hath 528. streates, 160. wells, foure great, and two small clockes, sixe great gates, and two small doores, eleuen stone bridges, twelue small hills, ten appoynted market places, thirteene common hothouses,[79] ten Churches, within the Towne are thirtie wheeles of water-mills; it hath 132. tall ships,[80] two mightie Towne walls of hewen stone and earth, with very deepe trenches. The walls haue 180. Towers about them, and foure faire platformes, ten Apothecaries, ten Doctors of the common lawe, foureteene Doctors of Phisicke. From *Norenberg,* hee went to *Auspurg,* where at the breake of the day, he demaunded of his Spirit wherevpon the Towne tooke his name: this Towne (saith he) hath had many names, when it was first built, it was called *Vindelica:* secondly, it was called *Zizaria,* the yron bridge: lastly by the Emperour *Octauius Augustus,* it was called *Augusta,* and by corruption of language the *Germanes* haue named it *Auspurg.* Now for because that *Faustus* had been there before, he departed without visiting their monuments to *Rauenspurg,* where his Spirite certified him that the Citie had had seuen names, the first *Tyberia,* the second *Quadratis,* the third *Hyaspalis,* the fourth *Reginopolis,* the fiift *Imbripolis,* the sixt *Ratisbona,* lastly *Rauenspurg.* The scituation of the Citie pleased *Faustus* well, also the strong and sumptuous buildings: by the walls thereof runneth the Riuer of *Danubia,* in Dutch called *Donow,* into

78 fountain

79 public bathhouses

80 This Nuremberg navy is a puzzle. Spies has "132 Hauptmannschafft." Evidently we have either a mistranslation or a misprint.

the which not farre from the compasse of the Citie, falleth nerehand threescore other small Riuers and fresh waters. *Faustus* also liked the sumptuous stone bridge ouer the same water, with the Church standing thereon, the which was founded 1115. the name whereof, is called S. *Remedian:* in this towne *Faustus* went into the celler of an Inholder, and let out all the Wine and Beere that was in his Celler. After the which feat he returned vnto *Mentz*[81] in *Bauaria,* a right prince-[Page 41]ly Towne, the Towne appeared as if it were newe, with great streates therein, both of breadth and length: from *Mentz* to *Saltzburg,* where the Bishop is alwaies resident: here sawe he all the commodities that were possible to be seene, for at the hill he sawe the forme of *Abel*[82] made in Christall, an huge thing to looke vpon, that euery yeare groweth bigger and bigger, by reason of the freezing colde. From hence, hee went to *Vienna,* in *Austria:* this towne is of so great antiquitie, that it is not possible to finde the like: in this towne (said the Spirite) is more Wine then water, for all vnder the towne are wells, the which are filled euery yeare with wine, and all the water that they haue, runneth by the towne, that is the Riuer *Danubia.* From hence, hee went vnto *Prage,* the chiefe Citie in *Bohemia,* this is deuided into thrée partes, that is, olde *Prage,* new *Prage,* and little *Prage.* Little *Prage* is the place where the Emperours Court is placed vpon an exceeding high mountaine: there is a Castle, wherein are two fayre Churches, in the one he found a monument, which might well haue been a mirror to himselfe, and that was the Sepulchre of a notable Coniurer, which by his Magick had so inchanted his Sepulchre, that who so euer set foote thereon, should be sure neuer to dye in their beds. From the Castell he came downe, and went ouer the Bridge. This Bridge hath twentie and foure Arches. In the middle of this Bridge stands a very fayre monument, being a Crosse builded of stone, and most artificially carued. From thence, he came into the olde *Prage,* the which is separated from the new *Prage,* with an exceeding deepe ditch, and round about inclosed with a wall of Bricke.* Vnto this is adioyning the Iewes Towne, wherein are thirteene thousand

* B.M. has no period.

[81] Munich

[82] A later text in our possession has "a Bell."

men, women, and Children, all Iewes. There he viewed the Colledge and the Garden, where all manner of sauage Beasts are kept; and from thence, he fet[83] a compasse rounde about the three townes, whereat he wondred greatly, to see so mighty a Citie to stand all within the walles. From *Prage,* hee flewe into the ayre and bethought himselfe what hee might doe, or which way to take, so hee looked round about and beholde, he had espied a passing faire City which lay not farre from *Prage,* about some foure & twentie miles, and that was *Breslaw* in *Sclesia;* into which when he was entred, it seemed to him that hee had been in Paradise, so neate and cleane was the streates, and so sumptuous was their buildings. In this Citie he sawe not many wonders, except the Brasen Virgin that standeth on a Bridge ouer the water, & vnder ye which standeth a mil like a powder mil, which Virgin is made to do executiō vpon those disobediēt town-borne children y^t^ be so wilde, y^t^ their parents cānot [Page 42] bridle them; which when any such are found with some hainous offence, turning to the shame of their parents and kindred, they are brought to kisse this Virgin, which openeth her armes, the person then to bee executed, kisseth her, then doth she close her armes together with such violence, that she crusheth out the breath of the person, breaketh his bulke, and so dieth: but being dead, she openeth her armes againe, and letteth the partie fall into the Mil, where he is stamped in smal morsels, which the water carrieth away, so that not any parte of him is found againe. From *Breslaw* he went toward *Cracouia,* in the Kingdome of *Polonia,* where he beheld the *Academie,* the which pleased him wonderful well. In this Citie the King most commonly holdeth his Court at a Castel, in which Castell are many famous monuments. There is a most sumptuous Church in the same, in which standeth a siluer alter gilded, and set with rich stones, and ouer it is a conueiance full of all maner siluer ornaments belonging to the Masse. In the Church hangeth the iawe bones of an huge Dragon that kept the Rocke before the Castel was edified thereon. It is full of all maner munition, and hath alwaies victual for three yeare to serue 2000. men. Through the towne runneth a riuer called the *Vistula* or *Wissel,* where ouer is a faire woodden bridge. This water

[83] Made or fetched.

deuideth the towne and *Casmere,* in this *Casmere* dwelleth the Iewes being a small walled towne by themselues, to the number of 25000. men, women, and Children. Within one mile of the towne there is a salte mine, where they finde stones of pure salte of a 1000. pound, or 900. pound, or more in waight, and that in great quantitie. This salte is as black as the *Newcastle* coales when it comes out of the mines, but being beaten to powder, it is as white as snowe. The like they haue foure mile from thence, at a towne called *Buchnia.* From thence, *Faustus* went to *Sandetz,* the Captaine thereof was called *Don Spiket Iordan,* in this towne are many monuments as the tombe or sepulchre of Christ, in as ample maner as that is at *Ierusalem,* at the proper costs of a Gentleman that went thrice to *Ierusalem* from that place, and returned againe. Not far from that towne is a new towne, wherein is a Nunrie of the order of Saint *Dioclesian,* into which order may none come, except they be Gentlewomen, and well formed and faire to looke vpon, the which pleased *Faustus* well: but hauing a desire to trauaile farther, and to see more wonders, mounting vp towards the East, ouer many lands and prouinces, as into *Hungaria, Transiluania, Shede, Ingratz,*[84] *Sardinia,* and so into *Constantinople,* where the Turkish Emperor kept his Court. This Citie was surnamed by *Constantine* the founder thereof, being builded of very faire stone. In the same [Page 43] the great Turke hath three faire Pallaces, the wals are strong, the pinnacles are very huge, and the streetes large: but this liked not *Faustus,* that one man might haue so many wiues as he would. The Sea runneth hard by the Citie, the wall hath eleuen Gates: *Faustus* abode there a certaine time to see the manner of the Turkish Emperours seruice at his table, where hee saw his royall seruice to bee such, that hee thought if all the Christian Princes should banquet together, and euery one adorne the feast to the vttermost, they were not able to compare with the Turke for his table, and the rest of his Countrey seruice, wherefore it so spighted *Faustus,* that hee vowed to bee reuenged of him, for his pompe he thought was more fit for himselfe: wherefore as the Turke sate and eate, *Faustus* shewed him a little apish play: for rounde about

[84] 'Shede' and 'Ingratz.' Our search for these places on old maps has yielded nothing positive. Strabo has a Schedia, a village port in Lower Egypt.

the priuie Chamber, he sent foorth flashing flames of fire, in so much, that the whole company forsooke their meate and fled, except onely the great Turke himselfe, him *Faustus* had charmed in such sorte, that hee could neither rise nor fall, neither could any man pull him vp. With this was the Hall so light, as if the Sunne had shined in the house, then came *Faustus* in forme of a Pope to the great Turke, saying, all haile Emperour, now art thou honoured that I so worthily appeare vnto thee as thy *Mahumet* was wont to doe, herevpon he vanished, and forthwith it so thundred, that the whole Pallace shooke : the Turke greatly merueiled what this should bee that so vexed him, and was perswaded by his chiefest counsailers, that it was *Mahumet* his Prophet, the which had so appeared vnto them, wherevpon the Turke commaunded them to fal downe on their knees, and to giue him thankes for dooing them so great honor, as to shew himselfe vnto them ; but the next day *Faustus* went into the Castell where hee kept his Wiues and Concubines, in the which Castel might no man vpon paine of death come, except those that were appointed by the great Turke to doo them seruice, and they were all gelded, Which when *Faustus* perceiued, he said to his Spirit *Mephostophiles,* how likest thou this sport, are not these faire Ladies greatly to be pitied, that thus consume their youth at the pleasure of one onely man ? Why (quoth the Spirit) maiest not thou instead of the Emperor, imbrace his fairest Ladies, doe what thy heart desireth herein, and I will aide thee, and what thou wishest, thou shalt haue it performed : wherefore *Faustus* (being before this counsaile apt enough to put such matters in practize) caused a great fogge to bee round about the Castell, both within and without, and he himselfe appeared amongst the Ladies in all things as they vse to paint their *Mahumet,* at which sight, the Ladies fell on their knees, and [Page 44] worshipped him, then *Faustus* tooke the fairest by the hand, and led her into a chamber, where after his maner hee fell to dalliance, and thus he continued a whole day and night : and when hee had delighted himselfe sufficiently with her, hee put her away, and made his spirite bring him another, so likewise hee kept with her 24. houres play, causing his spirit to fetch him most dainty fare, and so hee passed way sixe daies, hauing each day his pleasure of a sundry Lady, and that of the fairest, all which time, the fog was so thick, and so stinking, that they within the house thought they had been in hell, for the time, and they without wondred thereat, in such sort, that they went to their praiers calling on their God *Mahumet,* and worshipping of his Image. Wherfore the sixt day *Faustus* exalted himselfe in the ayre, like to a Pope, in the sight of the great Turke and his people, and hee had no sooner departed the Castell, but the fogge vanished away, whence presently the Turke sent for his Wiues and Concubines, demanding of them if they knew the cause why the Castell was beset with a mist so long': they said, that it was the God *Mahumet* himselfe that caused it, and how he was in the Castell personally full sixe daies, and for more certaintie, he hath lien with sixe of vs these sixe nights one after another. Wherefore the Turke hearing this fell on his knees, and gaue *Mahumet* thanks, desiring him to forgiue him for being offended with his visiting his Castel and wiues those sixe dayes: but the Turke commanded that those whome *Mahumet* had laine by, should bee most carefully looked vnto, perswading himselfe (and so did the whole people that knewe of it) that out of their *Mahumet* should be raised a mighty generation, but first he demaunded of the sixe Ladies if *Mahumet* had had actuall copulation with them, according as earthly men haue, yea my Lorde quoth one, as if you had been there your selfe, you could not haue mended it, for hee lay with vs starke naked, kissed and colled vs, and so delighted me, y^t^ for my part, I would hee came two or three times a week to serue me in such sort againe. From hence, *Faustus* went to *Alkar,* the which before time was called *Chairam,* or *Memphis,*[85] in this Citie the Egiptian Souldane holdeth his Court. From hence the riuer *Nilus* hath his first head and spring, it is the greatest fresh-water riuer that is in the whole world, and alwaies when the Sunne is in *Cancer,* it ouerfloweth the whole land of *Ægypt:* then hee returned againe towards the North-east, and to the towne of *Ofen*[86] and *Sabatz*[87] in *Hungaria.* This *Ofen* is the chiefest Citie in *Hungaria,* and

[85] 'Chairam, or Memphis.' The confusion in names goes back to Schedel's *Chronik,* where there is a picture (fol. XXII) labeled Memphis vel Chayrum. The descriptive paragraph identifies the two places.

[86] Budapest

[87] Possibly Šabac in Jugoslavia, 39 miles west of Belgrade.

standeth in a fertile soyle, wherein groweth most excellent wine, and not farre from the Towne there is a wel, called *Zipzar,*[88] the water whereof changeth yron [Page 45] into Copper : here are mines of gold and siluer, and all maner of mettall, we *Germains* call this towne *Ofen,* but in the *Hungarian* speech it is *Start.*[89] In the towne standeth a very faire Castell, and very well fortified. From hence he went to *Austria,* and through *Slesia* into *Saxony,* vnto the townes of *Magdeburg* and *Liptzig,* and *Lubeck. Magdeburg* is a Bishoprick : in this Citie is one of the pitchers wherein Christ changed the water into wine at *Cana* in *Galile.* At *Liptzig* nothing pleased *Faustus* so well as the great vessell in the Castell made of wood, the which is bounde about with 24. yron hoopes, and euery hoope waieth 200. pound waight, they must goe vpon a ladder of 30. steps high before they can looke into it : hee saw also the new church-yard, where it is walled, and standeth vpon a faire plaine, the yard is 200. paces long, and round about in the inside of the wall, are goodly places seperated one from each other to see sepulchers in, which in the middle of the yard standeth very sumptuous : therein standeth a pulpit of white worke and golde. From hence hee came to *Lubeck* and *Hamburg,* where he made no abode, but away againe to *Erfort* in *Duringen,* where he visited the *Freskold,*[90] and from *Erfort* hee went home to *Wittenberg,* when he had seene and visited many a strange place, being from home one yeare and a halfe, in which time he wrought more wonders than are here declared.

How Faustus had a sight of Paradise. Chap. 23.

AFter this, Doctor *Faustus* set forth againe, visited these countries of *Spaine, Portugal, France, England, Scotland, Denmark, Sweden, Poland, Muscouy, India, Cataia,*[91] *Africa, Persia,* and lastly into *Barbaria* amongst the *Blacke mores,* and

[88] Logeman suggests that this name is erroneously derived from the German adjective "Zipser," i.e., of Zips, a district north of Budapest. The belief in the extraordinary virtues of Hungarian springs was widespread. The springs actually contained copper which was precipitated by the iron.

[89] 'Start.' An error copied by P.F. from Spies. The error goes back to Schedel's *Chronik* where 'start' is a misprint for 'statt,' city.

[90] Possibly 'frescade,' according to N.E.D. 'a cool walk; a shady alley.' Logeman suggests 'fresco' but neither conjecture explains the reference.

[91] Cathay

in all his wandring he was desirous to visit the auncient monuments and mighty hils, amongst the rest beholding the high hill called the *Treno Riefe,* was desirous to rest vpon it : from thence hee went into the Isle of *Brittany,* wherein hee was greatly delighted to see the faire water and warme Bathes, the diuers sorts of mettall, with many pretious stones, and diuers other commodities the which *Faustus* brought thence with him, hee was also at the *Orchades* behinde *Scotland,* where hee saw the tree that bringeth forth fruite, that when it is ripe, openeth and falleth into the water, whereof ingendreth a certaine kinde of Fowle or Birde : these Islands are in number 23. but 10. of them are not habitable, the other 13. are inhabited : from hence, he went to the hill of *Caucasus,* which is the highest in all that *Tropick,* it lieth nere ye borders [Page 46] of *Scythia,* hereon *Faustus* stoode and beheld many lands and kingdomes. *Faustus* being on such an high hill, thought to looke ouer all the world and beyond, for he ment to see Paradise, but he durst not commune with his Spirit thereof : and being on the hill of *Caucasus,* hee sawe the whole lande of *India* and *Scythia,* and towards the East as hee looked he sawe a mightie cleare strike[92] of fire comming from heauen vpon the earth, euen as it had béen one of the beames of the Sunne, he sawe in the valley foure mighty waters springing, one had his course towards *India,* the second towards *Ægypt,* the third & fourth towards *Armenia.* When he saw these, he would needes knowe of his Spirit what waters they were, and from whence they came. His Spirite gaue him gently an answere, saying ; it is Paradise that lieth so farre in the East, the garden that God himselfe hath planted with all maner of pleasure, and the firie streame that thou seest, is the walles or defence of the garden, but that cleare light that thou seest so farre off, is the Angell that hath the custodie thereof, with a fierie sworde : and although that thou thinkest thy selfe to bee hard by, thou hast yet farther thither from hence, then thou hast euer been : the water that thou seest deuided in foure partes, is the water that issueth out of the Well in the middle of Paradise. The first is called *Ganges* or *Phison,* the second, *Gihon* or *Nilus,* the third *Tigris,* and the fourth *Euphrates,* also thou seest that hee standeth vnder *Libra* and *Aries* right vp towards the

92 streak

Zenith, and vpon this firie wall standeth the Angell *Michael* with his flaming sword to keep the tree of life the which he hath in charge ; but the Spirite said vnto *Faustus,* neither thou, nor I, nor any after vs, yea all men whosoeuer are denied to visite it, or to come any nearer then we be.

Of a certaine Comet that appeared in Germanie, and how Doctor Faustus was desired by certaine friends of his to knowe the meaning thereof. Chap. 24.

IN *Germanie* ouer the Towne of S. *Eizleben*[93] was seene a mightie great Comet, whereat the people wondered ; but Doctor *Faustus* being there, was asked of certaine of his friends his iudgement or opinion in the matter. Wherevpon hee answered, it falleth out often by the course and change of the Sunne and Moone, that the Sunne is vnder the earth, and the Moone aboue ; but when the Moone draweth neere the change, then is the Sunne so strong that hee taketh away all the light of the Moone, in such sorte that he is as red as blood : [Page 47] and to the contrary, after they haue been together, the Moone taketh her light againe from him, and so increasing in light to the full, shee will be as red as the Sun was before, and changeth herselfe into diuers and sundry colours, of the which springeth a prodygious monster, or as you call it, a Comet, which is a figure or token appoynted of God as a fore-warning of his displeasure : as at one time hee sendeth hunger, plague, sword, or such like : being all tokens of his iudgement : the which Comet commeth through the coniunction of the Sun & Moone begetting a monster, whose father is the Sunne, and whose mother is the Moone, ☉ and ☽.

A question put foorth to Doctor Faustus, concerning the Starres. Chap. 25.

THere was a learned man of the towne of *Halberstat,* named *N. V. W.* inuited Doctor *Faustus* to his table, but falling into communication before supper was ready, they looked out of the windowe, and seeing many starres in the firmament, this man being a Doctor of Phisick and a good Astrologian, sayd :

[93] The S., usual abreviation for 'Saint,' is probably a misprint.

Doctor *Faustus,* I haue inuited you as my guest, hoping that you will take it in good part with me, and withall I request you to impart vnto me some of your experience in the Starres and Planets. And seeing a Starre fall, hee said : I pray you *Faustus,* what is the condition, qualitie, or greatnes of the Starres in the firmament': *Faustus* answered him : My friend and Brother, you see that the Starres that fal from heauen when they come on ye earth they be very smal to our thinking as cādles, but being fixed in the firmament there are many as great as this Citie, some as great as a Prouince or Dukedome, other as great as the whole earth, other some farre greater then the earth : for the length & breadth of the heauens is greater than the earth twelue times, and from the height of the Heauens there is scarce any earth to be seene, yea the Planets in the heauens are some so great as this land, some so great as the whole Empire of *Rome,* some as *Turkie,* yea one so great as the whole world.

[Page 48] *Howe Faustus was asked a question concerning the Spirites that vexe men.* Chap. 26.

THat is most true (sayth hee to *Faustus*) concerning the starres and planets : but I pray you in what kinde or maner doe the spirites vse or vexe men so little by day, and so greatly by night': Doctor *Faustus* answered : because the spirits are by GOD forbidden the light, their dwelling is in darknesse, and the clearer the Sunne shineth, the further the Spirits haue their abiding from it, but in the night when it is darke, they haue their familiaritie and abiding neere vnto vs men. For although in the night we see not the Sunne, yet the brightnes thereof so lightneth the first mouing of the firmament as it doth y^t^ on earth in the day, by which reason we are able to see the stars and Planets in the night, euen so the rayes of the Sunne pearcing vpwards into the firmament, the Spirits abandon the place, and so come neere vs on earth in the darknes, filling our heads with heauy dreames and fond fantasies, with schriching[94] and crying in many deformed shapes : as sometimes when men go forth without light, there falleth to them a feare, that their hayre standeth an end, so many start in their sleepe thinking there is a Spirit by him, gropeth or feeleth for

[94] screaching

him, going round about the house in his sleep, & many such like fantasies : and all this is for because that in the night the Spirits are more familiarly by vs than we are desirous of their company, and so they cary vs, blinding vs and plaguing vs more than we are able to perceiue.

How Doctor Faustus was asked a question concerning the Starres that fall from Heauen, Chap. 27.

DOctor *Faustus* being demanded the cause why the Starres fell from Heauen, he answered : that is but our opinion ; for if one Starre fall, it is the great iudgement of God vpon vs, as aforewarning of some great thing to come : for when we thinke that a Star falleth, it is but as a sparke that issueth from a candle or a flame of fire, for if it were a substantiall thing, we should not so soone loose the sight of them as we doo. And likewise, if so be that we see as it were a streame of fire fall from the firmament, as oft it happeneth, yet are they no Starres, but as it were a flame of fire vanishing, but the Starres are substantiall, therefore are they firme and not falling : if [Page 49] there fall any, it is a signe of some great matter to come, as a scourge to a people or countrey, and then such Starre falling, the gates of heauen are opened, and the cloudes send foorth floods, or other plagues, to the dammage of the whole land and people.

How Faustus was asked a question as concerning thunder. Chap. 28.

IN the moneth of August, there was ouer *Wittenberg* a mighty great lightning and thunder, and as Doctor *Faustus* was iesting merily in the market place with certaine of his friends and companions being Phisit[i]ōs, they desired him to tel them the cause of that weather. *Faustus* answered : it hath beene commonly seene heretofore, that before a thunder-clap fell a showre of raine or a gale of winde, for commonly after a winde followeth a raine, and after a rayne a thunder-clap : such things come to passe when the foure windes meete together in the heauens, the ayrie cloudes are by force beatē against the fixed chrystallin firmament, but when the ayrie cloudes meet with the firmament they are congealed, and so strike & rush against the firmament, as great peeces of yce when they meet on the water, the eccho thereof soundeth in our eares, and that we call thunder, which indeede is none other than you haue heard.

The third and last part, of Doctor Faustus his mery conceits, shewing after what sort he practised Nicromancie in the Courts of great Princes, and lastly of his fearfull and pitifull ende.

How the Emperour Carolus quintus requested of Faustus to see some of his cunning, whereunto he agreed.
Chap. 29.

THe Emperour *Carolus* the fifth of that name was personally with the rest of his Nobles and gentlemen at the towne of *Inszbruck* where he kept his court, vnto the which also Doctor *Faustus* resorted, and being there well knowne of diuers Nobles & gentlemen, he was inuited into the court to meat, euen in the presence of the Emperour : whom when the Emperour saw, hee looked earnestly on him, thinking him by his looks to be some wonderfull fellow, wherfore he asked one of his Nobles whom he should be : who answered that he was called Doctor *Faustus.* Whereupon the Emperour held his peace [Page 50] vntill he had taken his repast, after which hee called vnto him *Faustus,* into the priuie chamber, whither being come, he sayd vnto him : *Faustus,* I haue heard much of thee, that thou art excellent in the black Arte, and none like thee in mine Empire, for men say that thou hast a familiar Spirit with thee & that thou canst do what thou list : it is therefore (saith the Emperour) my request of thee that thou let me see a proofe of thine experience, and I vowe vnto thee by the honour of mine Emperiall Crowne, none euill shall happen vnto thee for so dooing. Herevpon Doctor *Faustus* answered his Maiestie, that vpon those conditions he was ready in any thing that he could, to doe his highnes commaundement in what seruice he would appoynt him. Wel, then heare what I say (quoth the Emperour.) Being once solitarie in my house, I called to mind mine elders and auncesters, how it was possible for them to attaine vnto so great a degree of authoritie, yea so high, that wee the successors of that line are neuer able to come neere. As for example, the great and mighty monarch of the worlde *Alexander magnus,* was such a lanterne & spectacle to all his successors, as the Cronicles makes mention of so great riches, conquering, and subduing so many kingdomes, the which I and those that follow me (I feare) shall neuer bee able to attaine vnto : wherefore, *Faustus,* my hearty desire is that thou wouldst vouchsafe to let me see that *Alexander,* and his Paramour, the which was praysed to be so fayre, and I pray thee shew me them in such sort that I may see their personages, shape, gesture & apparel, as they vsed in their life time, and that here before my face ; to the ende that I may say I haue my long desire fulfilled, & to prayse thee to be a famous man in thine arte and experience. Doctor *Faustus* answered : My most excellent Lord, I am ready to accomplish your request in all things, so farre foorth as I and my Spirit are able to performe : yet your Maiestie shall know, that their dead bodies are not able substantially to be brought before you, but such Spirits as haue seene *Alexander* and his Paramour aliue, shall appeare vnto you in manner and forme as they both liued in their most florishing time : and herewith I hope to please your imperiall Maiestie. Then *Faustus* went a little aside to speake to his Spirit, but he returned againe presently, saying : now if it please your Maiesty you shall see them, yet vpon this condition that you demaund no question of them, nor speake vnto them, which the Emperour agreed vnto. Wherewith Doctor *Faustus* opened the priuy chamber doore, where presently entred the great and mighty Emperour *Alexander magnus,* in all things to looke vpon as if he had been a-[Page 51]liue, in proportion a strong thick set man, of a middle stature, blacke hayre, and that both thick and curled head and beard, red cheekes, and a broade face, with eyes like a *Basiliske,* hee had on a complet harnesse burnished and grauen exceeding rich to looke vpon ; and so passing towards the Emperour *Carolus,* he made lowe and reuerent curtesie : whereat the Emperour *Carolus* would haue stoode vp to receiue and greete him with the like reuerence, but *Faustus* tooke holde of him and would not permit him to doe it. Shortly after *Alexander* made humble reuerence and went out againe, and comming to the doore his Paramour met him, she comming in, she made the Emperour likewise reuerence, she was clothed in blew Veluet, wrought and embrodered with pearle and golde, she was also excellent fayre like Milke & blood mixed, tall and slender, with a face round as an Apple, and thus shee passed certaine times vp and downe the house, which the Emperour marking, sayd to himselfe: now haue I seene two persons, which my heart hath long wished for to beholde, and sure it cannot otherwise be, sayd he to himselfe, but that the Spirits haue changed themselues into these formes, and haue not deceiued me, calling to his minde the woman that raysed the Prophet *Samuel:* and for that the Emperour would be the more satisfied in the matter, he thought, I haue heard say, that behinde her necke she had a great wart or wenne, wherefore he tooke *Faustus* by the hand without any words, and went to see if it were also to be seen on her or not, but she perceiuing that he came to her, bowed downe her neck, where he saw a great wart, and hereupon shee vanished, leauing the Emperour and the rest well contented.

How Doctor Faustus in the sight of the Emperour coniured a payre of Harts hornes vpon a Knights head that slept out of a cazement. Chap. 30.

WHen Doctor *Faustus* had accomplished the Emperours desire in all things as he was requested, he went foorth into a gallerie, and leaning ouer a rayle to looke into the priuie garden, he saw many of the Emperours Courtiers walking and talking together, and casting his eyes now this way, now that way, he espyed a Knight leaning out at a window of the great hall; who was fast asleepe (for in those dayes it was hote) but the person shall bee namelesse that slept, for that he was a Knight, although it was done to [Page 52] a little disgrace of the Gentleman: it pleased Doctor *Faustus,* through the helpe of his Spirit *Mephostophiles,* to firme[95] vpon his head as hee slept, an huge payre of Harts hornes, and as the Knight awaked thinking to pul in his head, hee hit his hornes against the glasse that the panes therof flew about his eares. Think here how this good Gentleman was vexed, for he could neither get backward nor forward: which when the Emperour heard al the courtiers laugh, and came forth to see what was hapened, the Emperour also whē he beheld the Knight with so fayre

[95] fasten

a head, laughed heartily thereat, and was therewithall well pleased : at last *Faustus,* made him quite of his hornes agayne, but the Knight perceiued how they came, &c.

How the aboue mentioned Knight went about to be reuenged of Doctor Faustus. Chap. 31.

DOctor *Faustus* tooke his leaue of the Emperour and the rest of the Courtiers, at whose departure they were sory, giuing him many rewards and gifts : but being a league and a halfe from the Citie he came into a Wood, where he beheld the Knight that hee had iested with at the Court with other in harnesse, mounted on fayre palfrayes, and running with full charge towards *Faustus,* but he seeing their intent, ran towards the bushes, and before he came amongst the bushes he returned againe, running as it were to meet them that chased him, wherupon sodainly al the bushes were turned into horsemen, which also ran to incoũter with the Knight & his company, & comming to thẽ, they closed the Knight and the rest, & told them that they must pay their ransome before they departed. Whereupon the Knight seeing himselfe in such distresse, besought *Faustus* to be good to them, which he denied not, but let them lose, yet he so charmed them, that euery one, Knight & other for the space of a whole moneth did weare a payre of Goates hornes on their browes, and euery Palfray a payre of Oxe hornes on their head : and this was their penance appoynted by *Faustus,* &c.

How three young Dukes being together at Wittenberg to behold the Vniuersitie, requested Faustus to help them at a wish to the towne of Menchen in Bauaria, there to see the Duke of Bauaria his sonnes wedding. Chap. 32.

THree worthy young Dukes, the which are not here to bee named, but being students altogether at the Vniuersitie of *Wittenberg,* [Page 53] met on a time altogether, where they fell to reasoning concerning the pompe and brauery that would be at the Citie of *Menchen* in *Bauaria,* at the wedding of the Dukes Sonne, wishing themselues there but one halfe houre, to see the manner of their iollity : to whom one replied, saying to the other two Gentlemen, if it please you to giue mee the hearing, I will giue you good counsell that we may see the wedding, and be here againe to night, and this is my meaning; let vs send to Doctor *Faustus,* make him a present of some rare thing and so open our mindes vnto him, desiring him to assist vs in our enterprise, and assure ye he will not denie to fulfill our request. Hereupon they al concluded, sent for *Faustus,* tolde him their minde, and gaue him a gift, and inuited him to a sumptuous banquet, wherewith *Faustus* was well contented, and promised to further their iourney to the vttermost. And when the time was come that the Duke his sonne should be married, Doctor *Faustus* called vnto him the three young Gentlemen into his house, commaunding them that they should put on their best apparell, and adorne themselues as richly as they could, he tooke off his owne great large cloke, went into a gardē that was adioyning vnto his house, and set the three young Dukes on his cloke, and he himselfe sate in the middest, but hee gaue them in charge that in any wise they should not once open their mouthes to speak, or make answere to any man so soone as they were out, no not so much as if the Duke of *Bauaria* or his Son should speake to them, or offer them courtesie, they should giue no word or answere agayne, to the which they all agreed. These conditions being made, Doctor *Faustus* began to coniure, and on a sodayne arose a mightie winde, heauing vp the cloke, and so carried them away in the ayre, & in due time they came vnto *Menchen* to yᵉ Dukes Court, where being entred into the outmost court, the Marshall had espied them, who presently went to the Duke, shewing his Grace that all the Lords and gentlemen were already set at the table, notwithstanding, there were newly come three goodly Gentlemen with one seruant, the which stoode without in the court, wherefore the good old Duke came out vnto them, welcomming them, requiring what they were, & whence: but they made no answere at all, whereat the Duke wondred, thinking they were all foure dumbe; notwithstanding for his honor sake hee tooke them into his court, and feasted them. *Faustus* notwithstanding spake to thē, if any thing happen otherwise then wel, when I say, sit vp, thē fal you al on the cloke, & good inough: wel, the water being brought, & that they must wash, one of the three had so much maners as to desire [Page 54] his friend to wash first, which when *Faustus* heard, he said, sit vp, and all at once they got on the cloke, but he that spake fell off againe, the other two with Doctor *Faustus,* were againe presently at *Wittenberg,* but he that remayned, was taken and layde in Prison : wherefore the other two Gentlemen were very sorrowfull for their friend, but *Faustus* comforted them, promising that on the morrow he should also be at *Wittenberg.* Now all this while was this Duke taken in a great feare, and striken into an exceeding dump, wondring with himselfe that his hap was so hard to be left behinde, and not the rest, and now being locked & watched with so many keepers, there was also certaine of the guests that fell to reasoning with him to know what hee was, and also what the other were that were vanished away, but the poore prisoner thought with himselfe, if I open what they are, then it will be euill also with me : wherefore all this while he gaue no man any answere, so that he was there a whole day, and gaue no man a word. Wherefore the olde Duke gaue in charge, that the next morning they should racke him vntill he had confessed : which when the young Duke heard, hee began to sorrow and to say with himselfe, it may be that to morrowe, if Doctor *Faustus* come not to ayde me, then shall I be racked and grieuously tormented, in so much that I shall be constrayned by force to tell more than willingly I would doe : but he comforted himselfe with hope that his friends would intreat Doctor *Faustus* about his deliuerance, as also it came to passe, for before it was day, Doctor *Faustus* was by him, and he coniured them that watched him into such a heauy sleepe, that he with his charmes made open all the lockes in the prison, and therewithall brought the young Duke againe in safety to the rest of his fellowes and friends, where they presented *Faustus* with a sumptuous gift, and so they departed the one from the other, &c.

How Doctor Faustus borrowed monie of a Iew, and layd his own legge to pawne for it. Chap. 33.

IT is a common prouerb in *Germanie,* that although a Coniurer haue all things at commaundement, the day will come that hee shall not be worth a pennie : so is it like to fall out with Doctor *Faustus,* in promising the Diuel so largely: and as the Diuel is the author of lies, euen so hee led *Faustus* his minde, in practising of things to deceiue the people and blinding them, wherein hee tooke his whole delight, thereby to bring himselfe to riches, yet notwithstanding in the ende he [Page 55] was neuer the richer. And although that during foure and twentie yeares of his time that the diuel set him, hee wanted nothing; yet was he best pleased when hee might deceiue any bodie: for out of the mightiest Potentates Courtes in all those Countries, hee would send his Spirite to steale away their best cheare. And on a time being in his merriment where hee was banqueting with other Students in an Inne, whereunto resorted many Iewes, which when Doctor *Faustus* perceiued, hee was minded to play some merrie iest to deceiue a Iew, desiring one of them to lend him some money for a time, the Iewe was content, and lent *Faustus* threescore dollers for a moneth, which time being expired, the Iewe came for his money and interest, but Doctor *Faustus* was neuer minded to pay the Iewe againe: at length the Iewe comming home to his house, and calling importunately for his money, Doctor *Faustus* made him this answere: Iewe, I haue no money, nor know I how to pay thee, but notwithstanding, to the ende that thou maiest bee contented, I will cut off a lim of my bodie, bee it arme or leg, and the same shalt thou haue in pawne for thy money, yet with this condition, that when I shall pay thee thy money againe, then thou also giue mee my limme. The Iewe that was neuer friend to a Christian, thought with himself, this is a fellow right for my purpose, that will lay his limmes to pawne for money, hee was therewith very well content; wherefore Doctor *Faustus* tooke a sawe, and therewith seemed to cut off his foote (being notwithstanding nothing so) well, he gaue it to the Iewe, yet vpon this condition, that when he got money to pay, the Iewe should deliuer him his leg, to the ende hee might set it on againe. The Iewe was with this matter very well pleased, tooke his leg and departed: and hauing farre home, he was somewhat wearie, and by the way hee thus bethought him, what helpeth mee a knaues leg, if I should carrie it home, it would stinck, and so infect my house, besides it is too hard a peece of worke to set it on againe, wherefore what an asse was *Faustus* to lay so deare a pawne for so small a summe of money; and for my part, quoth the Iew to himselfe, this will neuer profit me any thing, and with these words he cast the leg away from him into a ditch. All this Doctor *Faustus* knewe right wel, therefore within three daies after he sent for the Iewe to make him payment of his 60. Dollers, the Iewe came, and Doctor *Faustus* demaunded his pawne, there was his money readie for him: the Iewe answered, the pawne was not profitable or necessarie for any thing and he had cast it away: but *Faustus* threatninglie replied, I will haue my [Page 56] leg againe, or else one of thine for it. The Iewe fell to intreating, promising him to giue him what money he would aske, if hee would not deale straightly[96] with him, wherefore the Iewe was constrained to giue him 60. Dollers more to be rid of him, and yet *Faustus* had his leg on, for he had but blinded the Iewe.

How Doctor Faustus deceiued an Horse-courser. Chap. 34.

IN like manner hee serued an Horse-courser at a faire called *Pheiffring,* for Doctor *Faustus* through his cunning had gotten an excellent fayre Horse, wherevpon hee rid to the Fayre, where hee had many Chap-men that offered him money: lastly, he sold him for 40. Dollers, willing him that bought him, that in any wise he should not ride him ouer any water, but the Horsecourser marueiled with himself that *Faustus* bad him ride him ouer no water, (but quoth he) I will prooue, and forthwith hee rid him into the riuer, presently the horse vanished from vnder him, and he sate on a bundell of strawe, in so much that the man was almost drowned. The horse-courser knewe well where hee lay that had solde him his horse, wherefore he went angerly to his Inne, where hee found Doctor *Faustus* fast a sleepe, and snorting on a bed, but the horsecourser could no longer forbeare him, tooke him by the leg and began to pull him off the bed, but he pulled him so, that he pulled his leg from his body, in so much that the Horse-courser fel down backwardes in the place, then began Doctor *Faustus* to crie with an open throate, he hath mur-

[96] rigorously

dered me. Hereat the Horse-courser was afraide, and gaue the flight, thinking none other with himselfe, but that hee had pulled his leg from his bodie; by this meanes Doctor *Faustus* kept his money.

How Doctor Faustus eate a lode of Hay. Chap. 35.

DOctor *Faustus* being in a Towne of *Germanie* called *Zwickaw,* where hee was accompanied with many Doctors and Masters, and going foorth to walke after supper, they met with a Clowne [97] that droue a loade of Hay. Good euen good fellowe said *Faustus* to the Clowne, what shall I giue thee to let mee eate my bellie full of Hay? the Clowne thought with himselfe, what a [Page 57] mad man is this to eate Hay, thought he with himselfe, thou wilt not eate much, they agreed for three farthings he should eate as much as he could: wherefore Doctor *Faustus* began to eat, and that so rauenously, that all the rest of his company fell a laughing, blinding so the poore clowne, that he was sory at his heart, for he seemed to haue eaten more than the halfe of his Hay, wherefore the clowne began to speake him faire, for feare he should haue eaten the other halfe also. *Faustus* made as though he had had pitie on the Clowne, and went his way. When the Clowne came in place where he would be, he had his Hay againe as he had before, a full loade.

How Doctor Faustus serued the twelue Students. Chap. 36.

AT *Wittenberg* before *Faustus* his house, there was a quarrell betweene seuen Students, and fiue that came to part the rest, one part being stronger than the other. Wherefore *Faustus* seeing them to bee ouermatched, coniured them all blinde, in so much that the one could not see the other, and yet hee so dealt with them, that they fought and smote at one another still, whereat all the beholders fell a laughing: and thus they continued blinde, beating one another, vntill the people parted them, and leade each one to his owne home: where being entred into their houses, they receiued their sight perfectly againe.

[97] A boor, rustic. A translation of the German "Bauer."

How Faustus serued the dronken Clownes.
Chap. 37.

DOctor *Faustus* went into an Inne, wherein were many tables full of Clownes, the which were tippling kan after kan of excellent wine, and to bee short, they were all dronken, and as they sate, they so sung and hallowed, that one could not heare a man speake for them; this angred Doctor *Faustus;* wherefore hee said to those that had called him in, marke my masters, I will shew you a merrie iest, the Clownes continuing still hallowing and singing, he so coniured them, that their mouthes stoode as wide open as it was possible for them to hold them, and neuer a one of them was able to close his mouth againe: by and by the noyse was gone, the Clownes notwithstanding looked earnestly one vpon another, and wist not what [Page 58] was happened; wherefore one by one they went out, and so soone as they came without, they were as well as euer they were: but none of them desired to goe in any more.

How Doctor Faustus solde fiue Swine for sixe Dollers a peece. Chap. 38.

DOctor *Faustus* began another iest, hee made him readie fiue fat Swine, the which hee solde to one for sixe Dollers a peece, vpon this condition, that the Swine-driuer should not driue them into the water. Doctor *Faustus* went home againe, and as the Swine had filed[98] themselues in the mudde, the Swine-driuer droue them into a water, where presently they were changed into so many bundels of straw swimming vpright in the water: the buier looked wishly[99] about him, and was sorrie in his heart, but he knewe not where to finde *Faustus,* so he was content to let all goe, and to lose both money and Hogs.

How Doctor Faustus played a merrie iest with the Duke of Anholt in his Court. Chap. 39.

DOctor *Faustus* on a time came to the Duke of *Anholt,* the which welcomed him very courteously, this was in the moneth

[98] defiled
[99] longingly, wistfully

of Ianuary, where sitting at the table, he perceiued the Dutchesse to be with childe, and forbearing himselfe vntill the meate was taken from the table, and that they brought in the banquetting dishes, said Doctor *Faustus* to the Dutchesse, Gracious Ladie, I haue alway heard, that the great bellied women doe alwaies long for some dainties, I beseech therefore your Grace hide not your mind from me, but tell me what you desire to eate, she answered him, Doctor *Faustus* now truely I will not hide from you what my heart dooth most desire, namely, that if it were now Haruest, I would eate my bellie full of ripe Grapes, and other daintie fruite. Doctor *Faustus* answered herevpon, Gracious Lady, this is a small thing for mee to doe, for I can doo more than this, wherefore he tooke a plate, and made open one of the casements of the windowe, holding it forth, where incontinent hee had his dish full of all maner of fruites, as red and white Grapes, Peares, and Apples, the which came from out of strange Countries, all these he presented the Dutchesse, saying: Madame, I [Page 59] pray you vouchsafe to taste of this daintie fruite, the which came from a farre Countrey, for there the Sommer is not yet ended. The Dutchesse thanked *Faustus* highly, and she fell to her fruite with full appetite. The Duke of *Anholt* notwithstanding could not with-holde to aske *Faustus* with what reason there were such young fruite to be had at that time of the yeare? Doctor *Faustus* tolde him, may it please your Grace to vnderstand, that the yere is deuided into two circles ouer the whole world, that when with vs it is Winter, in the contrary circle it is notwithstanding Sommer, for in *India* and *Saba*[100] there falleth or setteth the Sunne, so that it is so warme, that they haue twise a yeare fruite: and gracious Lorde, I haue a swift Spirit, the which can in the twinckling of an eye fulfill my desire in any thing, wherefore I sent him into those Countries, who hath brought this fruite as you see: whereat the Duke was in great admiration.

100 Sheba

How Doctor Faustus through his Charmes made a great Castle in presence of the Duke of Anholt. Chap 40.

DOctor *Faustus* desired the Duke of *Anholt* to walke a little forth of the Court with him, wherefore they went both together into the field, where Doctor *Faustus* through his skill had placed a mightie Castel : which when the Duke sawe, hee wondered thereat, so did the Dutchesse, and all the beholders, that on that hill, which was called the *Rohumbuel,* should on the sodaine bee so fayre a Castle. At last Doctor *Faustus* desired the Duke and the Dutchesse to walke with him into the Castle, which they denied not. This Castle was so wonderfull strong, hauing about it a great and deepe trench of water, the which was full of Fish, and all maner of water-foule, as Swannes, Duckes, Geese, Bitters, and such like. About the wall was fiue stone dores and two other dores : also within was a great open court, wherein were inchaunted all maner of wilde beasts, especiallie such as were not to bee found in *Germanie,* as Apes, Beares, Buffes, Antelopes, and such like strange beasts. Furthermore, there were other maner of beasts, as Hart, Hind, and wilde Swine, Roe, and all maner of land foule that any man could thinke on, the which flewe from one tree to another. After all this, he set his guestes to the table, being the Duke and the Dutchesse with their traine, for hee had prouided them a most sumptuous feast, both of meate and all maner of drinks, for he set nine messe of meate vpon the boord at once, and al this [Page 60] must his *Wagner* doe, place all things on the boord, the which was brought vnto him by the Spirit inuisiblie of all things that their heart could desire, as wild foule, and Venison, with all maner of daintie fish that could bee thought on, of Wine also great plentie, and of diuers sortes, as *French* wine, *Cullin* wine, *Crabatsher* wine, *Rhenish* wine, *Spanish* wine, *Hungarian* wine, *Watzburg* wine, Malmesie, and Sacke : in the whole, there were an hundred kannes standing rounde about the house. This sumptuous banquet the Duke tooke thankfullie, and afterwards hee departed homewards, and to their thinking they had neither eaten nor drunke, so were they blinded the whilest that they were in the Castle : but as they were in their Pallace they looked towards the Castle, and behold it was all in a flame of fire, and all those that beheld it wondred to heare so great a noyse, as if it were great Ordinance should haue been shot off ; and thus the Castle burned and consumed away cleane. Which done, Doctor *Faustus* returned to the Duke, who gaue him great thankes for shewing them of so great courtesie, giuing him an hundred Dollers, and libertie to depart or vse his owne discretion therein.

How Doctor Faustus with his companie visited the Bishop of Saltzburg his Wine-seller. Chap. 41.

DOctor *Faustus* hauing taken his leaue of the Duke, he went to *Wittenberg,* neere about Shrouetide, and being in companie with certaine Students, Doctor *Faustus* was himself the God *Bacchus,* who hauing well feasted the Students before with daintie fare, after the manner of *Germanie,* where it is counted no feast except all the bidden guests be drunke, which Doctor *Faustus* intending, said : Gentlemen and my guestes, will it please you to take a cuppe of wine with me in a place or seller whereunto I will bring you, and they all said willinglie wee will : which when Doctor *Faustus* heard, hee tooke them foorth, set either of them vpon an hollie wand, and so were coniured into the Bishop of *Saltzburg* his Seller, for there about grewe excellent pleasant Wine : there fell *Faustus* and his companie to drinking and swilling, not of the worst but of the best, and as they were merrie in the Seller, came downe to drawe drinke the Bishops butler : which when hee perceiued so many persons there hee cried with a loud voyce, theeues theeues. This spited Doctor *Faustus* wonderfullie, wherefore hee made euery [Page 61] one of his company to sit on their holly wand and so vanished away, and in parting Doctor *Faustus* tooke the Butler by the haire of the head and carried him away with them, vntill they came vnto a mightie high lopped[101] tree, and on the top of that huge tree he set the Butler, where he remained in a most fearefull perplexitie, and* Doctor *Faustus* departed to his house, where they tooke their *valete* one of another, drink-

* B.M. has 'aud.'

[101] trimmed

ing the Wine the which they had stolne in great bottels of glasse out of the Bishops * seller. The Butler that had held himselfe by the hand vpon the lopped tree all the night, was almost frozen with cold, espying the day, and seeing the tree of so huge great highnesse, thought with himselfe it is vnpossible to come off this tree without perill of death : at length he had espied certaine Clownes which were passing by, he cried for the loue of God helpe me downe : the Clownes seeing him so high, wondered what mad man would clime to so huge a tree, wherefore as a thing most miraculous, they caried tidings vnto the Bishop of *Saltzburg,* then was there great running on euery side to see a man in a huge tree, and many deuises they practised to get him downe with ropes, and being demaunded by the Bishop how hee came there, he said, that he was brought thither by the haire of the head of certaine theeues that were robbing of the Wine-seller, but what they were he knew not, for (said he) they had faces like men, but they † wrought like diuells.

How Doctor Faustus kept his Shrouetide. Chap. 42.

THere were seuen Students, and Masters that studied Diuinitie, *Iuris prudentia, & Medicina,* all these hauing consented were agreed to visite Doctor *Faustus,* and so to celebrate Shrouetide with him : who being come to his house hee gaue them their welcome, for they were his deare friends, desiring them to sit downe, where hee serued them with a very good supper of Hennes, fish, and other rost, yet were they but slightly cheared : wherefore Doctor *Faustus* comforted his guests, excusing himselfe that they stale vpon him so sodainely, that hee had not leisure to prouide for them so well as they were worthie, but my good friends (quoth he) according to the vse of our Countrie wee must drinke all this night, and so a draught of the best wine to bedward is commendable. For you know that in great Potentates Courts they vse as this night great feasting, the like will I [Page 62] doo for you : for I haue three great flagons of wine, the first is full of *Hungarian* wine, containing eight

* B.M. has 'Bishps.'
† B.M. has 'the.'

gallons, the second of *Italian* wine, containing seauen gallons, the third containing sixe gallons of *Spanish* wine, all the which we will tipple out before it bee day, besides, wee haue fifteene dishes of meate, the which my Spirite *Mephostophiles* hath fet so farre that it was cold before hee brought it, and they are all full of the daintiest things that ones heart can deuise, but (saith *Faustus*) I must make them hot againe: and you may beleeue mee Gentlemen, that this is no blinding of you, whereas you thinke that it is no naturall foode, verely it is as good and as pleasant as euer you eate. And hauing ended his tale, he commanded his boy to lay the cloth, which done, he serued them with fifteene messe of meate, hauing three dishes to a messe, the which were of all maner of Venison, and other daintie wild foule, and for wine there was no lacke, as *Italian* wine, *Hungarian* wine, and *Spanish* wine: and when they were all made drunke, and that they had almost eaten all their good cheare, they began to sing and to daunce vntill it was day, and then they departed each one to his owne habitation: at whose parting, Doctor *Faustus* desired them to bee his guests againe the next day following.

How Doctor Faustus feasted his guests on the Ash-wednesday. Chap. 43.

VPon Ashwednesday came vnto Doctor *Faustus* his bidden guests the Students, whom hee feasted very royallie, in so much that they were all full and lustie, singing and daunsing as the night before: and when the high glasses and goblets were caroused[102] one to another, Doctor *Faustus* began to play them some pretie iestes, in so much that round about the hall was heard most pleasant musick, and that in sundrie places, in this corner a Lute, in another a Cornet, in another a Citterne, Gitterne, Clarigolds, Harpe, Horne pipe: in fine, all maner of musicke was heard there at that instant, whereat all the glasses and goblets, cuppes and pots, dishes, and all that stoode on the boord began to daunce: then Doctor *Faustus* tooke ten stone pots, and* set them downe on the floare, where presently they began to daunce and to smite one against the other that the shiuers flewe round about the whole house,

* B.M. has 'add.'

[102] drunk or pledged

whereat the whole companie fell a laughing. Then he began another iest, hee set an Instrument on the table, and caused a monstrous greate Ape to come in amongst them, which Ape began to [Page 63] daunce and to skip, shewing them many mery conceipts. In this and such like pastime they passed away the whole day, where night being come, Doctor *Faustus* bade them al to supper, which they lightly agreeed vnto, for Students in these cases are easily intreated : wherefore he promised to feast them with a banquet of foule, and afterwards they would all goe about with a Maske, then Doctor *Faustus* put foorth a long pole out of the windowe, wherupon presently there came innumerable of birds and wild foule, and so many as came had not any power to flie away againe, but he tooke them and flang them to the students : who lightly pulled off the neceks of them, and being rosted they made their supper, which being ended they made themselues readie to the Maske. Doctor *Faustus* commanded euery one to put on a cleane shirt ouer his other clothes, which being done, they began to looke one vpon another, it seemed to each one of them they had no heads, and so they went forth vnto certaine of their neighbours, at which sight the people were wonderfully afraide. And as the vse of *Germanie* is, that wheresoeuer a Maske entreth, the good man of the house must feast them : so when these maskers were set to their banquet, they seemed againe in their former shape with heads, in so much that they were all knowne what they were : and hauing sat and well eate and drunke, Doctor *Faustus* made that euery one had an Asses head on, with great and long eares, so they fell to dansing and to driue away the time, vntill it was midnight, and then euery man departed home, and assoone as they were out of the house each one was in his naturall shape againe, and so they ended and went to sleepe.

How Doctor Faustus the day following was feasted of the Students, and of his merrie iestes with them while hee was in their companie.

Chap. 44.

THe last *Bacchanalia* was held on Thursday, where insued a great Snow, and Doctor *Faustus* was inuited vnto the students that were with him the day before, where they had prepared an excellent banquet for him : which banquet being ended, Doctor *Faustus* began to play his olde prankes, and forthwith were in the place thirteene Apes, that tooke hands and danced round in a ring together, then they fell to tumble and to vauting one ouer another, that it was most pleasant to behold, then they leaped out of the windowe and vanished away : then they set before Doctor *Faustus* a rosted Calues head : which one of [Page 64] the Students cut a peece off, and laid it on Doctor *Faustus* his trencher, which peece being no sooner layd downe, but the Calues head began to crie maynly out like a man, murther, murther, out alas what doest thou to me ! Whereat they were all amazed, but after a while considering of *Faustus* his iesting trickes they began to laugh, and then they pulled in sunder the Calues head and eat it vp. Whereupon Doctor *Faustus* asked leaue to depart, but they would in no wise agree to let him goe, except that he would promise to come againe : presently then *Faustus,* through his cunning, made a sleadge, the which was drawne about the house with foure fiery dragons : this was feareful for the students to beholde, for they saw *Faustus* ride vp and downe as though he should haue fiered and slayne al them in the house. This sport continued vntill midnight with such a noyse that they could not heare one another, and the heads of the students were so light, that they thought themselues to be in the ayre all that time.

How Doctor Faustus shewed the fayre Helena vnto the Students vpon the Sunday following. Chap. 45.

THe Sunday following came these students home to Doctor *Faustus* his owne house, and brought their meate and drinke with them : these men were right welcome guests vnto *Faustus,* wherfore they all fell to drinking of wine smoothly : and being merry, they began some of them to talke of the beauty of women, and euery one gaue foorth his verdit what he had seene and what hee had heard. So one among the rest said, I neuer was so desirous of any thing in this world, as to haue a sight (if it were possible) of fayre *Helena* of *Greece,* for whom the worthy towne of *Troie* was destroyed and razed downe to the ground, therefore sayth hee, that in all mens iudgement shee was more than commonly fayre, because that when she was stolne away from her husband, there was for her recouery so great blood-shed.

Doctor *Faustus* answered : For that you are all my friends and are so desirous to see that famous pearle of *Greece,* fayre *Helena,* the wife of King *Menelaus,* and daughter of *Tindalus* and *Læda,* sister to *Castor* and *Pollux,* who was the fayrest Lady in all *Greece :* I will therefore bring her into your presence personally, and in the same forme of attyre as she vsed to goe when she was in her chiefest flowres and pleasauntest prime of youth. The like haue I done for the Emperour *Carolus quintus,* at his desire I shewed him *Alexander* the great, and his Pa-[Page 65]ramour : but (sayd Doctor *Faustus*) I charge you all that vpon your perils you speake not a word, nor rise vp from the Table so long as she is in your presence. And so he went out of the Hall, returning presently agayne, after whome immediatly followed the fayre and beautiful *Helena,* whose beauty was such that the students were all amazed to see her, esteeming her rather to bee a heauenly than an earthly creature. This Lady appeared before thē in a most sumptuous gowne of purple Veluet, richly imbrodered, her hayre hanged downe loose as fayre as the beaten Gold, & of such length that it reached downe to her hammes, with amorous cole-black eyes, a sweete and pleasant round face, her lips red as a Cherry, her cheekes of rose all colour, her mouth small, her neck as white as the Swanne, tall and slender of personage, and in summe, there was not one imperfect part in her : shee looked round about her with a rouling Haukes eye, a smiling & wanton countenance, which neere hand inflamed the hearts of the students, but that they perswaded themselues she was a Spirit, wherefore such phantasies passed away lightly with them : and thus fayre *Helena* & Doctor *Faustus* went out agayne one with another. But the Students at Doctor *Faustus* his entring againe into the hall, requested of him to let them see her againe the next day, for that they would bring with them a painter and so take her counterfeit : which hee denied, affirming that hee could not alwayes rayse vp her Spirit, but onely at certaine times : yet (sayd he) I will giue you her counterfeit, which shall bee alwayes as good to you as if your selues should see the drawing thereof, which they receiued according to his promise, but soone lost it againe. The students departed from *Faustus* home euery one to his house, but they were not able to sleepe the whole night for thinking on the beauty of fayre *Helena.* Wherefore a man may see that the Diuel blindeth and enflameth the heart with lust oftentimes, that men fall in loue with Harlots, nay euen with Furies, which afterward cannot lightly be remoued.

How Doctor Faustus coniured away the foure wheeles from a clownes waggon. Chap. 46.

DOctor *Faustus* was sent for to the Marshall of *Brunswicke,* who was greatly troubled with the falling sicknes. Now *Faustus* had this vse, neuer to ride but walke foorth on foote, for hee could [Page 66] ease himselfe when his list, and as hee came neere vnto the towne of *Brunswicke,* there ouertooke him a Clowne with foure horses and an empty waggon, to whome Doctor *Faustus* iestingly to trie him, sayde : I pray thee good fellow let me ride a little to ease my weary legges ; which the buzzardly asse denied, saying : that his horses were also wearie, and he would not let him get vp. Doctor *Faustus* did this but to prooue the buzzard, if there were any curtesie to bee found in him if neede were.

But such churlishnes as is cōmonly found among clowns, was by Doctor *Faustus* well requited, euen with the like payment : for he sayd vnto him, Thou doltish Clown, voyde of all humanitie, seeing thou art of so currish a disposition, I will pay thee as thou hast deserued, for the foure wheeles of thy Waggon thou shalt haue taken from thee, let mee see then how canst thou shift : hereupon his wheeles were gon, his horses also fell downe to the ground, as though they had been dead : whereat the clowne was sore afright, measuring it as a iust scourge of God for his sinnes and churlishnes : wherefore all troubled, and wayling, he humbly besought Doctor *Faustus* to be good vnto him, confessing hee was worthy of it, notwithstanding if it pleased him to forgiue him, he would hereafter doo better. Which humilitie made *Faustus* his heart to relent, answering him on this maner, well, doe so no more, but when a poore weary man desireth thee, see that thou let him ride, but yet thou shalt not goe altogether cleare, for although thou haue agayne thy foure wheeles, yet shalt thou fetch them at the foure Gates of the Citie, so he threw dust on the horses, and reuiued them agayne, and the Clowne for his churlishnes was faine to fetch his wheeles, spending his time with wearinesse, where as before he might haue done a good deede, and gone about his busines quietly.

How foure Iuglers cut one anothers head off, and set them on agayne; and how Doctor Faustus deceiued them. Chap. 47.

DOctor *Faustus* came in the Lent vnto *Franckfort* Fayre, where his Spirit *Mephostophiles* gaue him to vnderstand that in an Inne were foure Iuglers that cut one anothers head off, and after their cutting off, sent them to the Barber to bee trimmed, which many people saw. This angred *Faustus,* (for he meant to haue himselfe the only Cocke in the diuels basket) & hee went to the place where they [Page 67] were, to behold them. And as these Iuglers were together, ready one to cut off the others head, there stoode also the Barbers ready to trim them, and by them vpon the table stoode likewise a glasse full of distilled water, and he that was the chiefest among them stood by it. Thus they began, they smote off the head of the first, and presently there was a Lilly in the glasse of distilled water, where *Faustus* perceiued this Lilly as it were springing, & the chiefe Iugler named it the tree of life, thus dealt he with the first, making the Barber wash and combe his head, & then he set it on againe, presently the Lilly vanished away out of the water, hereat the man had his head whole and sound againe; the like did they with the other two: and as the turne & lot came to the chiefe Iugler that he also should be beheaded, & that his Lilly was most pleasant, fayre, and florishing greene, they smote his head off, & when it came to be barbed, it troubled *Faustus* his conscience, in so much that he could not abide to see another doe any thing, for he thought himselfe to bee the principal coniurer in the world, wherfore Doctor *Faustus* went to y[e] table where as the other Iuglers kept that Lilly, & so he took a smal knife & cut off the stalke of the Lilly, saying to himself, none of thē should blind *Faustus*: yet no man saw *Faustus* to cut the Lilly, but when the rest of the Iuglers thought to haue set on their masters head, they could not, wherefore they looked on the Lilly, and found it a bleeding: by this meanes the Iugler was beguiled, and so died in his wickednes, yet not one thought that Doctor *Faustus* had done it.

How an old man the neighbour of Faustus, sought to perswade him to amend his euill life, and to fall vnto repentance. Chap. 48.

A Good Christian an honest and vertuous olde man, a louer of the holy scriptures, who was neighbour vnto Doctor *Faustus*: whē he perceiued that many students had their recourse in and out vnto Doctor *Faustus*, he suspected his euill life, wherefore like a friend he inuited Doctor *Faustus* to supper vnto his house, vnto the which hee agreed; and hauing ended their banquet, the olde man began with these words. My louing friend and neighbour Doctor *Faustus*, I haue to desire of you a friendly and Christian request, beseeching you that you wil vouchsafe not to be angry with me, but friendly resolue mee in my doubt, and take my poore inuiting in good part. To whome Doctor *Faustus* answered: My louing neighbour, I pray you say your minde. Thē began the old Patron to say: My good neighbour, you know in the [Page 68] beginning how that you haue defied God, & all the hoast heauen, & giuen your soule to the Diuel, wherewith you haue incurred Gods high displeasure, and are become from a Christian farre worse than a heathen person: oh consider what you haue done, it is not onely the pleasure of the body, but the safety of the soule that you must haue respect vnto: of which if you be carelesse, then are you cast away, and shall remaine in the anger of almighty God. But yet is it time enough Doctor *Faustus*, if you repent and call vnto the Lord for mercy, as wee haue example in the *Acts* of the Apostles, the eight Chap. of *Simon* in *Samaria*, who was led out of the way, affirming that he was *Simon homo sanctus*. This man was notwithstanding in the end conuerted, after that he had heard the Sermon of *Philip*, for he was baptized, and sawe his sinnes, and repented. Likewise I beseech you good brother Doctor *Faustus,* let my rude Sermon be vnto you a conuersion; and forget the filthy life that you haue led, repent, aske mercy, & liue: for Christ saith, *Come vnto me all ye that are weary & heauy loden, & I wil refresh you.* And in *Ezechiel: I desire not the death of a sinner, but rather that hee conuert and liue.* Let my words good brother *Faustus,* pearce into your adamant heart, and desire God for his Sonne Christ his sake, to forgiue you. Wherefore haue you so long liued in your Diuelish practises, knowing that in the olde and newe Testament you are forbidden, and that men should not suffer any such to liue, neither haue any conuersation with them, for it is an abomination vnto the Lord; and that such persons haue no part in the Kingdome of God. All this while Doctor *Faustus* heard him very attentiuely, and replyed. Father, your perswasions like me wonderous well, and I thanke you with all my heart for your good will and counsell, promising you so farre as I may to follow your discipline: whereupon he tooke his leaue. And being come home, he layd him very pensiue on his bed, bethinking himselfe of the wordes of the good olde man, and in a maner began to repent that he had giuen his Soule to the Diuell, intending to denie all that hee had promised vnto *Lucifer.* Continuing in these cogitations, sodainly his Spirit appeared vnto him clapping him vpon the head, and wrung it as though he would haue pulled the head from the shoulders, saying vnto him. Thou knowest *Faustus,* that thou hast giuen thy selfe body and soule vnto my Lord *Lucifer,* and hast vowed thy selfe an enemy vnto God and vnto all men; and now thou beginnest to harken to an olde doting foole which perswadeth thee as it were vnto God, when indeed it is too late, for that thou art the diuels, and hee hath good power presently to fetch [Page 69] thee: wherefore he hath sent me vnto thee, to tell thee, that seeing thou hast sorrowed for that thou hast done, begin againe and write another writing with thine owne blood, if not, then will I teare thee all to peeces. Hereat Doctor *Faustus* was sore afrayde, and sayd: My *Mephostophiles,* I will write agayne what thou wilt: wherefore hee sate him downe, and with his owne blood hee wrote as followeth : which writing was afterward sent to a deare friend of the sayd Doctor *Faustus* being his kinsman.

How Doctor Faustus wrote the second time with his owne blood and gaue it to the Diuell. Chap. 49.

I Doctor *Iohn Faustus,* acknowledge by this my deede and handwriting, that sith my first writing, which is seuenteene yeares, that I haue right willingly held, and haue been an vtter enemy vnto God and all men, the which I once againe confirme, and giue fully & wholly my selfe vnto the Diuel both body and soule, euen vnto the great *Lucifer :* and that at the ende of seuen yeares ensuing after the date of this letter, he shall haue to doe with me according as it pleaseth him, either to lengthen or shorten my life as liketh him : and herevpon I renounce * all perswaders that seeke to withdrawe mee from my purpose by the word of God, either ghostly or bodily. And further, I will neuer giue eare vnto any man, be he spirituall or temporall, that moueth any matter for the saluation of my soule. Of all this writing, and that therein contained, be witnesse, my own bloud, the which with mine own hands I haue begun, and ended.

Dated at Wittenberg the 25. of Iuly.

And presently vpon the making of this Letter, he became so great an enemie vnto the poore olde man, that he sought his life by all meanes possible ; but this godly man was strong in the holy Ghost, that he could not be vanquished by any meanes : for about two dayes after that hee had exhorted *Faustus,* as the poore man lay in his bed, sodainely there was a mightie rumbling in the Chamber, the which hee was neuer wont to heare, & he heard as it had been the groning of a Sowe, which lasted long : whereupon the good olde man began to iest, and mock, and saide : oh what Barbarian crie is this, oh fayre Bird, what foule musick is this of a faire Angell, that could not tarrie two dayes in his place′: [Page 70] beginnest thou † now to runne into a

* B.M. has 'renonnce.'
† B.M. has 'thon.'

poore mans house, where thou hast no power, and wert not able to keepe thine own two daies': With these and such like wordes the Spirit departed. And when hee came home *Faustus* asked him how hee had sped with the olde man: to whome the Spirit answered, the olde man was harnessed,[108] and that hee could not once lay holde vpon him: but he would not tell howe the olde man had mocked him, for the diuels can neuer abide to heare of their fall. Thus doth God defend the hearts of all honest Christians, that betake themselues vnder his tuition.

How Doctor Faustus made a marriage betweene two louers. Cap. 50

IN the Citie of *Wittenberg* was a student, a gallant Gentleman, named *N. N.* This Gentleman was farre in loue with a Gentlewoman, fayre and proper of personage. This Gentlewoman had a Knight that was a suiter vnto her, and many other Gentlemen, the which desired her in mariage, but none could obtaine her: So it was that this *N. N* was very well acquainted with *Faustus,* and by that meanes became a suiter vnto him to assist him in the matter, for he fell so farre in despayre with himselfe, that he pined away to the skinne and bones. But when he had opened the matter vnto Doctor *Faustus,* he asked counsell of his Spirit *Mephostophiles,* the which tolde him what to doe. Hereupon Doctor *Faustus* went home to the Gentleman, and bade him be of good cheare, for he should haue his desire, for he would helpe him to that hee wished for, and that this Gentlewoman should loue none other but him onely: wherefore Doctor *Faustus* so changed the minde of the Damsel by a practise he wrought, that she would doe no other thing but thinke on him, whome before she had hated, neither cared she for any man but him alone. The deuice was thus, *Faustus* commaunded this Gentleman that he should cloth himselfe in all his best apparel that he had and that he should goe vnto this gentlewoman, and there to shew himselfe, giuing him also a Ring, commanding him in any wise that he should daunce with her before he departed. Wherefore he followed *Faustus* his counsaile, went to her, and when they began to daunce

108 spiritually armed

they that were suiters began to take euery one his Lady in his hand, and this good Gentleman tooke her, whom before had so disdained him, and in the daunce hee thrust the Ring into her hand that Doctor *Faustus* had giuen him, the which shee no sooner toucht, but she fell immediatly in loue with him, beginning in the daunce to [Page 71] smile, and many times to giue him wincks, rouling her eyes, and in the end she asked him if he could loue her and make her his wife; hee gladly answered, hee was content: and hereupon they concluded, and were married, by the meanes and helpe of Doctor *Faustus,* for which hee receiued a good reward of the Gentleman.

How Doctor Faustus led his friends into his Garden at Christmas, and shewed them many strange sights in his 19. yeare. Chap. 51.

IN December, about Christmas in the Citie of *Wittenberg,* were many young Gentlewomen, the which were come out of the Countrey to make merry with their friends and acquaintance: amongst whome, there were certaine that were well acquainted with Doctor *Faustus,* wherefore they were often inuited as his guests vnto him, and being with him on a certaine time after dinner, hee led them into his Garden, where he shewed them all maner of flowers, and * fresh hearbs, Trees bearing fruit and blossomes of all sortes, insomuch that they wondered to see that in his Garden should bee so pleasant a time as in the middest of summer: and without in the streetes, and all ouer the Countrey, it lay full of Snowe and yce. Wherefore this was noted of them as a thing miraculous, each one gathering and carrying away all such things as they best liked, and so departed delighted with their sweete smelling flowers.

How Doctor Faustus gathered together a great armie of men in his extremitie agaynst a Knight that would haue iniured him on his iourney. Chap. 52

DOctor *Faustus* trauelled towards *Eyszleben,* and when he was nigh halfe the way, he espied seuen horsemen, and the

* B.M. has 'aud.'

chiefe of them hee knew to be the knight to whome he had plaied a iest in the Emperours Court, for he had set a huge payre of Harts hornes vpon his head : and when the knight now saw that he had fit opportunitie to be reuenged of *Faustus* he ran vpon him himselfe, & those that were with him, to mischiefe him, intending priuily to shoot at him : which when Doctor *Faustus* espied, he vanished away into the wood which was hard by them. But when the Knight perceiued that he was vanished away, he caused [Page 72] his men to stand still, where as they remayned they heard all manner of warlike instruments of musick, as Drummes, Flutes, Trumpets, and such like, and a certaine troupe of horsemen running towards them. Then they turned another way, and there also were assaulted on the same side : then another way, and yet they were freshly assaulted, so that which way soeuer they turned themselues, hee was encountred : in so much that when the Knight perceiued that he could escape no way, but that they his enemies layd on him which way soeuer hee offered to flie, he tooke a good heart and ranne amongst the thickest, and thought with himselfe better to die than to liue with so great an infamie. Therefore being at handy-blowes with them hee demaunded the cause why they should so vse them : but none of them would giue him answere, vntill Doctor *Faustus* shewed himself vnto the Knight, where withall they inclosed him round, and Doctor *Faustus* sayde vnto him, Sir, yeelde your weapon, and yourselfe, otherwise it will goe hardly with you. The Knight that knew none other but that he was inuironed with an hoast of men, (where indeede they were none other than Diuels) yeelded : then *Faustus* tooke away his sworde, his piece, and horse, with all the rest of his companions. And further hee said vnto him ; Sir, the chiefe General of our armie hath commaunded to deale with you according to the law of Armes, you shall depart in peace whither you please : and then he gaue the Knight an horse after the maner, and set him theron, so he rode, the rest went on foote, vntill they came to their Inne, where being alighted, his Page rode on his horse to the water, and presently the horse vanyshed away, the Page being almost suncke and drowned, but he escaped : and comming home, the Knight perceiued his Page so be myred & on foote, asked where his horse was become? Who answered that he was vanished away: which when the Knight heard, he said, of a truth this is *Faustus* his doing, for he serueth me now as he did before at the Court, only to make me a skorne and a laughing stock.

How Doctor Faustus caused Mephostophiles to bring him seuen of the fayrest women that he could finde in all those countries he had traueiled in, in the 20. yeare. Chap. 53.

WHen Doctor *Faustus* called to minde,* that his time from day to day drew nigh, hee began to liue a swinish and Epicurish life, wherefore he commaunded his Spirit *Mephostophiles,* to bring him [Page 73] seuen of the fayrest women that he had seene in all the time of his trauel: which being brought, first one, and then another, he lay with them all, insomuch that he liked them so well, that he continued with them in all maner of loue, and made them to trauell with him in all his iourneies. These women were two *Netherlanders,* one *Hungarian,* one *English,* two *Wallons,* one *Francklander:* and with these sweete personages he continued long, yea euen to his last ende.

How Doctor Faustus found a masse of money when hee had consumed 22. of his yeares. Chap. 54.

TO the ende that the Diuell would make *Faustus* his onely heire, he shewed vnto him where he should goe and finde a mighty huge masse of money, and that hee should haue it in an olde Chappell that was fallen downe, halfe a mile distant from *Wittenberg,* there hee bade him to dig and he should finde it, the which he did, and hauing digged reasonable deepe, he saw a mighty huge serpent, the which lay on the treasure it selfe, the treasure it selfe lay like an huge light burning: but D. *Faustus* charmed the serpent that he crept into a hole, and when he digged deeper to get vp the treasure, he found nothing but coles of fire: there also he heard and saw many that were tormented, yet notwithstand-

* B.M. has 'miude.'

ing he brought away the coles, and when he was come home, it was al turned into siluer and gold, as after his death was found by his seruant, the which was almost about estimation, a thousand gilders.

How Doctor Faustus made the Spirit of fayre Helena of Greece his own Paramour and bedfellow in his 23. yeare. Chap. 55.

TO the ende that this miserable *Faustus* might fill the lust of his flesh, and liue in all manner of voluptuous pleasures, it came in his minde after he had slept his first sleepe, & in the 23. yeare past of his time, that he had a great desire to lie with fayre *Helena* of *Greece,* especially her whom he had seene and shewed vnto the students of *Wittenberg,* wherefore he called vnto him his Spirit *Mephostophiles,* cōmanding him to bring him the faire *Helena,* which * he also did. Wherupō he fel in loue with her, & made her his common Concubine & bedfellow, for she was so beautifull and delightful a peece, that he could not be one [Page 74] houre from her, if hee should therefore haue suffered death, shee had so stolne away his heart : and to his seeming, in time she was with childe, and in the end brought him a man childe, whome *Faustus* named *Iustus Faustus :* this childe tolde Doctor *Faustus* many things that were to come, and what strange matters were done in forraine countries : but in the end when *Faustus* lost his life, the mother and the childe vanished away both together.

How Doctor Faustus made his Will, in the which he named his seruant Wagner to be his heire. Chap. 56.

DOctor *Faustus* was now in his 24. and last yeare, and hee had a prety stripling to his seruant, the which had studied also at the Vniuersitie of *Wittenberg :* this youth was very well acquainted with his knaueries and sorceries, so that hee was hated as well for his owne knaueries, as also for his Masters : for no man would giue him entertainement into his seruice, because of his vnhappines, but *Faustus :* this *Wagner* was so well beloued with *Faustus,* that hee vsed him as his

* B.M. has 'whic.'

sonne : for doo what hee would his master was alwayes therewith well content. And when the time drewe nigh that *Faustus* should end, hee called vnto him a Notary and certaine masters the which were his friends and often conuersant with him, in whose presence he gaue this *Wagner* his house and Garden. Item, hee gaue him in ready money 1600. gilders. Item, a Farme. Item, a gold chayne, much plate, and other housholde stuffe. This gaue he al to his seruant, and the rest of his time he meant to spend in Innes and Students company, drinking and eating, with other Iollitie : and thus hee finished his Will for that time.

How Doctor Faustus fell in talke with his seruant touching his Testament, and the couenants thereof. Chap. 57.

NOw, when this Will was made, Doctor *Faustus* called vnto him his seruant, saying : I haue thought vpon thee in my Testament, for that thou hast beene a trusty seruant vnto me and a faithfull, and hast not opened my secrets : and yet further (sayd he) aske of me before I die what thou wilt, and I will giue it vnto thee. His [Page 75] seruant* rashly answered, I pray you let mee haue your cunning. To which Doctor *Faustus* answered, I haue giuen thee all my bookes, vpon this condition, that thou wouldst not let them bee common, but vse them for thine owne pleasure, and studie carefully in them. And doest thou also desire my cunning? That maiest thou peraduenture haue, if thou loue and peruse my bookes well. Further (sayd Doctor *Faustus*) seeing that thou desirest of me this request, I will resolue thee : my spirit *Mephostophiles* his time is out with me, and I haue nought to commaund him as touching thee, yet will I helpe thee to another, if thou like well thereof. And within three dayes after he called his seruant vnto him, saying : art thou resolued? wouldst thou verily haue a Spirit? Then tell me in what maner or forme thou wouldst haue him? To whome his seruant answered, that hee would haue him in the forme of an Ape : whereupon presently appeared a Spirit vnto him in maner and forme of an Ape, the which leaped about the house. Then sayd *Faustus*, see, there hast thou thy request, but yet he will not obey thee

* B.M. has 'seruaut.'

vntill I be dead, for when my Spirit *Mephostophiles* shall fetch me away, then shal thy Spirit be bound vnto thee, if thou agree : and thy Spirit shalt thou name *Akercocke,* for so is he called : but all this is vpon condition that thou publish my cunning, and my merry conceits, with all that I haue done (when I am dead) in an hystory : and if thou canst not remember all, thy Spirit *Akercocke* will helpe thee : so shall the great actes that I haue done be manifested vnto the world.

How Doctor Faustus hauing but one moneth of his appoynted time to come, fell to mourning and sorrowe with himselfe for his diuelish exercise. Chap. 58.

TIme ranne away with *Faustus,* as the houre glasse, for hee had but one moneth to come of his 24. yeares, at the end whereof he had giuen himselfe to the Diuell body and soule, as is before specified. Here was the first token, for he was like a taken murtherer or a theefe, the which findeth himselfe guiltie in conscience before the Iudge haue giuen sentence, fearing euery houre to die : for hee was grieued, and wayling spent the time, went talking to himselfe, wringing of his hands, sobbing and sighing, hee fell away from flesh, and was very leane, and kept* himselfe close : neither could he abide to see or heare of his *Mephistophiles* any more.

[Page 76] *How Doctor Faustus complayned that hee should in his lusty time and youthful yeares die so miserably.* Chap. 59.

THis sorrowfull time drawing neere so troubled Doctor *Faustus,* that he began to write his minde, to the ende he might peruse it often and not forget it, and is in maner as followeth.

Ah *Faustus,* thou sorrowful and wofull man, now must thou goe to the damned company in vnquenchable fire, whereas thou mightest haue had the ioyfull immortalitie of the soule, the which thou now hast lost. Ah grosse vnderstanding and wilfull will, what seazeth on my limmes other than a robbing of my life': Bewayle with me my sound & healthfull body,

* B.M. has 'kpt.'

wit and soule, bewayle with me my sences, for you haue had your part and pleasure as well as I. Oh enuie and disdaine, how haue you crept both at once into me, and now for your sakes I must suffer all these torments? Ah whither is pitie and mercy fled': Vpon what occasion hath heauen repayed me with this reward by sufferance to suffer me to perish': Wherefore was I created a man': The punishment that I see prepared for me of my selfe now must I suffer. Ah miserable wretch, there is nothing in this world to shew me comfort: then woe is me, what helpeth my wayling.

Another complaint of Doctor Faustus. Chap. 60.

OH poore, wofull and weary wretch: oh sorrowfull soule of *Faustus,* now art thou in the number of the damned, for now must I waite for vnmeasurable paynes of death, yea far more lamentable than euer yet any creature hath suffered. Ah senceles, wilful & desperate forgetfulnesse! O cursed and vnstable life! O blinde and carelesse wretch, that so hast abused thy body, sence and soule! O foolish pleasure, into what a weary labyrinth hast thou brought mee, blinding mine eyes in the clearest day': Ah weake heart! O troubled soule, where is become thy knowledge to comfort thee': O pitifull weariness! Oh desperate hope, now shall I neuer more be thought vpon! Oh, care vpon carefulnesse, and sorrowes on heapes: Ah grieuous paynes that pearce my panting heart, whom is there now that can deliuer me': Would God that I knew where to hide me, or into what place to creepe or flie. Ah, woe, woe is me, be where I will, yet am I taken. Herewith poore [Page 77] *Faustus* was so sorrowfully troubled, that he could not speake or vtter his minde any further.

How Doctor Faustus bewayled to thinke on Hell, and of the miserable paynes therein prouided for him.

NOw thou *Faustus,* damned wretch, howe happy wert thou if as an vnreasonable beast thou mightest die without soule, so shouldest thou not feele any more doubts': But nowe the diuell will take thee away both body and soule, and set thee in an vnspeakable place of darkenesse: for although others soules haue rest and peace, yet I poore damned wretch must suffer all manner of filthy stench, paines, colde, hunger, thirst, heate, freezing, burning, hissing, gnashing, and all the wrath and curse of God, yea all the creatures that God hath created are enemies to mee. And now too late I remember that my Spirit *Mephostophiles* did once tell mee, there was a great difference amongst the damned ; for the greater the sinne, the greater the torment : for as the twigges of the tree make greater flame than the trunke thereof, and yet the trunke continueth longer in burning ; euen so the more that a man is rooted in sinne, the greater is his punishment. Ah thou perpetuall damned wretch, now art thou throwne into the euerlasting fiery lake that neuer shall be quenched, there must I dwell in all manner of wayling, sorrow, misery, payne, torment, griefe, howling sighing, sobbing, blubbering, running of eies, stinking at nose, gnashing of teeth feare to the eares, horror to the conscience, and shaking both of hand and foote. Ah that I could carry the heauens on my shoulders, so that there were time at last to quit me of this euerlasting damnation ! Oh who can deliuer me out of these fearful tormēting flames, yᵉ which I see prepared for me ': Oh there is no helpe, nor any man that can deliuer me, nor any wayling of sins can help me, neither is there rest to be found for me day nor night. Ah wo is me, for there is no help for me, no shield, no defence no comfort. Where is my hold ': knowledge dare I not trust : and for a soule to God wards that haue I not, for I shame to speake vnto him : if I doo, no answere shall be made me, but hee will hide his face from me, to the end that I should not beholde the ioyes of the chosen. What meane I then to complaine where no helpe is ': No, I know no hope resteth in my gronings. I haue desired that it should bee so, and God hath sayd *Amen* to my misdoings : for now I must haue shame to comfort me in my calamities.

[Page 78] *Here followeth the miserable and lamentable ende of Doctor Faustus, by the which all Christians may take an example and warning.* Chap. 62.

IN the 24. yeare Doctor *Faustus* his time being come, his Spirit appeared vnto him, giuing him his writing againe, and commaunding him to make preparation, for that the diuel would fetch him agaynst a certaine time appoynted. D. *Faustus* * mourned and sighed wonderfully, and neuer went to bed, nor slept winke for sorrow. Wherefore his Spirit appeared againe, comforting him, and saying: My *Faustus,* be not thou so cowardly minded; for although that thou losest thy body, it is not long vnto the day of Iudgement, and thou must die at the last, although thou liue many thousand yeares. The Turkes, the Iewes, & many an vnchristian Emperour, are in the same condemnation: therefore (my *Faustus*) be of good courage, and be not discomforted, for the diuel hath promised that thou shalt not be in paines as the rest of the damned are. This and such like comfort he gaue him, but he tolde him false, and agaynst the saying of the holy Scriptures. Yet Doctor *Faustus* that had none other expectation but to pay his debts with his owne skinne, went on the same day that his Spirit sayd the diuel would fetch him, vnto his trusty and dearest beloued brethren and companions, as Masters, and Batchelers of Arte, and other students more the which had often visited him at his house in merriment: these he entreated that they would walke into the Village called *Rimlich,* halfe a mile from *Wittenberg,* and that they would there take with him for their repast part of a small banquet, the which they all agreed vnto: so they went together, and there held their dinner in a most sumptuous maner. Doctor *Faustus* with them (dissemblingly) was merry, but not from the heart: wherefore he requested † them that they would also take part of his rude supper: the which they agreed vnto: for (quoth hee) I must tell you what is the Victulers due:[104] and when they sleeped (for drinke was in their heads) then Doctor *Faustus* payed and discharged the shot, and bound the students and the Masters to goe with him into another roume, for he had many wonderfull matters to tell them: and when they were entred the roume as he requested, Doctor *Faustus* sayd vnto them, as hereafter followeth.

* B.M. has *'Fanstus.'*
† B.M. has the last e upside down.

104 In early use, one who provisioned a trading vessel in return for a share in the transaction was called a victualler. The phrase here seems to mean, "I must tell you what I have done for which I must give the devil his due."

[Page 81] *An Oration of Faustus to the Students.* Chap. 63.

MY trusty and welbeloued friends, the cause why I haue inuited you into this place is this : Forasmuch as you haue knowne me this many yeares, in what maner of life I haue liued, practising al maner of coniurations and wicked exercises, the which I haue obtayned through the helpe of the diuel, into whose diuelish fellowship they haue brought me, the which vse the like Arte and practise, vrged by the detestable prouocation of my flesh, my stiffe necked and rebellious will, with my filthy infernall thoughts, the which were euer before me, pricking mee forward so earnestly, that I must perforce haue the consent of the diuell to ayde me in my deuises. And to the end I might the better bring my purpose to passe, to haue the Diuels ayd and furtherance, which I neuer haue wanted in mine actions, I haue promised vnto him at the ende and accomplishing of 24. yeares, both body and soule, to doe therewith at his pleasure : and this day, this dismall day those 24. yeares are fully expired, for night beginning my houre-glasse is at an end, the direfull finishing whereof I carefully expect : for out of all doubt this night hee will fetch mee, to whome I haue giuen my selfe in recompence of his seruice, both body and soule, and twice confirmed writings with my proper blood. Now haue I called you my welbeloued Lords, friends, brethren, and fellowes, before that fatall houre to take my friendly farewell, to the end that my departing may not hereafter be hidden from you, beseeching you herewith courteous, and louing Lords and brethren, not to take in euil part any thing done by mee, but with friendly commendations to salute all my friends and companions wheresoeuer : desiring both you and them, if euer I haue trespassed against your minds in any thing, that you would all heartily forgiue me : and as for those lewd practises the which this full 24. yeares I haue followed, you shall hereafter finde them in writing : and I beseech you let this my lamentable ende to the residue of your liues bee a sufficient warning, that you haue God alwayes before your eies, praying vnto him that he would euer defend you from the temptation of the diuell, and all his false deceipts, not falling altogether from God, as I wretched and vngodly damned creature haue done, hauing denied and defied Baptisme, the Sacraments of Christs body, God himselfe, all heauenly powers, and earthly men, yea, I haue denied such a God, that desireth not to haue one lost. Neither let the [Page 80] euill fellowship of wicked companions misselead you as it hath done me: visit earnestly and oft the Church, warre and striue continually agaynst the Diuell with a good and stedfast beliefe on God, and Iesus Christ, and vse your vocation in holiness. Lastly, to knitte vp my troubled Oration, this is my friendly request, that you would to rest, & let nothing trouble you: also if you chance to heare any noise, or rumbling about the house, be not therwith afrayd, for there shal no euil happen vnto you: also I pray you arise not out of your beds. But aboue all things I intreate you, if you hereafter finde my dead carkasse, conuay it vnto the earth, for I dye both a good and bad Christian; a good Christian, for that I am heartely sorry, and in my heart alwayes praye for mercy, that my soule may be deliuered: a bad Christian, for that I know the Diuell will haue my bodie, and that would I willingly giue him so that he would leaue my soule in quiet: wherefore I pray you that you would depart to bed, and so I wish you a quiet night, which vnto me notwithstanding will be horrible and fearefull.

This Oration or declaration was made by Doctor *Faustus,* & that with a hearty and resolute minde, to the ende hee might not discomfort them: but the Students wondered greatly thereat, that he was so blinded, for knauery, coniuration, and such like foolish things, to giue his body and soule vnto the diuell: for they loued him entirely, and neuer suspected any such thing before he had opened his mind to them: wherefore one of thē sayd vnto him; ah, friend *Faustus,* what haue you done to conceale this matter so long from vs, we would by the help of good Diuines, and the grace of God, haue brought you out of this net, and haue torne you out of the bondage and chaynes of Sathan, whereas nowe we feare it is too late, to the vtter ruine of your body and soule? Doctor *Faustus* answered, I durst neuer doo it, although I often minded, to settle my selfe vnto godly people, to desire counsell and helpe, as once mine olde neighbour counsailed mee, that I shoulde follow his learning, and leaue all my coniurations, yet when

I was minded to amend, and to followe that good mans counsell, then came the Diuell and would haue had me away, as this night he is like to doe, and sayd so soone as I turned againe to God, hee would dispatch mee altogether. Thus, euen thus, (good Gentlemen, and my deare friends) was I inthralled in that Satanicall band, all good desires drowned, all pietie banished, al purpose of amendmēt vtterly exiled, by the tyranous threatnings of my deadly enemy. But when the Students heard his words, they gaue him counsaile to doo naught else but call vpon God, desiring [Page 81] him for the loue of his sweete Sonne Iesus Christes sake, to haue mercy vpon him, teaching him this forme of prayer. O God bee mercifull vnto me, poore and miserable sinner, and enter not into iudgement with me, for no flesh is able to stand before thee. Although, O Lord, I must leaue my sinfull body vnto the Diuell, being by him deluded, yet thou in mercy mayest preserue my soule.

This they repeated vnto him, yet it could take no holde, but euen as *Caine* he also said his sinnes were greater than God was able to forgiue; for all his thought was on his writing, he meant he had made it too filthy in writing it with his owne blood. The Students & the other that were there, when they had prayed for him, they wept, and so went foorth, but *Faustus* taryed in the hall: and when the Gentlemen were laid in bed, none of them could sleepe, for that they attended to heare if they might be priuy of his ende. It happened between twelue and one a clock at midnight, there blewe a mighty storme of winde against the house, as though it would haue blowne the foundation thereof out of his place. Hereupon the Students began to feare, and got out of their beds, comforting one another, but they would not stirre out of the chamber: and the Host of the house ran out of doores, thinking the house would fall. The Students lay neere vnto that hall wherein Doctor *Faustus* lay, and they heard a mighty noyse and hissing, as if the hall had beene full of Snakes and Adders: with that the hall doore flew open wherein Doctor *Faustus* was, then he began to crie for helpe, saying: murther, murther, but it came foorth with halfe a voyce hollowly: shortly after they heard him no more. But when it was day, the Students that had taken no rest that night, arose and went into the hall in the which they left Doctor *Faustus,* where notwithstanding they found no *Faustus,* but all the hall lay besprinckled with blood, his braines cleauing to the wall : for the Diuel had beaten him from one wall against another, in * one corner lay his eyes, in another his teeth, a pitifull and fearefull sight to beholde. Then began the Students to bewayle and weepe for him, and sought for his body in many places : lastly they came into the yarde where they found his bodie lying on the horse dung, most monstrously torne, and fearefull to beholde, for his head and all his ioynts were dasht in peeces.

The forenamed Students and Masters that were at his death, haue obtayned so much, that they buried him in the Village where he was so grieuously tormented. After the which, they returned to *Wittenberg,* & comming into the house of *Faustus,* they found ye seruant of *Faustus* very [Page 80] sad, vnto whom they opened all the mat[t]er, who tooke it exceeding heauilie. There found they also this history of Doctor *Faustus* noted, and of him written as is before declared, all saue onely his ende, the which was after by the students thereto annexed : further, what his seruant had noted thereof, was made in another booke. And you haue heard that he held by him in his life the Spirit of fayre *Helena,* the which had by him one sonne, the which he named *Iustus Faustus,* euen the same day of his death they vanished away, both mother and sonne. The house before was so darke, that scarce any body could abide therein. The same night Doctor *Faustus* appeared vnto his seruant liuely, and shewed vnto him many secret things the which hee had done and hidden in his life time. Likewise there were certaine which saw Doctor *Faustus* looke out of the window by night as they passed by the house.

And thus ended the whole history of Doctor *Faüstus* his coniuration, and other actes that he did in his life ; out of the which example euery Christian may learne, but chiefly the stiffenecked and high minded may thereby learne to feare God, and to be careful of their vocation, and to be at defiance with all diuelish workes, as God hath most precisely forbidden, to the end we should not inuite the diuell as a guest, nor giue

* B.M. has 'in in.'

him place as that wicked *Faustus* hath done : for here we haue a feareful example of his writing, promise, and end, that we may remember him : that we goe not astray, but take God alwaies before our eies, to call alone vpon him, and to honour him all the dayes of our life, with heart and hearty prayer, and with al our strength and soule to glorifie his holy name, defying the Diuell and all his works, to the end we may remayne with Christ in all endlesse ioy : Amen, Amen, that wish I vnto euery Christian heart, and Gods name to bee glorified. Amen.

FINIS.

Here followeth the contents *of this Booke.*

* The pagination refers to the original printed book. The Contents was set all in roman type, not in black letter.

FINIS.

V

THE EARLIER FAUST DRAMAS AND PUPPET PLAYS

FAUST DRAMAS AND PUPPET PLAYS[1]

THE earliest known dramatic version of the Faust legend is that of the English dramatist, Christopher Marlowe: *The Tragicall History of D. Faustus.* Some evidence and argument has been advanced, pointing to the existence of a German Faust play prior to Marlowe's work.[2] It has even been argued that such a play was a source for both the "Spies Faustbuch" and Marlowe's play. The possibility that such a play existed cannot be said to be disproved, but unfortunately, if it did exist, we know practically nothing about it and modern authorities in the field have not, in general, been convinced by the arguments advanced. The starting point of the dramatic history of the Faust material still remains Marlowe's play.

The source used by Marlowe for his *Faustus* was the English translation of the "Spies Faustbuch," i.e., the English Faust book. The date of the writing is not absolutely certain, but it cannot be earlier than 1588 nor later than 1593. Two texts of the play are extant, one printed in 1604 and the other in 1616.[3] Both of these are undoubtedly corrupted by the interpolation of material not originally found in Marlowe.

In the last two decades of the sixteenth century, travelling troupes of English actors, the so-called "English Comedians," began to extend their activities to the

[1] For a detailed discussion of the subject see W. Creizenach, *Versuch einer Geschichte des Volksschauspiels vom Doctor Faust.* Halle, 1878.

[2] For a discussion of this point of view, see Walz, "A German Faust Play of the Sixteenth Century." *Germanic Review*, III (1928), 1 ff. The arguments for an independent German Faust play prior to Marlowe are generally based on a comparative study of Marlowe's play and later German plays, as far as we know them; on material in Marlowe's play not found in the "Spies Faustbuch"; and on parts of the "Spies Faustbuch" in which proponents of the theory find a more dramatic quality.

[3] The latest scholarly edition of Marlowe's *Dr. Faustus* is that by Frederick S. Boas, London, 1932. The preface contains a detailed discussion of the sources and transmission of the text.

continent. During the following century it became a common custom for English companies to make a tour of the German-speaking countries or to appear at some court at the request of the sovereign. The influence of these travelling companies was decidedly beneficial to the German stage in that they established an actors' caste and standards of stagecraft. Through them the productions of the English stage were made known to the German public—their earliest productions were done in English, only the comic character, the clown, speaking German. Gradually they began to produce the English plays—sadly mutilated, to be sure—in German, and in time they staged original German plays. With the gradual addition of German actors to these troupes and finally the formation of native German troupes, the cycle of development was complete and the groundwork necessary for the promotion of German dramatic production laid.

The first performance of a Faust play on the Continent, of which we have definite knowledge, was staged by an English company in Graz in 1608.[4] It is more than probable that this was a performance of Marlowe's play, or an adaptation of it. The English actors must have been familiar with the play and certainly would have included it in a repertoire to be given in German-speaking countries. Here indeed was a play "made to order" for their purpose and there can be no doubt that it became a favorite offering. We know of the following further performances during the seventeenth century: Dresden, 1626; Prague, 1651; Hannover, 1661; Lüneburg, 1666; Danzig, 1668; Munich, 1679; Bremen, 1688; Basle, 1696. The brevity of this list is evidence rather of our lack of definite information than of the actual frequency of the performances. In

[4] There is a possibility that an English company put on a Faust play in Frankfurt a. M. in 1592. The truth of this has not, however, been established. Cf. Goedeke, *Grundriss*, Vol. II, p. 525. No. 5.

the first scholarly investigation of the Faust legend (Neumann, *Disquisitio historica de Fausto praestigiatore,* 1683) we are told: "So this magician spent his life obscurely enough and would be even less known if he had not been presented on the stage so often." In the 1684 edition of Grimmelshausen's *Simplicissimus*[5] occurs the following: "What is more eagerly acted, played and seen than the history of the accursed archconjurer Doctor John Faust, because a number of devils are always introduced and represented in all kinds of disgusting doings." There is no doubt, therefore, of the popularity of the play during the seventeenth century, and this popularity continued throughout the following century.

The eighteenth century, however, developed certain tendencies which were not without important influence on the dramatic history of the Faust legend. The educated classes of this "Age of Enlightenment" began to turn away from the mummery, superstition and vulgarity which had come to form such a large part of the play. The powerful influence of Gottsched, professor at Leipzig and during the third decade of the century practically literary dictator of Germany, was exerted to turn the stage away from such nonsense and toward French models. The result was that Faust was gradually crowded from the legitimate stage and into the puppet theater. The first puppet performance of which we know was in 1746. The last performance of the old Faust play on the regular stage seems to have been in Hamburg in 1770. On the puppet stage the play maintained its popularity, especially among the lower classes, until down into the nineteenth century. In fact, one can see performances still.

Not a single text of the play as it was presented on the regular stage has survived. It existed only in

[5] Cf. Grimmelshausen, *Simplicissimus.* Edited by Adelbert Keller. Stuttgart, 1854. I, 271.

manuscript copies in the possession of the different companies of actors and was subject to arbitrary changes as the exigencies of the various troupes might demand. By the time Goethe's masterpiece had created an interest in all that pertained to Faust, these manuscripts were unfortunately lost. All we know about the character of the play during the more than a century and a half preceding Goethe's *Faust* comes from three sources. We have occasional indirect information about performances. Thus the diary of Georg Schröder describes the performance in Danzig in 1668. There have survived a number of theater programs which cast much light on what had happened in the development of the play. We have, finally, a goodly number of texts of the puppet plays. These, to be sure, are of a much later date. But they retain in varying degrees traces of the older state of the play and therefore permit us to draw inferences concerning the older dramas.

While there is general agreement that the Marlowe play is the basis of the German Faust play, it must not be assumed that Marlowe's text was necessarily closely followed even in the early years of its transplanting. It will be remembered that the original performances were, with the exception of the clowns' parts, in English. In "putting the play across," therefore, the actors found the poetic qualities and the finer nuances of motivation, as present in Marlowe, no particular asset. Action and spectacle and the comic element were the features that were important. So it is undoubtedly true that the play with which Germany became acquainted was, if not from the beginning then certainly from an early point in its history, a very much corrupted version of Marlowe—sadly corrupted indeed from any literary and artistic point of view.

In considering the development of the play, it must

also be remembered that to these travelling companies, there was nothing sacred about the text. It was a vehicle pure and simple, subject to any changes that the changing taste of the public or the necessities of the company, as determined by the composition of the troupe and the equipment at its disposal, might suggest. Features characteristic of and essential to the play and therefore expected by the public would of course be retained. But shifting of emphasis and the addition of new features from time to time or from company to company were the logical outcome of the whole general attitude of the age.

One source of change in the play was the local Faust tradition as it had spread throughout Germany. For example, the motif of the choice of a devil on the basis of his speed is not found in the English Faustbook nor in Marlowe's "Faustus." It had early become a part of the legend in Germany, however, and in due time became a part of the German Faust play.

The motif of the Prologue in Hell, which is found in a number of versions of the Faust play, was not in Marlowe's play, nor was it a part of the Faust tradition. Such prologues were, however, not unknown in the drama of the period and the appearance of the motif in the Faust play is no doubt an example of the transfer of typical features of the drama of the time to our play.

The tendency to develop the spectacular and the comic was, as has already been pointed out, inherent in the history of the play in Germany from the beginning. Towards the end of the seventeenth and the beginning of the eighteenth century, this tendency was much emphasized and affected by Italian influence working for the most part through Vienna. The Faust plays of the eighteenth century in their emphasis on spectacular magic feats and transformations and in the entirely new attitude towards the comic element are striking examples of this influence. Particularly important in this development was the Viennese actor Stranitzky.[6]

The early trend had been to introduce the comic element loosely. There would be introduced scenes in which Pickelhäring, through his dialect, crass jokes, and local hits, amused the audience. But these scenes had no real connection with the plot of the play itself. In fact, their content was at times left altogether to the inventiveness of the actor himself. The Viennese influence tended to bring the Harlekin or Hans Wurst (by these names, as also Caspar, Crispin, etc., he came to be called in the eighteenth century) organically into the play, to give him a definite part in the action and to throw him into direct contrast with the main characters of the play. In fact, he became a sort of parody of Faust and second in importance only to the worthy Doctor himself, who in the end was dragged off to hell, while the clown had wit enough to cheat the devil.

The development thus indicated explains the opposition of Gottsched and his followers to the Faust play as it existed in the first half of the eighteenth century.

The material presented in the following pages illustrates the three types of evidence as to the character of the stage play: a translation of the passage from the diary of Georg Schröder; theatre programs from Bremen, Hamburg and Frankfurt a. M.; and a sample puppet play. The theatre programs printed have been selected because they indicate the development of the Faust action between the years 1690-1767. There are a number of others extant but they add nothing to the information here given. The choice of a puppet play was a more difficult matter. Geissler in his *Gestaltungen des Faust,* München, 1927, selected the composite text of Karl Simrock. Most of the German scholars believe that the *Ulmer Puppenspiel* repre-

[6] Vid. Creizenach, op. cit., p. 105 ff.

sents the earliest form of the puppet play which has come down to us. For that reason we are including in our collection the Ulm play.

Marlowe's play is so readily accessible in any college library that it has not seemed worth while to include it in this collection.

The sample puppet play, and the source material for Lessing's Faust reprinted in the following section, are presented in the original German without translation. The language and vocabulary are sufficiently modern to be understood readily by the student. Notes on unusual expressions have been furnished.

I. Description of a Faust Performance in Danzig in 1668. Found in the Diary of Georg Schröder, Councilman of Danzig.[7]

First Pluto comes out of hell and summons one devil after the other—the tobacco devil, the bawdy devil, and among others the cunning devil—and gives them orders to deceive people to the best of their ability. Following this it develops that Dr. Faust, discontented with ordinary wisdom, acquires books on magic and conjures the devils into his service. In doing so he investigates their speed and wishes to choose the speediest. It is not enough for him that they be as quick as stags, or clouds, or the wind; he wishes one who is as quick as the thoughts of man. And after the canny devil has represented himself as meeting this requirement, Faust demands that he serve him for twenty-four years, in return for which Faust would surrender himself to the devil. This the canny devil will by no means do, but he refers the proposal to Pluto, and when the latter is agreed, the canny devil enters into a compact with Faust, who signs a contract in blood.

[7] Cf. Creizenach, op. cit., p. 5.

Later a hermit tries to warn Faust, but in vain. All Faust's conjurings turn out well. He causes Charlemagne to appear to him, and likewise the beautiful Helen, with whom he has his pleasure. Finally his conscience awakes and he counts the hours until the clock strikes twelve. Then he addresses his servant and warns him to abstain from magic. Soon Pluto comes and sends his devils to fetch Dr. Faust. This is done and they throw him into the air and tear him to pieces. It is also presented how he is tormented in hell, where he is drawn up and down and these words of fire are seen : Accusatus est, judicatus est, condemnatus est (he has been accused, judged and condemned).

II. Announcement of a Performance of Faust in Bremen.[8]

"The Life and Death of the great archconjurer Dr. John Faust, excellently presented, with Pickelhäring comedy, from beginning to end." The following scenes are offered for the admiration of the public: Pluto rides in the air on a dragon. Then Faust appears and conjures the spirits. Pickelhäring wants to gather money but is tormented by all sorts of magic birds in the air. Following this, Dr. Faust gives a banquet at which the centerpiece (épergne) is transformed into all kinds of wonderful figures, so that human beings, dogs, cats, and other animals come out of a pastry and fly through the air. Then a fire breathing raven, in flight, announces to Faust his approaching death and Faust is carried away by the spirits. Hell is pictured, adorned with beautiful fireworks. Finally, the whole action is once more presented in shadow pictures, in connection with which there is a masquerade of six per-

[8] Cf. Creizenach, op. cit., p. 6f. The performance was by a company of "Saxon high German comedians," probably in the ninth decade of the seventeenth century. The spectacular features advertised point towards the beginning of the Italian influence.

sons, a Spaniard, two jugglers, a schoolmaster, a farmer and a farmer's wife, who put on an especially humorous dance. . .

III. Announcement of a Performance in Hamburg.[9]

The court players of His Royal Highness, the King of Poland and Elector of Saxony, and of the Prince of Brunswick, Lüneburg and Wolfenbüttel, and of the Prince of Schleswig-Holstein will present today, by permission of the authorities, a German play, entitled: The impious life and terrible end of the world renowned archconjurer Dr. John Faust. The following features will form part of the production:

A great courtyard in the palace of Pluto on the rivers Lethe and Acheron in Hades. Charon comes sailing in his boat on the river and with him on a fiery dragon appears Pluto, accompanied by his whole hellish retinue and spirits.

Dr. Faust's study and library. An attractive celestial spirit sings the following affecting aria to the accompaniment of soft music:

Faust! what hast thou undertaken?
Oh, alas! what hast thou done?
Hast thou all good sense forsaken?
Thinkest thou no more upon
The eternal grief and pain,
And the bliss ne'er known again?

Does the prick of sinful longing
Far outweigh your soul's delight?
Wouldst thou be to hell belonging
When thou shouldst in heaven abide?

[9] July 7, 1738, by Johann Neuber, husband of the actress Karolina Neuber, and, with her, director of the famous Neuber troupe. To please Gottsched, Frau Neuber had burned Harlekin or Hans Wurst publicly on the Leipzig stage in 1737 as a sign that henceforth Hans Wurst and all he stood for was banished from the stage!!! The program is printed in Geissler, *Gestaltungen des Faust*, München, 1927, Vol. I, pages 222-223.

Holdest thou the sinner's groan
Dearer than the heavenly throne?

Is there naught your mind can alter?
Oh, so gaze on heaven above
If perchance its bounteous water
May arouse in you God's love.
Let it work upon your heart
And in heaven seek your part.

A raven comes out of the air and fetches Dr. Faust's signature.

Hans Wurst comes by chance upon his master, Dr. Faust, as he is engaged in conjuring. He has to stand still and cannot move from the spot until he has taken off his shoes. The shoes dance together merrily.

An impertinent courtier, who makes fun of Dr. Faust, gets horns on his forehead in sight of all.

A peasant buys a horse from Dr. Faust and as soon as he rides it, the horse changes into a bundle of hay. The peasant wants to call Dr. Faust to account for this, Faust pretends to be asleep, the peasant pulls at him and tears out his leg.

Hans Wurst wants to have a lot of money and, to please him, Mephistophiles permits him to cause a shower of gold.

Beautiful Helen, to the accompaniment of pleasant music, sings to Dr. Faust an aria which he does not like, because in it she prophesies his destruction.

Dr. Faust takes leave of his servant Christopher Wagner. Hans Wurst also clears out and the spirits carry away Dr. Faust during a display of fireworks.

The palace of Pluto in Hades is again seen. The furies have Dr. Faust and hold a ballet around him because they have succeeded in bringing him to their realm.

The rest will be pleasanter to see than to read about.

IV. Announcement of a Performance of Faust in Frankfurt a.M.[10]

With the gracious permission of the very noble and wise Council, the High German Comedians located here will again open their theater today and present the familiar but none the less favorite tragedy entitled Ex doctrina Interitus, or Unfortunate Learning, presented in the life and wretched death of Dr. John Faust. With Hans Wurst, a servant tormented by many kinds of spirits.—Noteworthy scenes which are presented: (1) Pluto appears, travelling through the air on a dragon. (2) Hans Wurst comes into Faust's magic circle and is tormented by the spirits. (3) Mephistophiles comes flying through the air into Faust's room. (4) Faust shows the following to the Duke of Parma: the torments of Tantalus; the vulture of Tityos; the stone of Sisyphus; the death of Pompey. (5) A woman is publicly changed into a fury. (6) To the accompaniment of a ballet of spirits, Faust is torn to pieces by the furies. In conclusion there is a ballet and a merry comedy.

V. Announcement of a Performance in Frankfurt a.M.[11]

With the gracious permission of the very noble and wise Council of the imperial, electoral, and commercial free city of Frankfurt, the newly built stage will be opened today under the direction of Mr. Joseph von Kurz. There will be presented a grand mechanical comedy, old, world famous, often staged and presented in various ways. But it is to be presented by us today

[10] Cf. Creizenach, op. cit., p. 10. The performance was given in 1742 by a company of German actors, directed by Walleroti.

[11] Cf. Creizenach, op. cit., p. 11. The performance was given in October, 1767, under the directorship of Joseph Felix von Kurz.

in such fashion that the like will hardly have been seen put on by other companies. Entitled: In doctrina interitus or The infamous life and terrible end of the world famed and universally known archconjurer Dr. John Faust, professor of theology at Wittenberg. According to the epigram:

> Multi de stygia sine fronte palude jocantur
> Sed vereor fiat, ne jocus iste focus.

That is:

> Many but jest at hell and scoff at fears,
> Until their brazen laughter 's turned to tears.

Together with Crispin, a dismissed students' fag, a traveller evilly beset by spirits, the tormented comrade of Mephistopheles, an unfortunate aerial traveller, a laughable settler of his debts, a natural wizard and a foolish night watchman. Here follow the individual attractions, mechanical contrivances, transformations and scenes. (1) Faust's learned discussion in his study as to whether the study of theology or of nigromancy is preferable. (2) Faust's remarkable conjuration in a dark wood at night, at which appear amid thunder and lightning various hellish monsters, spirits, and furies, among whom is Mephistopheles. (3) Crispin, in the magic circle, performs laughable tricks with the spirits. (4) Faust's personal contract with hell, which is fetched through the air by a raven. (5) Crispin impudently opens a book in Dr. Faust's library and little devils come out of it. (6) Faust's journey through the air with Mephistopheles. (7) Crispin receives from Mephistopheles a fiery rain of gold. (8) Faust, at the court of the Duke of Parma, presents various noteworthy scenes from biblical and profane history, viz., (1) How Judith cuts off the head of Holofernes on a bed in his tent. (2) How Delilah robs the mighty Samson of his hair and the Philistines overcome Samson. (3) The martyrdom of Titius,[12] whose entrails the ravens devour out of his body. (4) The camp of Goliath who is slain by little David with a stone from a sling. (5) The destruction of Jerusalem, surely a fine spectacle. (9) Faust will make merry with the councillors of the Prince of Parma and conjure horns on the head of one of them. (10) Shows a cemetery or graveyard with many epitaphs and inscriptions. Faust wants to excavate the bones of his dead father and misuse them in his magic, but he is urged to penitence by his father's spirit. (11) Faust is converted, but is again seduced by Mephistopheles through various illusions, in which the mournful cemetery is changed into a pleasure garden. (12) Faust recognizes the deception when it is too late. The pleasant park is turned into an open hell and the despairing Faust, after a plaint in verse, is carried to hell by the furies amid thunder and lightning. (13) A ballet of furies. (14) Mephistopheles, to the accompaniment of fireworks, draws Faust into the jaws of hell. (15) A great finale of fireworks.

VI. The Ulm Puppetplay[1]

Doktor Johann Faust
Schauspiel in zwei Theilen

Erster Theil
Vorspiel

Charon : Pluto !
Pluto : Ho !
Charon : So !
Pluto : Was so ?
Charon : Ich begehre, nicht länger dein Sklave zu seyn.
Pluto : Was für ein Sklav ?

[12] Probably 'Tityos.'

[1] The text is taken from Scheible's *Kloster,* Vol. V, pp. 783-805.

Charon: Dein höllischer Galeerensklav. Verbessere meine Gasche,[2] oder ich fahre nicht mehr.

Pluto: Wie Charon? du höllischer Galgenhund und mein Sklav, hab ich dir nicht genugsam deine Gasche verbessert? der du zuvor von einer verdammten Seele nicht mehr als einen Heller, jetzt aber einen Pfennig hast! Darum schwöre ich, du sollst fahren!

Charon: So will ich fahren. Aber lasz deine faulen Teufel nicht immer in der Hölle, sondern schicke sie in die obere Welt unter die sterblichen Menschen, lasz sie lernen alles Uebles thun. Vor diesem war mein altes Schiff mit Seelen beschwängert,[3] nun aber fahren die alten Hexen haufenweis hin und wieder. Wirst du aber nicht zu deinen faulen Teufeln sehen, so wird meine Schifffahrt nichts nützen.

Pluto: Du alter Diener des plutonischen Reichs, ich verschwöre[4] deinen Eifer, darum soll geschehen, wie du gesagt hast.

Charon: Nun will ich fröhlich seyn
Und will mich nicht mehr kränken,
Weil Pluto will durch Gunst
Mir Schiff voll Seelen schenken.

Pluto: Aber holla, ihr faule Teufel! wo seyd ihr? liegt ihr im Schlaf? Begehret ihr nicht, das höllische Reich zu vermehren? So gefallt ihr mir! darum, so vernehmt meinen Befehl und fahret in alle Welt und lehret sie alles Uebles thun: die Sekten untereinander falsch disputiren, das Vorderste zum Hintern kehren; die Kaufleute, falsche Gewicht, falsche Ellen führen; das Frauenzimmer[5] hoffärtig seyn, Unkeuschheit treiben; auf den Universitäten, wo die Studenten zusammenkommen, lehret sie fressen, saufen, schwören, zaubern, zanken und schlagen, dasz sie mit ihren Seelen zu unsrer Hölle fahren.

Teufel alle: Trage keinen Zweifel an unsrer Verrichtung,[6] mächtigster Pluto.

Pluto: Aber in dieser Gestalt könnt ihr nichts thun; drum

[2] 'Gasche,' i.e., Gage, pay.
[3] i.e. filled
[4] lit. 'confirm by oath,' the sense here seems to be 'recognize, appreciate.'
[5] women in general, the female sex
[6] Don't worry. We'll do our job. Have no doubts about our performance.

fort und verändert euch, so wird es recht nach meinem Willen gehen. Die Menschen sagen, der Teufel sey ein Tausendkünstler,[7] darum will ich auch meine List auf tausenderlei Arten gebrauchen. (*Die Teufel kommen wieder.*) So recht, in dieser Gestalt seyd ihr etwas leidlicher, drum fahret hin. Unsre Zusammenkunft soll seyn in dem Böhmerwald[8] unter der groszen Eiche, darum empfanget den Segen. Bah ! bah ! bah !

Geister alle : Bah ! bah ! bah ! (*Die Geister ab.*)

Actus I.

Faust : Kein Berg ohne Thal, kein Felsen ohne Stein, kein Studiren ohne Müh und Arbeit. Man sagt zwar im gemeinen Sprüchwort : *quot capita, tot sensus,* viel Köpf, viel Sinn. Der eine hat Lust zur Malerkunst, der andere zur Architektur ; dieser ist ein Poet, jener ein guter Orator, dieser ein guter Philosoph, jener ein guter Medicus. Dieser legt sich auf[9] das Studium *theologicum,* gedenket[10] dadurch Ehre und Ruhm zu erlangen, wie ich denn solches auch von meiner Kindheit an gethan, und durch Hülf meiner Präceptoren es so weit gebracht, dasz ich allhier in Wittenberg *summum gradum Doctoratus cum laude* empfangen habe. Aber was ist es ? ich bin ein Doctor und bleib ein Doctor. Habe aber viel mehr gehört und gelesen von der Planeten Eigenschaften und dasz der Himmel in *forma sphaerica* oder rund seyn soll ; aber Alles zu sehen und mit Händen zu greifen, möchte ich wünschen, deszwegen habe ich mich entschlossen, das Studium *theologicum* ein Zeitlang auf die Seite zu setzen und mich an dem Studio *magico* zu ergötzen.

Engel : Faust, fahre fort in dem Studio *theologico* und verlasz das Studium *nigromanticum,* oder du bist in Ewigkeit verloren.

Mephistopheles : Faust, fahre fort in dem Studio *nigromantico,* so wirst du der gelehrteste Doctor werden, so[11] jemalen in Asia, Afrika, Amerika und ganz Europa gelebt hat.

[7] jack of all trades
[8] The Bohemian mountains between Czechoslovakia and Bavaria.
[9] applies himself to
[10] has in mind
[11] 'so,' used as a relative pronoun = der or welcher.

Faust: Wie? was hör ich! Zwei widerstreitende Stimmen; eine zu meiner Rechten, die andere zur Linken. Die zur Rechten zur Theologie, die zur Linken zur Nigromantie. Zu meiner Rechten: was bist du für eine?

Engel: Ich bin ein guter Engel, von oben herab gesandt, der dir deine Seele bewahren und zur Seligkeit bringen soll.

Faust: Aber zu meiner Linken: wer bist du?

Mephistopheles: Ich bin ein Geist von der niedern Welt, und komme, dich über alle Menschen glückselig zu machen.

Faust: Ein Wunderding ist's, Fauste, du hast dich billig[12] zu erfreuen: die Engel vom Himmel kommen, dich zu trösten und die Geister aus der niedern Welt, dir zu dienen. Aber holla, ich verstehe: weilen[13] ich mir vorgenommen, die Nigromantie zu lieben und die Theologie auf die Seite zu setzen, wirst du zur Rechten mir nicht behülflich seyn; du aber, zur Linken, folge mir.

Mephistopheles: Ha, ha, ha, ha!

Engel: O weh, Fauste, sieh dich vor; wie schwer wird es dir seyn, wenn du deine Seel verscherzest und leidest Höllenpein.

Faust: Es ist geschehen, Fauste, leb hinfüro[14] glücklicher, als bishero geschehen ist. Ich will mich in mein Museum[15] verfügen und den Anfang meines lustigen Studiums machen; darum, Fauste, entsetze dich nicht, es geht nach deinem Willen. (*Ab.*)

Actus II.

Pickelhäring tritt mit seiner Bagasche[16] auf.

Pickelhäring: Ach ich armer Bärnhäuter,[17] wann[18] es mir nicht wehe thäte, ich gäb mir selbsten ein paar Dutzend Ohrfeigen. Ich wär werth, dasz man mich einsperren thät und gäb mir nichts zu fressen, als lauter gebratene Hühner

[12] 'du hast dich billig zu erfreuen,' you have every reason to rejoice.
[13] weil, because
[14] 'hinfüro', in the future.
'bishero,' in the past.
[15] study
[16] Bagage, baggage
[17] sluggard, lazybones
[18] wenn

und Grammetsvögel,[19] und nichts zu saufen als lauter spanischen Wein und Malvasier.[20] Wann ich daran gedenke an die guten Sachen, wo[21] ich bei meinem Vater, dem alten Eselskopf, gehabt, so möcht ich all mein Sach hinschmeiszen.[22] Es möcht mich aber einer fragen: warum bist du nicht bei deinem Vater geblieben, so gib ich zur Antwort: die Fasttäg haben mich vertrieben. Aber hört, wie es mir vor etlich Tagen so wunderlich gegangen. Ich habe mich auf der rechten Landstrasz verirrt und bin zu einem groszen Berg kommen; es war ein groszes Thor vor; ich meinte, es wär eine Garküchel.[23] Ich klopfte an, da kam ein garstiger, schmutziger Schelm und stank nach lauter Schwefel und Pech, wie ein Kohlenbrenner nach Rauch. Ich fragte, was das für ein Lusthaus wäre, dasz die Leute so riechen. Der Kerl rief mir bei meinem Namen und sagte: O Pickelhäring! woher? Der Teufel, dachte ich, soll ich dann so weit bekannt seyn? und fragte, wer er wäre? Er antwortete mir, sein Nam wäre Strohsack, und das sey die Hölle, er aber sey Thorwart, wenn[24] ich Lust habe, fremde Sachen zu sehen. Ich liesz mich überreden; da führt mich Domine Strohsack in ein groszes Zimmer, da saszen lauter Kerls auf niedern Stühlen; denen steckt man Trichter in Hals und schüttet ihnen lauter warm Bier ein, von Schwefel und Pech gemacht. Ich fragte Monsieur Strohsack, was das bedeute; er sagte mir, das sind die Vollsäufer, die in der Welt nicht genug getrunken: da gibt man ihnen genug. Dann sagte ich, wenn das lauter Gesundheiten seyn, so will ich lieber eine Flasche voll Merzen[25] trinken; die Kammer gefällt mir nicht. Wir kamen in die zweite Kammer, da waren nichts als Schuhnägel rund um geschlagen, da hings voller Juden. Ich verwunderte mich über so viel Speckfresser; da sagte Strohsack: mein ehrlicher Pickelhäring, wann Pluto etwan auf das heimlich Gemach geht, so braucht er allzeit einen zum Auswischen. Da fing ich überlaut an zu lachen, dasz man die Mausche[26] also

[19] Krammetsvögel, a kind of thrush.
[20] malmsey, a Greek wine
[21] which
[22] throw overboard
[23] a cheap eatinghouse
[24] 'wenn'— ob.
[25] A kind of beer, drunk in March.
[26] Mauschel, Jew

verwahrt, dasz sie nicht staubig werden. Ich fragte, ob auch Pickelhäring darinnen wären; nein, sprach Herr Strohsack, man leide keine, wegen des Gestanks; aber wenn ich Lust hätte zu bleiben, so wollt er mir ein ehrliches Quartier anschaffen. Ich bedankte mich des guten Willens, und war froh, dasz ich wieder heraus kam. Nun hat michs gehungert: wann ich nicht bald etwas bekommen hätte, so hätt ich mich selbsten aufgefressen. So liederlich gehts in der Lumpenhölle zu. Ich glaub, sie fressen gar nichts. Aber holla, was kommt da für ein Kerl.

Actus III.

Wagner und Pickelhäring

Wagner: Mein Herr Fauste hat mir befohlen, ich sollte mich um einen Jungen umsehen, der mir die Hausarbeit verrichten hilft. Es gibt solche Schlüffel[27] genug, aber sie legen sich lieber auf den Bettel, als dasz sie einem ehrlichen Herrn aufwarten.

Pickelhäring: Ja, hätt ich nur einen Herrn, ich wollte ihm wohl dienen. In der Schüssel oder Kanne[28] soll mein Fleisz nicht gespart werden.

Wagner: Aber siehe, da sah ich einen feinen Kerl; der ist wohl stark genug, wenn er dienen will als ein Jung.

Pickelhäring: Sollt mich der Kerl für einen Jungen ansehen; ich fresz wohl so viel als vier Jungen!

Wagner: Glück zu, mein Herr.

Pickelhäring: Wen wird er wohl meinen?

Wagner: Noch eins: Glück zu, mein Herr.

Pickelhäring: Tausend Schlapperment![29] der heiszt mich einen Herrn. Ich musz doch gleichwohl ein gutes Aussehen haben; aber ich musz doch mit ihm reden. Hört Ihr, Herr, was wollt Ihr da von mir haben?

Wagner: Sag mir, hast du nicht Lust, einem Herrn zu dienen?

Pickelhäring: Das ist ein Flegel![30] Zuvor hiesz es: Glück

[27] a burly fellow
[28] 'In der Schüssel oder Kanne,' in eating or drinking.
[29] i.e. Sapperment, the deuce.
[30] unmannerly fellow

zu, mein Herr, jetzt heiszts: Hast nicht Lust einem Herrn zu dienen? Du magst wohl froh.seyn, dasz ich nicht jähzornig bin, sonst würde sich meine wohlgeborne Hand an deinem allmächtigen Maul wohl vergriffen haben. Sagtest du nicht vom Herrn dienen?

Wagner: Ja, ich frage dich, ob du nicht Lust hast, einem Herrn zu dienen?

Pickelhäring: Das ist wahr, wenn ich noch lang rumlaufe, so werde ich nicht allein herrenlos, sondern auch hirnlos.

Wagner: Nun wohlan! ich will dir Dienst geben.

Pickelhäring: Du, mein Herr?

Wagner: Ja, ich.

Pickelhäring: Du kommst mir schier vor wie Monsieur Strohsack.

Wagner: Warum? du sollst bei mir keine Noth leiden.

Pickelhäring: Das wär recht; wann ich wollt Noth leiden, wär ich bei Herrn Strohsack blieben.

Wagner: Nein, an Essen und Trinken sollst du keine Noth haben.

Pickelhäring: Ja, das geht mir am meisten ab; wann du deine Parole hältst, so ist der Kauf richtig.

Wagner: Da hast du meine Hand. Komm, ich will dir zeigen, was du thun sollst.

Pickelhäring: Nun gehts drauf los; ist doch besser als so liederlich rumlaufen; weisz einer doch, an welchem Tisch er essen soll. (*Ab.*)

Actus IV.

Faust in seinem Zimmer allein.

Faust: Die Begierde, mein vorgenommenes Studium fortzusetzen, machen mich aller andern Sachen vergessend. Ich verlange keine andere Gesellschaft, als nur Ergötzlichkeit in den Büchern, zu lesen und zu sehen, ob ein Mensch vermag, die Luft zu ändern, dem Wind zu gebieten, die Wellen zu zwingen, die Erde zittern zu machen und andere unglaubliche Dinge zu vollbringen. Aber halt Faust, bedenke dich, dasz du den Herrn, der die Elemente und Alles erschaffen, nicht erzürnest, damit nicht du und die Elemente zugleich fallen. Aber wie? bin ich nicht bei meinem Verstand? Wär es etwas

Gefährliches? weisz ich davon abzustehen. Aber was willst du, Wagner?

Actus V.

Faust.—Zwei Studenten.—Wagner.

Wagner: Herr Doctor, es sind zwei Studenten drauszen, sie begehren mit Ihro Excellenz zu reden.

Faust: Studenten, sagst du? Es werden vielleicht Politici[31] von einem guten Freund seyn; lasse sie hereinkommen.

Wagner: Es soll verrichtet werden.

Faust: Alles was hier in Wittenberg lebt, ehret Fausten. Wünschen wollte ich, dasz mir die zwei Herren bei meinem Fürnehmen[32] behülflich seyn könnten.

Erster Student: Mit Erlaubnisz, wenn wir den Herrn Doctor etwa beunruhigen sollten.

Zweiter Student: Ich wünsche Ihro Excellenz alle Wohlfahrt, bitte es nicht übel zu nehmen, wofern wir dieselbe molestiren.

Faust: Habt Dank, meine Herrn; die Ankunft Ihrer Personen ist mir lieb und angenehm; darum bitte ich, Sie wollen vernehmen lassen, was Ihnen beliebt. Jung, Stühle her!

Erster Student: Es sey ohne Bemühung. Die Ursache, dasz wir Ihro Excellenz besuchen, ist, weilen wir vernommen, dasz Ihro Excellenz jetziger Zeit dem Studio magico nachhängen. Hier aber habe ich ein Buch wunderlicher Weise bekommen, welches *propter magicam artem* etwas Sonderliches in sich enthält, wie man die Sonne verfinstern, die Sterne stillstehend machen und dem Mond seinen Lauf benehmen könne. Wofern es dem Herrn Doctor beliebt, stehts zu Diensten.

Zweiter Student: Mit Erlaubnisz, Herr Doctor; meiner Schuldigkeit nach habe ich Ihro Excellenz hiemit aufwarten wollen. Hier habe ich unter meines Vaters Bibliothek einen sonderlichen Autoren gefunden, welcher dem Herrn Doctor in seinem neuen angefangenen Studio sehr dienlich. Ihro Excellenz kann nach Dero Gefallen selbigen gebrauchen,

[31] The word has no meaning applicable here. Something like "protégés" seems to be intended.

[32] Vornehmen

jedoch so, dasz für keine Seele Gefahr daraus entstehen möge.

Faust: Edle Herren, Sie machen mir mehr Freud, als jemals ein Cäsar gehabt. Ihr Herren machet mich gegen Euch höchst verpflichtet. Jetzt will ich meine bishero geübte Theologie auf die Seite setzen und mich mit diesen und dergleichen Büchern ergötzen.

Erster Student: Wohl, Herr Doctor; es sollte mir lieb seyn, dasz ich Ihnen ferner dienen könnte; bitte aber noch, der Herr Doctor wolle sich nicht darinnen vertiefen, denn es möchte Schaden bringen.

Zweiter Student: Dergleichen bitte ich auch Ihro Excellenz; denn der Teufel ist ein Tausendkünstler, die Menschen zu fangen und zu fällen.

Faust: Meine Herren, ich bedanke mich des guten Erinnerns; ich bitte, leben Sie ohne Sorg. Beliebt den Herren, ein wenig zu verziehen,[33] auf ein Gläschen Wein? ich werde es für die gröszte Ehre halten.

Erster Student: Wir bedanken uns gegen den Herrn Doctor und nehmen hiemit unsren Abschied.

Zweiter Student: Und ich deszgleichen bitte unterthänig um Vergebung; nehmen also hiemit unsren Abschied.

Faust: Leben die Herren wohl! Ihr Gedächtnisz soll stets bei mir verbleiben. Jetzt kann ich Alles das sagen, was einem gefällt, das des Menschen Herz. erfreut. Diese zwei Bücher will ich mit Fleisz durchlesen, und sollte gleich mein Leben darauf stehen. Dieses ist beschrieben[34] von dem spanischen Runzifar und dieses von dem spanischen Varth: zwei grosze Meister dieser Kunst. Die Bücher zu verstehen, will ich mich hin verfügen, ich will ein Sieger seyn und mag nicht unten liegen.

Actus VI.

Faust und Wagner.

Faust: O, mehr als zu viel Ergötzlichkeit hab ich in diesen Büchern gefunden. Es bleibt dabei, ich habe es mir vorgenommen, darum will ichs auch probiren. Holla, holla, Wagner!

[33] tarry
[34] geschrieben

Wagner: Hier bin ich, hochgeehrter Herr.

Faust: Höre und observire, was ich dir sage. In meiner Studirstube auf dem Tisch wirst du einen Zirkel, von Papier zusammen gelegt, finden und ein Stäblein; das bringe mir und sage Niemand etwas.

Wagner: Ich werde Dero Befehl fleiszig nachkommen.

Faust: Mein Herz ist ganz mit Freuden umgeben. Ha, ha, ha, wie wird es mir gefallen, wenn die höllischen Geister gezwungen werden, hieher zu kommen und meine Befehle zu erwarten! Aber hier kommt Wagner.

Wagner: Hier bring ich, was Sie zu bringen befohlen.

Faust: So mache dich geschwind von hier und wenn dich Jemand fragt, wo ich sey, so sage, ich sey auf etliche Tage verreist.

Wagner: Ich werde Alles in Acht nehmen, Herr Doctor. Ich hätt eben doch auch etwas lernen wollen. (*Ab.*)

Faust: Nun bin ich allein und kann ungehindert mein angefangenes Werk verrichten. Hier musz der Zirkel liegen und hier der Stab. Nun, Fauste, ehe du in den Zirkel gehest, fasse einen frischen Muth, sonst bist du in Ewigkeit verloren. Ja, mein Verlangen ist so grosz in mir, als eines Bräutigams, der zu seiner Braut gehen soll. Nun steh ich fest, wie ein Kolossus. Aber Fauste, nimm dich in acht, oder du wirst einen erbärmlichen Fall thun: die Haare steigen mir schier zu Berg. (*Steigt in den Zirkel und es wird gedonnert.*) Stehe ich, oder bin ich gefallen, denn mir war nicht anders, als wenn alle Elemente über mich zusammenfallen wollten. Es steht noch eines zu wagen und die höllischen Geister hervorzurufen: *Conjuro vos per omnes Deos, qui vos Kakadaemones sitis, ut statim appareates!* [35]

Actus VII.

Alle Teufel kommen.

Faust: Holla, dieser Sturm ist vorbei! Was bist du für einer?

Krummschal: Ich heisze Krummschal und musz auf deinen Befehl erscheinen.

[35] By all the Gods, I conjure you spirits of evil to appear at once.

Faust: Wie geschwind bist du?

Krummschal: Als wie ein Vogel in der Luft.

Faust: Hinweg du Höllenhund, du taugst mir nicht! — Aber wie heiszest du?

Vizibuzli: Ich bin ein fliegender Geist und heisze Vizibuzli, der Liebesteufel.

Faust: Wie geschwind bist du?

Vizibuzli: Als wie ein Pfeil vom Bogen.

Faust: Packe dich, du taugst mir nicht! — Aber sage mir, was bist du für einer?

Mephistopheles: Ich bin ein Luftgeist und heisze Mephistopheles, der geschwinde.

Faust: So sag mir, wie geschwind bist du?

Mephistopheles: So geschwind wie der Menschen Gedanken.

Faust: Das wär viel. Du taugst mir. Aber sage, willst du mir dienen?

Mephistopheles: Fauste, das steht nicht in meiner Macht; ist aber Pluto, der Höllengott, zufrieden, so bin ich bereit, dir zu dienen.

Faust: Nun wohlan, weil es in deiner Macht nicht steht, so fahre hin und bringe mir von deinem mächtigsten Pluto eine Antwort.

Mephistopheles: Es soll geschehen. (*Ab.*)

Faust: Morgen um 12 Uhr erwarte ich dich in meinem Museo. Wohlan, diesem ist genug gethan! In Wahrheit, ich habe mich einer groszen Sache unterfangen. Jetzt sehe ich die Wirkung dieser Bücher. Wohlan, ich verfüge mich nach Haus und warte des Geistes mit Verlangen.

(*Geht ab.*)

Ende des ersten Theils.

Zweiter Theil.

Actus I.

Wagner: Diesz ist ein leichtfertiger Schelm, der Pickelhäring; so oft ich ihm etwas befehle, so oft versteckt er sich. Ich will ihm noch einmal rufen. (*Er pfeift ihm.*)

Pickelhäring: Pfeif du nur, ich bin dein Jung nicht.

Wagner: Ich sage dir, komm hervor, oder ich will dich beim Herrn verklagen.

Pickelhäring : Zahl du eingefrorne Baurenkugel,[36] und so mit Gunst hab ich ausgeredt.

Wagner : Hier hab ich einen Jungen, Euer Excellenz.

Faust : Wenn ich dich aufnehmen will, willst du mir dienen ?

Pickelhäring : Das kann ich nicht wissen.

Faust : Komm her, lasz dich examiniren. Sag mir : wie heiszt dein Vater, deine Mutter, deine Brüder, deine Schwestern und wie heiszest du ?

Pickelhäring : Diesz ist viel gesagt in einem Athem. Mein Vater heiszt Stockfisch, meine Mutter heiszt Blatteisz,[37] die war allzeit voll Roger,[38] mein Bruder heiszt Weiszfisch, meine Schwester Barm,[39] und weil ich der schönste bin, so hat man mich eingesalzen, dasz ich nicht stank : und so heiszt man mich Pickelhäring.

Faust : Diesz ist ein lustiger Nam.

Pickelhäring : Hör du Schwarzbart ! Wie heiszt dein Vater, deine Mutter, dein Bruder, deine Schwester, und wie heiszest du ?

Faust : Du leichtfertiger Schelm, wer hat dich geheiszen, mich zu examiniren ?

Pickelhäring : Wer hat dir Schwarzbart befohlen, mich zu examiniren.

Wagner : Pickelhäring, sey nicht zu grob.

Faust : Nun, das sey dir verziehen. Wagner, nimm Pickelhäring zu dir und unterrichte ihn.

(*Wagner mit Pickelhäring ab.*)

Actus II.

Faust : Jetzt erinnere ich mich des Geists, welcher versprochen, von dem höllischen Regenten mir Antwort zu bringen.

Mephistopheles : Fauste ! In was für einer Gestalt soll ich erscheinen ?

Faust : Gleichwie ein Mensch.

Mephistopheles : Hier bin ich.

[36] 'Zahl du eingefrorne Baurenkugel,' a vulgar phrase probably equivalent to "Go to the devil."

[37] flatfish

[38] Probably 'Rogen,' roe.

[39] Probably Barme — Barbe. A barbel, a fish of the carp family.

Faust: Was bringst du für eine Antwort von deinem mächtigen Pluto?

Mephistopheles: Ja, mein Fauste, ich habe Befehl, dir zu dienen, aber du muszt dich mit dem höllischen Reich verbinden und nach verflossener Zeit mit Leib und Seel sein eigen seyn.

Faust: Und wie lange?

Mephistopheles: Vier und zwanzig Jahre, nicht länger.

Faust: Diesz waren auch meine Gedanken. Aber was ist dem mächtigsten Pluto mit meiner armen Seel gedient?

Mephistopheles: Gleichwie ihr Sterbliche einander nicht traut, also traut auch das höllische Reich nicht. Daher muszt du dich mir verschreiben.

Faust: Ists nichts anderes als dieses, so will ich schreiben.

Actus III.

Der Engel.—Faust.—Mephistopheles.

Engel: Nein, Faust, thu es nicht, der Kauf wird dir zu theuer, gedenk an das Gericht und an das höllisch Feuer.

Faust: Was ist das für eine Stimme? Es entzückt sich mein Geblüt. Mephistopheles!

Mephistopheles: Hier bin ich.

Faust: Hier finde ich mit romanischen Buchstaben geschrieben: Homo fuge! Wohin soll ich fliehen?

Mephistopheles: Wie, Fauste? bist du ein so gelehrter Doctor und verstehst die Worte nicht? Das ist: Mensch, fliehe in meine Arme, so bist du vor aller Gewalt sicher.

Faust: Es ist wahr und musz also heiszen. (*Schreibt.*) Da ist die Handschrift.

Mephistopheles: Gut, aber der Name musz darunter.

Faust: Es soll gleich geschehen.

Engel: Faust, gib die Handschrift nicht von dir, oder du bist in Ewigkeit verloren.

Faust: Hinweg du falsche Stimme! hier hast du meine Handschrift, nun gebrauch ich mich deiner Dienste.

Mephistopheles: Alles was du begehrst, sollst du von mir verlangen.

Engel: O Fauste! o weh! dein Seel fängt an zu sinken; du muszt in Ewigkeit im Schwefelpfuhl ertrinken. (*Ab.*)

Actus IV.

Mephistopheles und Faust.

Faust: Sage mir, Mephistopheles, ob es sich also verhält, dasz an dem Hof des ungekrönten Königs in Prag ein so stattlicher Hof gehalten werde?

Mephistopheles: Es ist nicht anders, als dasz derselbe in aller Freud und Herrlichkeit lebet und liebet sehr die Künste.

Faust: Weil mir allhie in Wittenberg die Zeit etwas traurig fallen will, so bin ich gesinnt, mich an dessen Hof zu begeben, darum sey fertig und bereit.

Mephistopheles: Wenn es dir beliebt, sage nur, wie ich dich hinbringen soll.

Faust: Nach meinem Gefallen fein langsam durch die Luft.

Actus V.

König.—Edelmann.—Faust.—Mephistopheles.

König: Den Thron dieses Königreichs beherrschen Wir bereits schon eine geraume Zeit in Glückseligkeit, dasz wir auch sagen müssen, Fortuna trage uns auf den Flügeln.

Edelmann: Euer Majestät vergönnen; wie ich vernommen, so solle ein vortrefflicher Künstler allhier angekommen seyn, Namens Doctor Johann Faust, in solcher Wissenschaft erfahren, wie man seit die Welt steht, nie gesehen hat.

König: Nun, so wollen wir ihn auch sehen.

Edelmann: Wenn es Eurer Majestät gefällt, so will ich ihn alsbald anhero[40] bringen.

Faust: Lange lebe der König, er beherrsche seinen Thron in erwünschtem Frieden. Sie verzeihen mir, dasz ich mich erkühnt, Dero königlichen Hof zu besuchen.

König: Seyd uns willkommen, Herr Doctor: Saget, seyd Ihr ein Künstler, wie von Euch gesagt wird, dasz Ihr könnt sehen lassen, was man von Euch verlangt.

Faust: Ihro Majestät demüthigst aufzuwarten, Sie haben zu befehlen.

[40] here

König: Herr Doctor, Wir haben viel von *Alexandro magno* gelesen. Könnt Ihr durch Eure Kunst so viel zu wege bringen, dasz wir denselben sammt seiner Gemahlin sehen können, doch ohne Schaden.

Faust: Ohne allen Schaden und Gefahr kann es seyn.—Mephistophele! geschwind bringe beide hervor.

Mephistopheles: Hier seyn sie.

König: Wir haben gelesen, dasz Padamera[41] einen schwarzen Flecken am Hals, auf der linken Seite gehabt.

Faust: Eure Majestät werdens auch finden.

König: In Wahrheit, es ist also; aber lasz sie wieder hingebracht werden, woher sie kamen.

Faust: Mephistophele! bring sie wieder hinweg!

König: Herr Doctor, Wir sehen, dasz Sie in Ihrer Kunst gut erfahren. Anjetzo kommt und folget uns zur Tafel, alldorten könnt Ihr uns Mehreres zeigen. (*Sie gehen ab.*)

Actus VI.

Faust.—Wagner und Mephistopheles.

Faust: Nun sind wir wieder in Wittenberg angelangt. Sag mir, Wagner, wie hast du dich und Pickelhäring seit meiner Abreise verhalten?

Wagner: Hochgeehrtester Herr Doctor, was mich anbelangt, so soll keine Klag kommen, beim Pickelhäring hätts wohl besser seyn können. (*Ab.*)

Faust: Mephistopheles, lege dich zu meinen Füszen, denn ich habe dich nothwendige Sachen zu fragen.

Mephistopheles: Hier lieg ich schon.

Faust: Sage mir von dem Gefängnisz der Hölle, von dem Abgrund der Verdammten und von der Qual der Verstoszenen.

Mephistopheles: Du fragst, was die Hölle sey? Sie wird auch die brennende Höll genannt, da Alles brennet und glühet, und verzehret sich doch nicht. So heiszt die Hölle auch eine ewige Pein, die weder Hoffnung, noch Ende hat, da man weder die Herrlichkeit Gottes, noch die Sonne erblicken kann.

Faust: Ist denn ganz und gar keine Erlösung?

41 Apparently a corruption of Marlowe's "paramour."

Mephistopheles: Nein, ganz und gar nicht. Diejenigen, so einmal von Gottes Gnade verstoszen sind, müssen ewig brennen.

Faust: Wenn du an meiner Statt von Gott als ein Mensch erschaffen wärest, was wolltest du thun, dasz du Gott und den Menschen gefielest?

Mephistopheles: Ich wollte mich gegen Gott biegen, so lang als ich einen menschlichen Athem in mir hätte; ich wollte mich befleiszen, meinen Schöpfer nicht zum Zorn gegen mich zu reitzen; seine Gebote wollt ich halten so viel möglich, dasz ich nach meinem Absterben die ewige Seligkeit gewisz erlangen möchte.

Faust: So sage mir auch vom Himmel und von den Auserwählten.

Mephistopheles: Es ist mir verboten, dir solches zu offenbaren.

Faust: Dieses verlange ich am meisten von dir zu wissen.

Mephistopheles: Ich kann es aber nicht thun.

Faust: Du sollst es aber thun.

Mephistopheles: So flieh ich. (*Ab.*)

Faust: Fliehest du? O erbarmenswürdiger Fauste; hast du Gnade nicht, die Seligkeit zu wissen! So bin ich denn verloren mit meiner Kunst? O meiner armen Seele! Ich will Gnade bei dem Himmel suchen und die gelernte Kunst sammt allen Teufeln verfluchen; ich will auf meine Kniee niederfallen und Gott um Verzeihung bitten. (*Geht ab.*)

Mephistopheles: Es ist in unsrem Reich erschollen,[42] dasz Faust umkehrt und auf dem Weg der Buszfertigkeit meinen Klauen entgehen will;—da, hier liegt er auf seinen Knieen. Pfui, schäme dich!

Faust: Weiche von mir, Höllengespenst, vermaledeite Furie!

Mephistopheles: Wie? soll denn alle meine Müh, so ich mit dir gehabt, vergeblich seyn? O Pluto, komme zu Hülf! Faust, hier hast du Kron und Scepter! Man wird dir mehr Reverenz erzeigen als *Alexandro magno* und *Julio Caesari.*

Faust: Meinest du, weil ich die heilige Theologie verlassen, ich müszte bei dir verharren? Nein, du kannst bei mir nichts richten, darum verlasse mich!

[42] rumored

Mephistopheles: Wie? will nichts helfen? Durch Schönheit der Weiber sind schon oft tapfere Helden gefallen; es soll dir auch also ergehen. (*Zu Faust.*) Sieh her, Faust, die griechische Schönheit Helena, um welcher willen Troja ist zerstöret worden!

Faust: Ist das die Helena aus Griechenland?

Mephistopheles: Sie winkt dir.

(*Faust umarmt sie.*)

Faust: Was für eine wunderschöne Creatur!

Mephistopheles: Ach, Fauste! sie macht dich glückselig.

Faust: Macht sie mich glückselig?

Mephistopheles: Ja, Faust, und über alle Menschen glückselig.

Faust: Ist das die schöne Helena? Komm her, ich will dein Paris seyn! (*Geht mit ihr ab.*)

Actus VII.

Faust und mehrere Studenten.

Faust: Ihr Herren, die Ehre, so Ihr mir gönnt, zur schlechten Mahlzeit zu kommen, ist grosz; ich bitte Sie wollen vorlieb nehmen.

Erster Student: Mein Herr Doctor, die Ehre, so wir genieszen, ist grosz.

(*Hier wird gedonnert.*)

Zweiter Student: Was mag wohl das Donnerwetter bedeuten?

Faust: Ich fürchte, das wird nichts Gutes bedeuten.

Erster Student: Ach, das erschreckt mich!

Faust: Ist es wohl so? Ach! ach!

Zweiter Student (*für sich:*) Was bedeutet dieses, dasz er so traurig wird?

Faust: Ach! ach! ach!

Erster Student: Helft! helft! Herr Faust will etwas wanken! [43]

Erster und Zweiter Student: Der Himmel bewahre vor Unglück!

[43] is staggering

Faust: O, ihr Herren erschreckt selbst, wenn ich mein schändliches Leben erzähle. Es begab sich vor 24 Jahren, dasz mein Eifer und groszes Verlangen zu der abscheulichen Nigromantie mich so weit gebracht, meine edle Theologie zu verlassen. Alsdann hab ich mich verführen lassen, mich dem leidigen Teufel mit Leib und Seel zu verschreiben. O Schmerz! O Angst! die Jahre sind aus, die Stunde ist da, allwo ich die gemachte Schuld bezahlen musz!

Erster Student: O Herr Doctor, es ist übel gethan! Er kehre um zu Gott, er kann noch Errettung seiner Seele finden.

Faust: Ach ihr Herren, Euer Trost wär gut! aber es ist zu spät: das Gute hab ich verworfen und das Böse gethan. Holla, Wagner!

Zweiter Student: Nun wohlan! kann es nicht mehr anders seyn: wir verlassen ihn, mich kommt ein Grausen an!

(*Die Studenten ab.*)

Wagner: Hier bin ich.

Faust: Sag mir, um welche Zeit ists?

Wagner: Es wird allbereits um 11 Uhr seyn.

Faust: Ach wie schrecklich werde ich in meinem Gewissen gepeinigt! Wagner, bewahre dich hinfüro vor falscher Lehr, die du bisher von mir gesehen. Geh von hier und leg dich nieder, und wenn du gefragt wirst, wo ich hinkommen sey, so sage, dasz ich ein verfluchtes Ende genommen! (*Es schlägt 11 Uhr.*) Jetzt bin ich von allen Menschen in dieser Welt verlassen. Göttliche Hülfe ist von mir gewichen. Ach weh und aber weh! Ach, Fauste musz versinken!

(*Es schlägt 1 Viertel.*)

Mephistopheles: Fauste, *praepara te!*

Faust: Ach, Faust, *praepara te!* Ach, Faust, bereite dich! Ach Höllenangst, ich erschreck, dasz ich nicht weisz, wohin!

(*Es schlägt 2 Viertel.*)

Mephistopheles: Fauste! *accusatus es!*

Faust: Faust ist schon verklagt! Womit soll ich mich entschuldigen, wenn der strenge Richter hervortritt und das Buch aufschlagen wird? Schamroth musz ich stehen, weil ich keinen Erlöser, noch Advokaten habe!

(*Es schlägt 3 Viertel.*)

Mephistopheles: Fauste, *judicatus es!*

Faust: *Judicatus* ist Faust! ist schon von dem strengen

Richter verurtheilt! Der Stab ist schon gebrochen; keine Erlösung ist für Faust zu finden!

Ach weh, und aber weh!
Ich werde vorgestellt
Vor Gottes Richterstuhl:
Das Urtheil ist gefällt!

Mephistopheles: Fauste, *in perpetuum damnatus es!*

Faust: In perpetuum damnatus es! Faust ist in alle Ewigkeit verloren! O weh, Finsternisz! In dieser Nacht bellet der Hund, mein schwarzes Gewissen! O, alle Menschen, jung und alt, nehmt doch ein Exempel an dem unglücklichen Faust und lasset euch durch die Weltfreuden nicht so sehr verführen! Aber ach! die Sanduhr meines Lebens ist ausgelaufen und ich musz in ein ewiges Land, da Heulen und Zittern seyn wird. O, ewig verloren seyn! Ewiger Abgrund des Verderbens, du donnerst mir ewige Marter zu und durchwühlst mir mein vermaledeites Herz. Weh mir! schon jetzt stürmen die Qualen auf meine bebende Seele!

(*Die Hölle eröffnet sich. Feuerwerk geht an.*)

Faust: Brecht, Himmel, Sterne kracht!
Spritzt schwefelblaue Flammen,
Ihr Lichter jener Welt,
Ihr Berge fallt zusammen,
Und werft den ganzen Grund
Der harten Erde ein!
O weh! ich sinke schon
Und fühl der Hölle Pein!

(*Die Hölle eröffnet sich. Die Teufel holen Fausten dahin ab.*)

VI

LESSING AND FAUST

LESSING AND FAUST[1]

AFTER Christopher Marlowe the first literary man of prominence to interest himself positively in the Faust tradition was the German dramatist and critic G. E. Lessing (1729–1781). Lessing was probably familiar with the stage play as early as his student days but the impulse to modernize and deepen the content of the play doubtless came from a performance of the Schuch troupe which he saw in Berlin in 1754. The earliest evidence which we have that he was working on a Faust play is in a letter from Moses Mendelssohn dated Nov. 19, 1755.

Lessing worked intermittently on Faust for twenty years. Whether he ever actually composed a complete Faust drama is exceedingly doubtful. There is evidence that his plans changed from time to time and that he had at least two and possibly three different versions of the story in mind, none of which, so far as we know, was ever finished. The story told by Lessing's brother Karl and by Hauptmann von Blankenburg about the loss of Lessing's manuscript is not, necessarily, a proof that Lessing had completed his drama.

All that remains of the work by Lessing's own hand is the scene published in the 17th "Literaturbrief" on Feb. 16, 1759, and the Berlin scenario, composed at about the same period, which was published after Lessing's death. The two fragments together with the reports of Hauptmann von Blankenburg and J. J. Engel suffice to give the student a fairly definite idea of one of the versions which Lessing had in mind.

[1] For a detailed discussion of Lessing's work on Faust, and a collection of all the pertinent documentary evidence, see Petsch, *Lessings Faustdichtung*, Heidelberg, 1911.

Compare further the excellent introduction to "D. Faust" by Waldemar Oehlke in *Lessings Werke*, ed. Petersen and Olshausen, Vol. X, pp. 204-211.

The contributions toward a loftier conception of the Faust problem become clear when one compares the puppet plays or Marlowe's play with the plot reported by Engel. The most important innovation is the change in the attitude toward the pursuit of wisdom. In Marlowe and in the puppet plays Faust's too great intellectual curiosity is looked upon as a sin. The same is true of the Faust books. In Lessing's plot the desire for knowledge and the search for truth are regarded as among the highest ideals of humanity. Lessing's Faust cannot be damned to eternal punishment. This alone would have assured Lessing a place in the development of the story. The attempt to rationalize the tradition by adopting the dream motive, a device borrowed from Voltaire and Calderon, is a second addition; and a third, the ennobling of Faust's character which placed the whole drama on a higher plane. By these changes in the traditional treatment of the theme Lessing rescued the old story from threatened oblivion, uncovered some of its latent possibilities, and paved the way for Goethe.

I. Extract from the XVII. Literaturbrief [2]

Dass aber unsre alten Stücke wirklich sehr viel Englisches gehabt haben, könnte ich Ihnen mit geringer Mühe weitläuftig beweisen. Nur das bekannteste derselben zu nennen; „Doktor Faust" hat eine Menge Szenen, die nur ein Shakespearesches Genie zu denken vermögend gewesen. Und wie verliebt war Deutschland, und ist es zum Teil noch, in seinen „Doktor Faust"! Einer von meinen Freunden [3] verwahret

[2] The most recent reprints are to be found in *Lessings Werke*, Petersen and Olshausen, Vol. IV, pp. 58-60; Geissler, *Gestaltungen des Faust*, I, pp. 297-299; Petsch, *Lessings Faustdichtung*, pp. 34-36. The passage is an extract from the famous seventeenth "Literaturbrief" (February 16, 1759) in which Lessing takes Professor Gottsched to task for attempting to Frenchify the German theater. Lessing himself suggests that the English drama is more in conformity with German taste and genius.

[3] The scene that follows is by Lessing himself.

einen alten Entwurf dieses Trauerspiels, und er hat mir einen Auftritt daraus mitgeteilet, in welchem gewiss ungemein viel Grosses liegt. Sind Sie begierig ihn zu lesen? Hier ist er! —Faust verlangt den schnellsten Geist der Hölle zu seiner Bedienung. Er macht seine Beschwörungen; es erscheinen derselben sieben; und nun fängt sich die dritte Szene des zweiten Aufzugs an.

Faust und sieben Geister.

Faust: Ihr? Ihr seid die schnellesten Geister der Hölle?

Die Geister alle: Wir.

Faust: Seid ihr alle sieben gleich schnell?

Die Geister alle: Nein.

Faust: Und welcher von euch ist der schnelleste?

Die Geister alle: Der bin ich!

Faust: Ein Wunder! dass unter sieben Teufeln nur sechs Lügner sind.—Ich muss euch näher kennen lernen.

Der erste Geist: Das wirst du! Einst!

Faust: Einst! Wie meinst du das? Predigen die Teufel auch Busse?

Der erste Geist: Jawohl, den Verstockten.—Aber halte uns nicht auf.

Faust: Wie heissest du? Und wie schnell bist du?

Der erste Geist: Du könntest eher eine Probe, als eine Antwort haben.

Faust: Nun wohl. Sieh her; was mache ich?

Der erste Geist: Du fährst mit deinem Finger schnell durch die Flamme des Lichts—

Faust: Und verbrenne mich nicht. So geh auch du, und fahre siebenmal ebenso schnell durch die Flammen der Hölle, und verbrenne dich nicht.—Du verstummst? Du bleibst? —So prahlen auch die Teufel? Ja, ja; keine Sünde ist so klein, dass ihr sie euch nehmen liesset.—Zweiter, wie heissest du?

Der zweite Geist: Chil; das ist in eurer langweiligen Sprache: Pfeil der Pest.

Faust: Und wie schnell bist du?

Der zweite Geist: Denkest du, dass ich meinen Namen vergebens führe?—Wie die Pfeile der Pest.

Faust: Nun so geh, und diene einem Arzte! Für mich bist du viel zu langsam.—Du dritter, wie heissest du?

Der dritte Geist: Ich heisse Dilla; denn mich tragen die Flügel der Winde.

Faust: Und du vierter?—

Der vierte Geist: Mein Name ist Jutta, denn ich fahre auf den Strahlen des Lichts.

Faust: O ihr, deren Schnelligkeit in endlichen Zahlen auszudrücken, ihr Elenden—

Der fünfte Geist: Würdige sie deines Unwillens nicht. Sie sind nur Satans Boten in der Körperwelt. Wir sind es in der Welt der Geister; uns wirst du schneller finden.

Faust: Und wie schnell bist du?

Der fünfte Geist: So schnell als die Gedanken des Menschen.

Faust: Das ist etwas!—Aber nicht immer sind die Gedanken des Menschen schnell. Nicht da, wenn Wahrheit und Tugend sie auffordern. Wie träge sind sie alsdann!—Du kannst schnell sein, wenn du schnell sein willst; aber wer steht mir dafür, dass du es allezeit willst? Nein, dir werde ich so wenig trauen, als ich mir selbst hätte trauen sollen. Ach!—(*Zum sechsten Geiste.*) Sage du, wie schnell bist du?—

Der sechste Geist: So schnell als die Rache des Rächers.

Faust: Des Rächers? Welches Rächers?

Der sechste Geist: Des Gewaltigen, des Schrecklichen, der sich allein die Rache vorbehielt, weil ihn die Rache vergnügte.—

Faust: Teufel! du lästerst, denn ich sehe, du zitterst.—Schnell, sagst du, wie die Rache des—Bald hätte ich ihn genennt! Nein, er werde nicht unter uns genennt!—Schnell wäre seine Rache? Schnell?—Und ich lebe noch? Und ich sündige noch?—

Der sechste Geist: Dass er dich noch sündigen lässt, ist schon Rache!

Faust: Und dass ein Teufel mich dieses lehren muss!—Aber doch erst heute! Nein, seine Rache ist nicht schnell, und wenn du nicht schneller bist, als seine Rache, so geh nur.—(*Zum siebenten Geiste.*)—Wie schnell bist du?

Der siebente Geist: Unzuvergnügender Sterbliche, wo auch ich dir nicht schnell genug bin——

Faust: So sage; wie schnell?

Der siebente Geist: Nicht mehr und nicht weniger, als der Übergang vom Guten zum Bösen.—

Faust: Ha! du bist mein Teufel! So schnell als der Übergang vom Guten zum Bösen!—Ja, der ist schnell; schneller ist nichts als der!—Weg von hier, ihr Schnecken des Orkus! Weg!—Als der Übergang vom Guten zum Bösen! Ich habe es erfahren, wie schnell er ist! Ich habe es erfahren! usw.——

Was sagen Sie zu dieser Szene? Sie wünschen ein deutsches Stück, das lauter solche Szenen hätte? Ich auch!

II. The Berlin Scenario.[4]

VORSPIEL.

In einem alten Dome. Der Küster und sein Sohn, welche eben zu Mitternacht geläutet oder läuten wollen.

Die Versammlung der Teufel, unsichtbar auf den Altären sitzend und sich über ihre Angelegenheiten beratschlagend. Verschiedne ausgeschickte Teufel erscheinen vor dem Beelzebub, Rechenschaft von ihren Verrichtungen zu geben. Einer, der eine Stadt in Flammen gesetzt, ein andrer, der in einem Sturme eine ganze Flotte begraben, werden von einem dritten verlacht, dass sie sich mit solchen Armseligkeiten abgegeben. Er rühmt sich, einen Heiligen verführt zu haben, den er beredet, sich zu betrinken, und der im Trunke einen Ehebruch und einen Mord begangen. Dieses gibt Gelegenheit, von Fausten zu sprechen, der so leicht nicht zu verführen sein möchte. Dieser dritte Teufel nimmt es auf sich, und zwar, ihn in vier und zwanzig Stunden der Hölle zu überliefern.

„Itzt," sagt der eine Teufel, „sitzt er noch bei der nächtlichen Lampe und forschet in den Tiefen der Wahrheit.

Zuviel Wissbegierde ist ein Fehler; und aus einem Fehler

[4] The scenario is reprinted in *Lessings Werke,* Petersen and Olshausen, Vol. X, pp. 212-214; Geissler, op. cit., I, pp. 300-302; Petsch, op. cit., pp. 37-39. It was published after Lessing's death by his brother Karl, in 1784. Petsch (op. cit., p. 16) believes that it goes back to about the same time as the seventeenth "Literaturbrief."

können alle Laster entspringen, wenn man ihm zu sehr nachhänget."

Nach diesem Satze entwirft der Teufel, der ihn verführen will, seinen Plan.

ERSTER AUFZUG.

Erster Auftritt.

(Dauer des Stückes: von Mitternacht zu Mitternacht.)

Faust unter seinen Büchern bei der Lampe. Schlägt sich mit verschiednen Zweifeln aus der scholastischen Weltweisheit. Erinnert sich, dass ein Gelehrter den Teufel über des Aristoteles Entelechie zitiert haben soll. Auch er hat es schon vielfältigemal versucht, aber vergebens. Er versucht es nochmals (eben ist die rechte Stunde) und lieset eine Beschwörung.

Zweiter Auftritt.

Ein Geist steigt aus dem Boden, mit langem Barte, in einen Mantel gehüllet.

G.: Wer beunruhiget mich? Wo bin ich? Ist das nicht Licht, was ich empfinde?

Faust erschrickt, fasset sich aber und redet den Geist an. Wer bist du? Woher kömmst du? Auf wessen Befehl erscheinest du?

G.: Ich lag und schlummerte und träumte, mir war nicht wohl, nicht übel; da rauschte, so träumte ich, von weitem eine Stimme daher; sie kam näher und näher; „Bahall!" „Bahall!" hörte ich und mit dem dritten „Bahall" stehe ich hier!

F.: Aber wer bist du?

G.: Wer ich bin? Lass mich besinnen! Ich bin—ich bin nur erst kürzlich, was ich bin. Dieses Körpers, dieser Glieder war ich mir dunkel bewusst; itzt etc.

F.: Aber wer warst du?

G.: Warst du?

F.: Ja; wer warst du sonst, ehedem?

G.: Sonst? ehedem?

F.: Erinnerst du dich keiner Vorstellungen, die diesem gegenwärtigen und jenem deinem hinbrütenden Stande vorhergegangen? —

G.: Was sagst du mir? Ja, nun schiesst es mir ein — Ich habe schon einmal ähnliche Vorstellungen gehabt. Warte, warte, ob ich den Faden zurückfinden kann.

F.: Ich will dir zu helfen suchen. Wie hiessest du?

G.: Ich hiess — Aristoteles. Ja, so hiess ich. Wie ist mir?

Er tut, als ob er sich nun völlig erinnerte, und antwortet dem Faust auf seine spitzigsten Fragen. Dieser Geist ist der Teufel selbst, der den Faust zu verführen unternommen.

Doch, sagt er endlich, ich bin es müde, meinen Verstand in die vorigen Schranken zurückzuzwingen. Von allem, was du mich fragest, mag ich nicht länger reden als ein Mensch, und kann nicht mit dir reden als ein Geist. Entlass mich; ich fühl' es, dass ich wieder entschlummre etc.

Dritter Auftritt.

Er verschwindet, und Faust, voller Erstaunen und Freude, dass die Beschwörung ihre Kraft gehabt, schreitet zu einer andern, einen Dämon heraufzubringen.

Vierter Auftritt.

Ein Teufel erscheinet.

Wer ist der Mächtige, dessen Rufe ich gehorchen muss! Du? Ein Sterblicher? Wer lehrte dich diese gewaltige Worte?

III. Extract from Letter of Staatsrat Gebler of Vienna to Friedrich Nicolai.[5]

Ich wünsche, dass Ew. Hochedelgeboren Hoffnung wegen der Erscheinung des Lessingschen Dr. Fausts zutreffen möge. Mir hat unser grosser, aber zu wenig gegen das Publikum

[5] The passage is reprinted in Petsch, op. cit., pp. 44-45. The date of the letter is Dec. 9, 1775. Gebler was an Austrian statesman and dramatist. Nicolai was a writer, publisher, and bookdealer in Berlin. Both were friends of Lessing.

freigebiger Freund auf mein Befragen mündlich anvertraut, dass er das Sujet zweimal bearbeitet habe, einmal nach der gemeinen Fabel, dann wiederum ohne alle Teufelei, wo ein Erzbösewicht gegen einen Unschuldigen die Rolle des schwarzen Verführers vertritt. Beide Ausarbeitungen erwarten nur die letzte Hand.

IV. Extract from Friedrich Müller's Account of His Meeting with Lessing in Mannheim, 1777.[6]

Bei dieser Gelegenheit erzählte der Tröstliche[7] mir, dass er zwei Schauspiele vom Faust angelegt, beide aber wieder liegen gelassen habe, das eine, sagte er, mit Teufeln, das andere ohne solche, nur sollten in dem letzten die Ereignisse so sonderbar auf einander folgen, dass bei jeder Scene der Zuschauer würde genötigt gewesen sein, auszurufen : das hat der Satan so gefügt.

V. Captain von Blankenburg on Lessing's Lost "Faust".[8]

Sie wünschen, mein teurester Freund, eine Nachricht von dem verloren gegangenen Faust des verstorbenen Lessing zu erhalten ; was ich davon weiss, teile ich Ihnen um desto lieber mit, da, mit meinem Willen, nicht eine Zeile, nicht eine Idee dieses grossen, und immer noch nicht genug gekannten, ja oft sogar mutwillig verkannten Mannes verloren gehen sollte. Verloren, gänzlich verloren könnte zwar vielleicht sein Faust nicht sein ; ——und zu fürchten ist denn auch nicht, dass, wenn ein anderer mit dieser Feder sich sollte schmücken wollen, der Betrug nicht entdeckt werden würde ; denn was man von den Versen des Homer und den Ideen des Shakespeare sagt, gilt mit ebenso vielem Rechte von den Arbeiten Lessings, und der verloren gegangene Faust gehört zu diesen ;

6 The passage is reprinted in Petsch, op. cit., p. 45. Müller was a poet, painter, and engraver, generally referred to in the history of the Storm and Stress period as "Maler Müller."

7 i.e. Lessing.

8 Reprinted in *Lessings Werke,* Petersen and Olshausen, Vol. X, pp. 216-218 ; Geissler, op. cit., I, 302-304 ; Petsch, op. cit., pp. 46-47. Friedrich von Blankenburg, an officer and writer, was a friend of Lessing's.

aber wer weiss, wann und wie, und ob das Publikum jemals etwas von diesem Werke zu Gesichte bekömmt? und so teilen Sie ihm denn einstweilig mit, was ich weiss.

Dass Lessing vor vielen Jahren schon an einem Faust gearbeitet hatte, wissen wir aus den Literaturbriefen. Aber, soviel mir bekannt ist, unternahm er die Umarbeitung—vielleicht auch nur die Vollendung—seiner Arbeit zu einer Zeit, wo aus allen Zipfeln Deutschlands Fauste angekündigt wurden, und sein Werk war, meines Wissens, fertig. Man hat mir mit Gewissheit erzählt, dass er, um es herauszugeben, nur auf die Erscheinung der übrigen Fauste gewartet habe.—Er hatte es bei sich, da er von Wolfenbüttel eine Reise nach Dresden machte; hier übergab er es in einem Kästchen, in welchem noch mehrere Papiere und andere Sachen waren, einem Fuhrmann, der dieses Kästchen einem seiner Verwandten in Leipzig, dem Kaufmann Hrn. Lessing,[9] einliefern, und dieser sollte es dann weiter nach Wolfenbüttel besorgen. Aber das Kästchen kam nicht; der würdige Mann, an welchen es geschickt werden sollte, erkundigte sich sorgfältig, schrieb selbst deswegen an Lessing usw. Aber das Kästchen blieb aus—und der Himmel weiss, in welche Hände es geraten, oder wo es noch versteckt ist?—Es sei, wo es wolle, hier ist mindestens das Skelett von seinem Faust!

Die Szene eröffnet sich mit einer Konferenz der höllischen Geister, in welcher die Subalternen dem Obersten der Teufel Rechenschaft von ihren auf der Erde unternommenen und ausgeführten Arbeiten ablegen. Denken Sie, was ein Mann, wie Lessing, von diesem Stoffe zu machen weiss!—Der letzte, welcher von den Unterteufeln erscheint, berichtet: dass er wenigstens einen Mann auf der Erde gefunden habe, welchem nun gar nicht beizukommen sei; er habe keine Leidenschaft, keine Schwachheit; in der nähern Untersuchung dieser Nachricht wird Fausts Charakter immer mehr entwickelt; und auf die Nachfragen nach allen seinen Trieben und Neigungen antwortet endlich der Geist: er hat nur einen Trieb, nur eine Neigung; einen unauslöschlichen Durst nach Wissenschaften und Kenntnis—„Ha!" ruft der Oberste der Teufel aus, „dann ist er mein, und auf immer mein, und sicherer mein,

[9] Lessing's brother Karl, by way of correction, states that the box was to be taken to Wolfenbüttel by a Brunswick bookdealer named Gebler.

als bei jeder andern Leidenschaft!"—Sie werden ohne mein Zutun fühlen, was alles in dieser Idee liegt; vielleicht wäre sie ein wenig zu bösartig, wenn die Auflösung des Stückes nicht die Menschheit beruhigte. Aber urteilen Sie selbst, wieviel dramatisches Interesse dadurch in das Stück gebracht, wie sehr der Leser bis zur Angst beunruhigt werden müsse.—Nun erhält Mephistophiles Auftrag und Anweisung, was und wie er es anzufangen habe, um den armen Faust zu fangen; in den folgenden Akten beginnt—und vollendet er, dem Scheine nach, sein Werk; hier kann ich Ihnen keinen bestimmten Punkt angeben; aber die Grösse, der Reichtum des Feldes, besonders für einen Mann wie Lessing, ist unübersehlich.— —Genug, die höllischen Heerschaaren glauben ihre Arbeit vollbracht zu haben; sie stimmen im fünften Akte Triumphlieder an—wie eine Erscheinung aus der Oberwelt sie auf die unerwartetste und doch natürlichste und doch für jeden beruhigendste Art unterbricht: „Triumphiert nicht," ruft ihnen der Engel zu, „ihr habt nicht über Menschheit und Wissenschaft gesiegt; die Gottheit hat dem Menschen nicht den edelsten der Triebe gegeben, um ihn ewig unglücklich zu machen; was ihr sahet und jetzt zu besitzen glaubt, war nichts als ein Phantom.—"

So wenig, mein teuerster Freund, dies auch, was ich Ihnen mitteilen kann, immer ist, so sehr verdient es, meines Bedünkens, denn doch aufbewahrt zu werden. Machen Sie nach Belieben Gebrauch davon!—etc.

v. Blankenburg.

Leipzig,
am 14ten Mai 1784.

VI. Engel's Account of Lessing's Faust.[10]

An den Herausgeber des Theatralischen Nachlasses.[11]

Es ist ganz wahr, liebster Freund, dass Ihr seliger vortrefflicher Bruder mir verschiedene seiner Ideen zu theat-

[10] Reprinted in *Lessings Werke,* Petersen and Olshausen, Vol. X, pp. 218-221; Geissler, op. cit., I, 305-309; Petsch, op. cit., pp. 48-50. Johann Jakob Engel was professor at the Joachimsthaler Gymnasium in Berlin. Lessing's brother Karl has the following to say about this account: „Unser Freund, Herr Professor Engel zu Berlin, mit dem mein Bruder zu verschiedenenmalen

ralischen Stücken mitgeteilt hat. Aber das ist nun schon so lange her; die Pläne selbst waren so wenig ausgeführt oder wurden mir doch so unvollständig erzählt, dass ich nichts mehr in meinem Gedächtnis davon zusammenfinde, was des Niederschreibens, geschweige denn des öffentlichen Bekanntmachens, wert wäre. Von seinem Faust indessen, um den Sie mich vorzüglich fragen, weiss ich noch dieses und jenes; wenigstens erinnere ich mich im allgemeinen der Anlage der ersten Szene und der letzten Hauptwendung derselben.

Das Theater stellt in dieser Szene eine zerstörte gotische Kirche vor, mit einem Hauptaltar und sechs Nebenaltären. Zerstörung der Werke Gottes ist Satans Wollust; Ruinen eines Tempels, wo ehemals der Allgütige verehrt ward, sind seine Lieblingswohnung. Eben hier also ist der Versammlungsort der höllischen Geister zu ihren Beratschlagungen. Satan selbst hat seinen Sitz auf dem Hauptaltar; auf die Nebenaltäre sind die übrigen Teufel zerstreut. Alle aber bleiben dem Auge unsichtbar; nur ihre rauhen misstönenden Stimmen werden gehört. Satan fordert Rechenschaft von den Taten, welche die übrigen Teufel ausgeführt haben; ist mit diesen zufrieden, mit jenen unzufrieden.—Da das wenige, dessen ich mich aus dieser Szene erinnere, so einzeln und abgerissen, ohne alle Wirkung sein würde, so wage ich's, die Lücken dazwischen zu füllen und die ganze Szene hieherzuwerfen.—

Satan: Rede, du erster! Gib uns Bericht, was du getan hast!

Erster Teufel: Satan! Ich sah eine Wolke am Himmel; die trug Zerstörung in ihrem Schoss: da schwang ich mich auf zu ihr, barg mich in ihr schwärzestes Dunkel und trieb sie und hielt mit ihr über der Hütte eines frommen Armen, der bei seinem Weibe im ersten Schlummer ruhte. Hier zerriss ich die Wolke und schüttete all' ihre Glut auf die Hütte, dass die lichte Lohe emporschlug und alle Habe des Elenden ihr Raub ward.—Das war alles, was ich vermochte, Satan. Denn ihn selbst, seine jammernden Kinder, sein Weib: die riss Gottes Engel noch aus dem Feuer, und als ich den sah— entfloh ich.

sich sehr ausführlich darüber unterhalten, hat daher die Güte gehabt, auf mein vielmaliges Bitten, mir alles das, was er davon weiss, zu schreiben." (Cf. Petsch, op. cit., p. 47).

[11] i.e., to Karl Lessing.

Satan: Elender! Feiger! — Und du sagst, es war eines Armen, es war eines Frommen Hütte?

Erster Teufel: Eines Frommen und eines Armen, Satan. Jetzt ist er nackt und bloss und verloren.

Satan: Für uns! Ja, das ist er auf ewig. Nimm dem Reichen sein Gold, dass er verzweifle, und schütt' es auf den Herd des Armen, dass es sein Herz verführe: dann haben wir zwiefachen Gewinn! Den frommen Armen noch ärmer machen, das knüpft ihn nur desto fester an Gott.— — Rede, du zweiter! Gib uns bessern Bericht!

Zweiter Teufel: Das kann ich, Satan.— Ich ging aufs Meer und suchte mir einen Sturm, mit dem ich verderben könnte, und fand ihn: da schallten, indem ich dem Ufer zuflog, wilde Flüche zu mir hinauf, und als ich niedersah, fand ich eine Flotte mit Wuchrern segeln. Schnell wühlt' ich mich mit dem Orkan in die Tiefe, kletterte an der schäumenden Woge wieder gen Himmel— —

Satan: Und ersäuftest sie in der Flut?

Zweiter Teufel: Dass nicht einer entging! Die ganze Flotte zerriss ich, und alle Seelen, die sie trug, sind nun dein.

Satan: Verräter! Diese waren schon mein. Aber sie hätten des Fluchs und Verderbens noch mehr über die Erde gebracht; hätten an den fremden Küsten geraubt, geschändet, gemordet; hätten neue Reize zu Sünden von Weltteil zu Weltteil geführt: und das alles — das ist nun hin und verloren! — O, du sollst mir zurück in die Hölle, Teufel: du zerstörst nur mein Reich.— — Rede, du dritter! Fuhrst auch du in Wolken und Stürmen?

Dritter Teufel: So hoch fliegt mein Geist nicht, Satan: ich liebe das Schreckliche nicht. Mein ganzes Dichten ist Wollust.

Satan: Da bist du nur um so schrecklicher für die Seelen!

Dritter Teufel: Ich sah eine Buhlerin schlummern; die wälzte sich, halb träumend, halb wachend in ihren Begierden, und ich schlich hin an ihr Lager. Aufmerksam lauscht' ich auf jeden Zug ihres Atems, horcht' ihr in die Seele auf jede wollüstige Phantasie; und endlich — da erhascht' ich glücklich das Lieblingsbild, das ihren Busen am höchsten schwellte. Aus diesem Bilde schuf ich mir eine Gestalt, eine schlanke, nervigte, blühende Jünglingsgestalt: und in der— —

Satan. (schnell) : Raubtest du einem Mädchen die Unschuld ?

Dritter Teufel : Raubt' ich einer noch unberührten Schönheit — den ersten Kuss. Weiter trieb ich sie nicht.— Aber sei gewiss ! Ich hab' ihr nun eine Flamme ins Blut gehaucht ; die gibt sie dem ersten Verführer preis, und diesem spart' ich die Sünde. Ist dann erst sie verführt — —

Satan : So haben wir Opfer auf Opfer ; denn sie wird wieder verführen.— Ha, gut ! In deiner Tat ist doch Absicht.— Da lernt, ihr ersten ! ihr Elenden, die ihr nur Verderben in der Körperwelt stiftet ! Dieser hier stiftet Verderben in der Welt der Seelen ; das ist der bessere Teufel.— — Sag' an, du vierter ! Was hast du für Taten getan ?

Vierter Teufel : Keine, Satan.— Aber einen Gedanken gedacht, der, wenn er Tat würde, alle jene Taten zu Boden schlüge.

Satan : Der ist ? —

Vierter Teufel : Gott seinen Liebling zu rauben.— Einen denkenden, einsamen Jüngling, ganz der Weisheit ergeben ; ganz nur für sie atmend, für sie empfindend ; jeder Leidenschaft absagend, ausser der einzigen für die Wahrheit ; dir und uns allen gefährlich, wenn er einst Lehrer des Volks würde — den ihm zu rauben, Satan !

Satan : Trefflich ! Herrlich ! Und dein Entwurf ?—

Vierter Teufel : Sieh, ich knirsche ; ich habe keinen.— Ich schlich von allen Seiten um seine Seele ; aber ich fand keine Schwäche, bei der ich ihn fassen könnte.

Satan : Tor ! hat er nicht Wissbegierde ?

Vierter Teufel : Mehr als irgendein Sterblicher.

Satan : So lass ihn nur mir über ! Das ist genug zum Verderben.— —

Und nun ist Satan viel zu voll von seinem Entwurfe, als dass er noch den Bericht der übrigen Teufel sollte hören wollen. Er bricht mit der ganzen Versammlung auf ; alle sollen ihm zur Ausführung seiner grossen Absichten beistehn. Des Erfolgs hält er bei den Hilfsmitteln, die ihm Macht und List geben, sich völlig versichert. Aber der Engel der Vorsehung, der unsichtbar über den Ruinen geschwebt hat, verkündiget uns die Fruchtlosigkeit der Bestrebungen Satans, mit den feierlich, aber sanft gesprochenen Worten, die aus der Höhe herabschallen : „Ihr sollt nicht siegen !"——

So sonderbar, wie der Entwurf dieser ersten Szene, ist der Entwurf des ganzen Stücks. Der Jüngling, den Satan zu verführen sucht, ist, wie Sie gleich werden erraten haben, Faust ; diesen Faust begräbt der Engel in einen tiefen Schlummer und erschafft an seiner Stelle ein Phantom, womit die Teufel so lange ihr Spiel treiben, bis es in dem Augenblick, da sie sich seiner völlig versichern wollen, verschwindet. Alles, was mit diesem Phantome vorgeht, ist Traumgesicht für den schlafenden wirklichen Faust : dieser erwacht, da schon die Teufel sich schamvoll und wütend entfernt haben, und dankt der Vorsehung für die Warnung, die sie durch einen so lehrreichen Traum ihm hat geben wollen.—Er ist jetzt fester in Wahrheit und Tugend als jemals. Von der Art, wie die Teufel den Plan der Verführung anspinnen und fortführen, müssen Sie keine Nachricht von mir erwarten : ich weiss nicht, ob mich hier mehr die Erzählung ihres Bruders oder mehr mein Gedächtnis verlässt ; aber wirklich liegt alles, was mir davon vorschwebt, zu tief im dunkeln, als dass ich hoffen dürfte, es wieder ans Licht zu ziehen.

Ich bin usw.

J. J. Engel

INDEX

INDEX

M

T

Z

For Product Safety Concerns and Information please contact our EU representative GPSR@taylorandfrancis.com
Taylor & Francis Verlag GmbH, Kaufingerstraße 24, 80331 München, Germany

www.ingramcontent.com/pod-product-compliance
Lightning Source LLC
Chambersburg PA
CBHW061921130726
47908CB00016B/536

* 9 7 8 1 1 3 8 9 8 2 5 8 1 *